— *Things*

The hen flings a single pebble aside
with her yellow, reptilian foot.
Never in eternity the same sound—
a small stone falling on a red leaf.

The juncture of twig and branch,
scarred with lichen, is a gate
we might enter, singing.

The mouse pulls batting
from a hundred-year-old quilt.
She chewed a hole in a blue star
to get it, and now she thrives. . . .
Now is her time to thrive.

Things: simply lasting, then
failing to last: water, a blue heron's
eye, and the light passing
between them: into light all things
must fall, glad at last to have fallen.

SIMPLY LASTING

writers on

JANE KENYON

Edited by Joyce Peseroff

Graywolf Press

SAINT PAUL, MINNESOTA

Publication of this volume is made possible in part by a grant provided by the Minnesota State Arts Board, through an appropriation by the Minnesota State Legislature; a grant from the Wells Fargo Foundation Minnesota; and a grant from the National Endowment for the Arts, which believes that a great nation deserves great art. Significant support has also been provided by the Bush Foundation; Target, with support from the Target Foundation; the McKnight Foundation; and other generous contributions from foundations, corporations, and individuals. To these organizations and individuals we offer our heartfelt thanks.

MINNESOTA
STATE ARTS BOARD

NATIONAL
ENDOWMENT
FOR THE ARTS

Published by Graywolf Press
2402 University Avenue, Suite 203
Saint Paul, Minnesota 55114
All rights reserved.

www.graywolfpress.org

Published in the United States of America

ISBN 1-55597-429-5

2 4 6 8 9 7 5 3 1
First Graywolf Printing, 2005

Library of Congress Control Number: 2005925168

Cover design: Christa Schoenbrodt. Studio Haus

Cover art: Don McCrae, Fo2PiX

Cover photograph: © Ken Williams

Acknowledgments

David Barber, "Constance," © 1994 by The Poetry Foundation. Reprinted by permission of the Editor of POETRY.

Wendell Berry, "Sweetness Preserved," from *Bright Unequivocal Eye,* © 2000 by Peter Lange Publishing, Inc. Reprinted by permission of Peter Lange Publishing.

Robert Bly, "A Few Lines about Jane," from *New Hampshire Arts.* © 1995, 2004 by Robert Bly. Reprinted with permission.

Robert Bly, "The Yellow Dot," from *Morning Poems* by Robert Bly. © 1997 by Robert Bly. Reprinted by permission of HarperCollins Publishers Inc.

Paul Breslin, "Jane Kenyon's 'Manners Toward God': Gratitude and the 'Anti-urge,'" from *Bright Unequivocal Eye,* © 2000 by Peter Lange Publishing, Inc. Reprinted by permission of Peter Lange Publishing.

Hayden Carruth, from "Poets on the Fringe," © 1980 by *Harper's.* Reprinted with permission of the author.

Alfred Corn, "Plural Perspectives, Heightened Perceptions," from *The New York Times Book Review.* © 1991 by Alfred Corn. Reprinted with permission.

Michael Dirda, "The Gift of Being Simple," © 1996, *The Washington Post.* Reprinted with permission.

Deborah Garrison, "Simply Lasting," from *The New Yorker.* © 1996 by Deborah Garrision. Reprinted with permission of the author.

Donald Hall, "Ghost in the House," from *Unholy Ghost: Writers on Depression,* © 2003 by Donald Hall. Reprinted with permission of the author.

Robert Hass, from *Poet's Choice: Poems for Everyday Life,* © 1998 by Robert Hass. Reprinted with permission of the author.

Laban Hill, "Jane Kenyon," from American Writers Supplement VII, ed. by Jay Parini, Charles Scribner's Sons, © 2001, Charles Scribner's Sons. Reprinted by permission of The Gale Group.

Marie Howe, "Jane Kenyon's *Constance,*" from *Agni.* © 1994 by Marie Howe. Reprinted with permission.

Galway Kinnell, "How Could She Not," from *Poets & Writers.* © 1995, 2004 by Galway Kinnell. Reprinted with permission of the author.

Peter D. Kramer, "Unequivocal Eye," from *Psychiatric Times.* © 1994 by Peter D. Kramer. Reprinted with permission of the author.

Alice Mattison, "Let it Grow in the Dark like a Mushroom," from *Bright Unequivocal Eye,* © 2000 by Peter Lange Publishing, Inc. Reprinted by permission of Peter Lange Publishing.

Wesley McNair, "A Government of Two," reprinted from *Mapping the Heart* by permission of Carnegie Mellon University Press. © 2003 by Wesley McNair.

Constance Merrit, "Jane Kenyon, *Otherwise,*" reprinted from *Prairie Schooner,* volume 72, number 1 (Spring 1998) by permission of the University of Nebraska Press. © 1997 by the University of Nebraska Press.

Carol Muske, "The Boat of Quiet Hours," from *The New York Times Book Review.* © 1987 by Carol Muske-Dukes. Reprinted with permission.

Gregory Orr, "Our Lady of Sorrows," from *Bright Unequivocal Eye,* © 2000 by Peter Lange Publishing, Inc. Reprinted by permission of Peter Lange Publishing.

Molly Peacock, "A Comfort Poem," © 1999 by Molly Peacock, is reprinted by permission of the author.

Robert Pinsky, "Tidings of Comfort and Dread: Poetry and the Dark Beauty of Christmas," from *The New York Times Book Review.* © 1994 by Robert Pinsky. Reprinted with permission.

Haines Sprunt Tait, "Intimations of Mortality," © 2000 by Haines Sprunt Tait. Reprinted with permission.

John H. Timmerman, "The Poet at Work," *Jane Kenyon: A Literary Life.* © 2002 Wm. B. Eerdmans Publishing Co., Grand Rapids, MI. Used by permission.

John Unterecker, "Shape-Changing in Contemporary Poetry," from *The Michigan Quarterly Review.* © 1988 by John Unterecker. Reprinted with permission.

Jean Valentine, "Elegy for Jane Kenyon," from *Columbia.* © 1996 by Jean Valentine. Reprinted with permission of the author.

Jean Valentine, "Jane Kenyon 1947–1995," from *PSA Poetry Pilot.* © 1995 by Jean Valentine. Reprinted with permission of the author.

Contents

Introduction

Jane Kenyon was an artist at the height of her power when, six months after a bone marrow transplant, she died of leukemia in April 1995. Her poems, those "brief musical cries of the spirit," moved thousands who heard them, and thousands more who read the four volumes praised by reviewers. Bill Moyers interviewed her for the Emmy Award–winning documentary, "A Life Together." Composers set her work to music. She wrote newspaper columns for and about her neighbors in Wilmot, New Hampshire, as well as essays on gardening and mountain climbing. She visited the Bennington Writing seminars to read and talk about her favorite poets. Her verse grew ever more discursive, ambitious, and complex. That there will be no more writing by Jane Kenyon is one of the terrible losses that might have been otherwise.

I first met Jane Kenyon in 1972, one of two poets accepted that year as Junior Fellows in the newly minted University of Michigan Society of Fellows. The program offered artists and scholars three luxurious years of thinking and writing, with few responsibilities or requirements other than residence in Ann Arbor. In the 1970s Jane's hair was straight, and she wore black-framed glasses she would later exchange for contact lenses. But her voice was the same modulated music you can hear in her later readings. I was invited to join her workshops with Gregory Orr, which had started the year before; she and Don took me to a Michigan football game; we attended Society dinners (Don was a Senior Fellow) and campus poetry readings; we became friends. A year after I returned to Massachusetts, Don and Jane moved to New Hampshire. I might have been the only soul within a hundred miles, other than Don, she'd known from her Ann

Arbor days; lucky for me, a two-hour drive brought Jane to Cambridge for bookstores, tacos and beer, or me to the farmhouse for generous meals and hours of talk. She nicknamed us the country mouse and the city mouse, though I—a native New Yorker, and a fine example of urban provincialism—was drawn to her sophistication and perfect manners. Together we worked on *Green House,* a literary magazine we'd planned while still in Michigan. We divided editorial duties, and educated ourselves in the details of layout, production, and distribution. We published friends and discovered strangers; our goal was to provide a forum for poets who didn't know each other, and whose work could not usually be found in the same magazine, to find common readers. Over three years of the magazine's existence, we tested and refined our notions of what made a good poem. When *From Room to Room* was published in 1978, Jane Kenyon was firmly part of a New England literary community.

Jane was witty, inventive, fun. She discovered that lengths of gutter made perfect pans for baking French bread. She patiently leveled and set in sand the large brick patio patterned behind her house. She also told me how much she enjoyed reading ads for extravagant handbags in the Sunday *New York Times,* and once we went to Bloomingdale's in Chestnut Hill for a free cosmetic consultation and makeover. When we met at the Mall of New Hampshire, halfway between Lexington and Wilmot, to exchange poems and news, Jane bought earrings and scarves in fine fabrics. Later we chose books for my daughter and her five grandchildren, including *The Stupids Die,* a title she adored, and the Margaret Wise Brown's *The Runaway Bunny,* whose theology—"It's like the love of God!"—made her weep. She loved Mahler and Motown, Dutch paintings and poker-playing-dog placemats, Beethoven and Mel Brooks, lotions and baths.

Once while Jane was working on *Twenty Poems of Anna Akhmatova,* she took me to Vera Sandomirsky Dunham's home on Long Island. Jane was choosing, with Vera's advice, several more poems to translate. I remember thick black volumes of Akhmatova's work like a complete edition of the *O.E.D.,* and how Vera read aloud several poems in Russian. I also remember Vera Dunham's oft-repeated, "This is impossible! It cannot be done!" after her reading: no poem in English, she believed, could properly render Akhmatova's sound, or her intricate form. For a while it did seem as if that day she would go no further. Then she sat with Jane, providing a literal translation, answering Jane's questions concerning connotation and tone, and explaining historical details such as what the "tree-lined drive" in "Tale of the Black Ring" might look like. The Dunhams' guest bathroom was scarlet, and before we left, Jane nudged me to notice Vera's full-length Russian sable coat in the hall closet. Later, Jane was ambitious to translate Akhmatova's masterpiece "Requiem," but, whether because of Vera's husband's illness, or Vera's, or her own, she never did. Perhaps she knew she had learned what her master had to teach her: a precise way of describing great emotional intensity through imagery as plain as a white stone in a deep well, or a winter glove put on the wrong hand.

If I had to pick one perfect, exemplary day I spent with Jane, it would be in late spring, 1993. She was visiting the college where I taught to take part in a twentieth- anniversary reading for Alice James Books. I joined her that morning at Symphony Hall (she and Don had season tickets for the BSO's Thursday open rehearsal). Over and over the singer repeated her gorgeous aria; Jane's pleasure was palpable. After the rehearsal we had lunch—probably in the Cinderella restaurant that served students delicious home-cooked pasta by day and became a tony boite at night—on our way to the original Filene's Basement, where Jane sorted through bins of sassy shoes, hunting for bargains. Then came the reading, old poems and new ones from *Constance,* which would be published later that year. It's possible that she read "No Steps," and I remember her saying that she'd written it partly for the pleasure of getting "ziplock plastic bag" into the language of a poem. An audience of students, faculty, fellow readers, and Boston friends filled the room—intent on every word—applauded, and bought books.

The tone of those books was often bleak. Jane enjoyed the things of this world, but there's a terrifying longing for the void in her poems—desire for oblivion, for *nada,* paralysis, immobility, or effacement in sleep's "frail wicker coracle." The newborn welcomed by shouts in "Caesarian" is shocked by light and noise. Entrance into the world is disordered (outside in, inside out), an introduction to the abyss. Kenyon's poems interrogate the abyss: why live, when life is suffering? Like Akhmatova, Kenyon knows trouble, the shadow between "love's tense joys and red delights."

Yet throughout the body of her work, things—a stone warmed by sun, a wood thrush, a clothes pin, a long gray hair, hay bales, rushing water, peonies—answer existential doubt and dread. Whether gifts of the Holy Ghost, or "thoughts/in an unconflicted mind," they are preceptors. Kenyon's poems are not didactic but they always show us where to look. In "Depression in Early Winter," it's at a crescent of bare ground; in "Portrait of a Figure Near Water" it's a stone trough; in "Let Evening Come," it's everything. "Go to the pine to learn from the pine," Basho wrote four centuries ago; Kenyon's work is a twentieth-century response. What adds pressure to these poems is the landscape in which so many of these objects reside. Fields, woods, ponds and streams, hayrick, shed, farmhouse, inn, general store—Kenyon describes a rural life that is fading fast. The whip-poor-will, dispossessed by men making hay, may be dispossessed for good, if fields become real estate. Kenyon's poems argue for the preservation of an ecology as strongly as anything by Gary Snyder, if more subtly. For how can we give the world our steady attention if its natural objects disappear?

Man-made objects, other than domestic ones—the snowplow, school clothes and satchels, the wineglass weary of holding wine—often conduct disquiet and grief rather than joy. Even music and books—the Chopin and Nabokov that pained her father, and the Keats she loves but cannot bear to read him—may be charged with suffering. Surely there is something of Wordsworth in Kenyon's gaze. Wordsworth saw nature's beauty as proof of God's hand in creation; by delighting in the scent of roses, plush of moss, play of sky and clouds, man learns to love his creator. But Kenyon doesn't write just about beautiful things. The hen's foot is "reptilian," snow and rain can be violent, the mouse leaves behind its shit and smell. So why this feeling of joy when Kenyon writes, "Now is her time to thrive"? Whether Kenyon's eyes are on the sparrow or the skunk, we are persuaded to invest them with complete attention, as Kenyon's words—and possibly the Word—have. We may live in the abyss, God may be distant, indifferent, or dead, there maybe no earthly reason to lift an arm from a chair—all the same, Kenyon does the work of discovering all that this world is made of.

She didn't much like cities or suburbs, places where it was possible to overhear and yet avoid a neighbor's pain. Jane didn't avoid anything. The intimacy of voice in a Jane Kenyon poem erases the line between her vision and the reader's. The structure of her sentences reveals a mind in motion—a strategy learned from Elizabeth Bishop, but employed differently. Kenyon, avoiding nothing, doesn't insist on conclusion. The ellipse—something she admired in Louis Simpson's poems—indicates the end of one thought before it flows into another. Kenyon's poems seem lifted directly from the poet's consciousness.

She once described writing poetry as taking off her clothes in front of everyone, which implies exhibitionism, seduction, frankness, and bravery. These are qualities necessary to a voice essentially alone, confronting space both infinite and eternal. One needs quiet, solitude, and belief in the importance of perception in order to measure the progress of a beating heart.

"One of the functions of poetry is to keep the memory of people and places and things and happenings alive," Kenyon said to Bill Moyers during an interview. This is true of collections like this one as well. I recognize that any volume about Jane Kenyon must be incomplete, since even as I type these words, someone is writing a paper, an article, a review, or a poem in response to Kenyon's life and work. That is both joy and pain, as is the fact that I can no longer speak to Jane, though she still speaks to me—and to each reader—through words that are "simply lasting."

I want to thank Donald Hall for his continuous support, suggestions, and help during my work on this project. I would also like to thank Roland Goodbody, curator of the Milne Special Collections and Archives at the University of New Hampshire, for his assistance with Kenyon's papers. Jessica DelGizzi's vigilance and patience in the production of this manuscript was invaluable. As always, thanks to Jeff and Elizabeth White for their presence.

Joyce Peseroff
Lexington, MA
August 2004

— *Personal Essays, Letters, Poems, and One Interview*

ALICE MATTISON

"Let It Grow in the Dark like a Mushroom": Writing with Jane Kenyon

In a fireproof box in my study are letters the poet Jane Kenyon wrote me between the time we met in 1979 and her death, at the age of forty-seven, in 1995. I wrote to Jane first thing every Monday morning, when I could hardly bear being a writer. Jane wrote less often, but often enough. I look at a letter of hers from May 28, 1985. She was trying to place her second book of poems, *The Boat of Quiet Hours,* and waiting for her newly published book of translations from Akhmatova to arrive. For two and a half years she and Joyce Peseroff and I had been meeting several times a year to work on writing together.

> I've been overly busy and underly inspired. . . .
> Still no word from Knopf. Still no book of translations. If being an adult means that one can postpone gratification, I must be very grownup by now. Is it wrong to want fame and fortune? Probably. Better just want to be good. But let's get paid, too.

Later in the letter she speculates on when we'll be able to hold a workshop meeting:

> Last time I knew, Joyce's parents were coming to visit her during the time we were going to meet. And Lucy is going to

be here from June 7–17th. So what's to become of our schedule I don't know.

I <u>need</u> to get together. I'm feeling discouraged and dry.

A postcard from November 10, 1986:

Monday

Dear Alice,

I'm still torturing these poems, consulting your letter about them each in its turn.

I couldn't get the ribbon in my typewriter to move this morning. I had a <u>tantrum</u>, a <u>meltdown</u>. I can hardly believe it.

I talked to Joyce; she sounded fine. Tired and possessed, but fine.

Hope you are working <u>freely</u>.

Love, J.

Though we lived in different places and worked in solitude for long periods, Jane and I—and Jane and Joyce and I—became writers together, partners and friends, to a degree I hadn't imagined and hadn't known I wanted. Being writers as a group—thinking of two other people as colleagues or coworkers rather than rivals, even friendly rivals—was quite different from going about that business alone. I think we taught ourselves, together, how to live as writers, and a fair amount about how to write.

Jane's feelings were intense, her perceptions acute, and she was honest. It would have been impossible to be her friend without acknowledging pain, often the pain in small things—though sometimes Joyce and I teased her about discovering pain everywhere. Once, greatly moved, Jane told me of seeing a man leave a hospital with a woman's coat on his arm. Surely he was newly bereaved, as Jane assumed, but I mischievously invented a different explanation: perhaps he was taking his wife's coat to the dry cleaners while she was in the hospital for a facelift. In Jane's poem about the incident, "Coats," there's no doubt: "The sunglasses he wore could not/ conceal his wet face, his bafflement." Jane was often depressed, and her depression did not lead her to feel sorry for herself nearly as frequently as she felt sorry for others; I sometimes found myself trying vainly to deflect Jane's deep sympathy about a problem that I didn't mind much.

Above all, or so it seemed to me, Jane tried to live decently as the self she found herself to be—as a writer, and also as a person whose depression sometimes made her unable to act. Being a writing colleague of Jane Kenyon's meant that certain issues, certain questions, were always on the agenda. I think I became a different person from the one I'd have been without her. I want to speak here about what we gave one another in our workshop, as I remember it, and what I learned from knowing Jane.

In the 1970s and in my thirties, I was living with my husband in New Haven, writing poems, teaching part-time, and looking after three young sons. I had a couple of old friends who were poets, but on the whole I was alone, writing and revising, sending manuscripts out. Then one of my poet friends told me about a new magazine called *Green House,* edited by Joyce Peseroff—a poet I'd once met whose work I admired—and someone I didn't know named Jane Kenyon. I began reading *Green House,* which printed a couple of my poems in 1977. In the following issue, one of Jane Kenyon's poems, "From the Back Steps," appeared. I liked it enormously, responding, I imagine, to its frankness about feelings one would rather not have:

> The cat lolls in the shade
> under the parked car, his head
> in the wheel's path.
> I bury the thing I love.

When Alice James Books, already Joyce Peseroff's publisher, published *From Room to Room* by Jane Kenyon, I sent for it and read it with delight.

I too had a manuscript of poems, and Alice James Books had seen it more than once. Alice James is a cooperative press. In those days it was located in Cambridge, Massachusetts, and nearly all the work of running it was done by the poets it published. Anyone whose manuscript was accepted—mostly women—joined the cooperative, attended meetings, helped out in the office, and took charge of her own book's publication. In 1979 I submitted my much-rejected manuscript in a new version, and then, by chance, was asked to give a short poetry reading in Cambridge during the period when manuscripts were being considered.

At a crowded book fair, I was asked to be last of a large group of readers, and I sat beside my husband, waiting for my turn and watching in dismay as the audience grew smaller with each reading. Even the poets didn't stay. Just before my reading, people began to enter the room. In my nervousness I decided they were just passing through, but not finding a second door out, they sat down. I gave my reading and then the newcomers crowded around me, shaking my hand and introducing themselves. They were the Alice James poets, I gradually realized, and they had come on purpose to hear me. They were mostly shorter than I'd imagined them, and one of them told me later that they had thought *I'd* be bigger than I am. A woman a few inches taller then me, with lots of wild curly hair, said her name in a low, calm voice: she was Jane Kenyon.

My book was accepted and I began attending meetings of the cooperative and putting in time in the office, taking the train to Cambridge from Connecticut every couple of weeks. Jane lived at a distance in the other direction, and her book had been out for a while. She was becoming less active in the cooperative, and I didn't see her often.

When the first copies of my book arrived at the Alice James office, in February of 1980, I rushed to Cambridge to see them. In the office I found Jane, who was spending a few hours there before nervously taking a plane to Long Island, where she was meeting Vera Dunham, the Russian woman with whose help Jane translated Akhmatova. I don't remember whether Jane imitated Vera's gruff voice and tragic intonation that afternoon, but I heard her do it—her admiration as notable as her amusement—many times later. "It eez impossible! It cannot be done! Let us begin!" Quite possibly Jane didn't imitate Vera, or even tell me where she was going; she might have thought it sounded like bragging.

I was pleased that Jane was afraid of airplanes, as I was, and impressed that she was flying anyway. We set out to spend our time usefully, filling book orders we found in a drawer. Later it turned out that we'd misunderstood the process, and all the books we mailed out had already been sent. Somewhere are twenty or so people with duplicate copies of Alice James books, souvenirs of the day Jane Kenyon and I became friends.

That spring I suggested to some people who ran a reading series in New Haven, where I live, that they invite Jane Kenyon and Joyce Peseroff. They asked if I also knew Donald Hall. (I've always been proud of the fact that I admired Jane's work before I knew she was married to Don.) I hadn't met him, but I supplied his address, and two readings were arranged, one by Jane and Joyce and one by Don, to take place at an old barn in Hamden once used by Eli Whitney. Donald Hall grew up in Hamden; his mother and her friends attended both readings, and Joyce worried about the blunt language in some of her poems. After Jane and Joyce's reading we all ate strawberry shortcake at my house. Don's reading, a week later, was attended by everybody from the Yale literati to his old elementary school teachers. Jane and I sat together, talking freely and intimately as we waited for him to begin. Ease had come to us quickly, I remember thinking.

When Jane invited my family and me to visit them at Eagle Pond during our vacation, I was excited. In those years, Edward and the kids and I spent two weeks every August in a rented cabin in southern New Hampshire, and starting in 1980, we always visited the farm one afternoon. Don would give us tours of the house and barn, or we'd drink lemonade on the shore of Eagle Pond. Edward and Don obligingly entertained the children, giving Jane and me a chance to walk and talk by ourselves. Jane and I would also walk and talk in New Haven whenever she and Don came to visit his mother.

We began writing letters. Looking over some from those first years, I see that Jane wrote to me more formally than she did later, but already with directness and openness about her feelings and her work. In a letter written on March 29, 1982, not long after the death of her father, she speaks of a trip to England, where she "finished the really depressive phase of grieving." (It's the trip she described in "Travel: After a Death.") In her letter she wrote,

> I've been working on a sequence of poems in memory of my
> father . . . terribly costly for me . . . not finished. Almost
> all in iambic pentameter, which I am having to learn as one
> learns to drive a car or ride a bike. It begins to get easier—the
> technical end of it. The emotional end is about the same.

Jane's letters always contained more about the rest of life than about writing, however. At the end of this one, she says "The other day I took an axe to the snowbank on top of the crocus-bed . . . still four feet high, it was. I went nuts, chopping and yelling, 'Go away!' Took it down at least twelve inches!"

A letter from June 23 of that year apparently responds to a note of congratulation from me, though I don't remember what about. She said, "I tell you I know who my friends are: when something good happens they're not mean about it. You, and dear Joycie, are pleased for me..I know that." Later in the letter (which was written in longhand),

> Our youngest cat is on top of my typewriter. I can see his
> long hair (he's shedding) dragging into the works. . . . I
> just had the thing serviced because it would only type num-
> bers! Maybe it was trying to tell me something . . . I should
> change careers, or go straight to the racetrack.

During Thanksgiving weekend of 1982, when Jane and Don were visiting Mrs. Hall and Jane invited me there for tea, she proposed that the two of us meet with Joyce, who'd been Jane's friend for years, to talk about writing. Joyce was low, Jane thought, which may or may not have been true; Jane was always deciding that her friends were in need. Jane needed help, she said, because she was afraid her iambics seemed old-fashioned. I too was having difficulties. Just as my youngest child started first grade, a full-time teaching job opened at the college where I taught as an adjunct, but I was rejected for it. I was hurt and troubled, but also felt that I now had permission to make writing my chief business—a frightening idea. I had begun writing fiction, but was full of doubts about it.

We three met as a workshop in Joyce's house, in Lexington, Massachusetts, in January of 1983. Later we sometimes gathered at Eagle Pond Farm, sometimes at my house, and twice at the Lord Jeffrey Inn in Amherst (where Don kept us company when we weren't working), but we met most often at Joyce's. We'd begin just after lunch, work through the afternoon—pausing for coffee and dessert—then go out to a Chinese restaurant. In the evening we'd chat with Joyce's husband, Jeff, and go to bed early, Jane and I sleeping on cots in his study. In the morning we'd work again. Exhausted, I'd take Amtrak home in the afternoon.

Before each meeting, we mailed one another copies of all our new work. At the workshop, we'd take turns reading out poems aloud. (When I began to bring stories, I read those aloud, and when I twice brought novels to the workshop, I read aloud a lot more of them than you'd think.) Then we'd try to figure out what was wrong, and make suggestions. We did a lot of specific pencil-on-paper work right there. I think I remember that in the first meeting we considered Jane's poem "Trouble with Math in a One-Room Country School." She'd been ready to abandon it, she claimed, for want of a preposition. She was describing an enraged schoolteacher pulling the little girl Jane, whom she'd caught talking, out of her classroom. (We never asked whether anything in a poem or story had really happened, but

I think this incident did.) At the end of the poem comes the wonderful line about the change that comes with the loss of illusion: "I . . . hardened my heart against authority." Jane wanted to be true to the drama of the story, but she also wanted to tell it without repeating prepositions. How was she to describe the teacher leading her from the classroom to a closet? She'd already used "from" and she didn't want the double preposition "out of." I am afraid I remember this conversation because I was the one who came up with the answer: "through." The line remains, "And led me roughly through the class." Jane liked "through" because it had only one syllable, a syllable she hadn't employed before, but also because it made the humiliation worse. She wrote down the word with a satisfied flourish. After that first workshop, I took the train home and stepped into Edward's arms saying "I'm healed." I'd put behind me the disappointment about the teaching job. I was going to be a writer. The train pulled out and I realized I'd left my wallet on the seat.

In all our meetings we worked hard on diction, trying to be brief and clear. From Don, through Jane, we picked up a horror of dead metaphors and excess articles and prepositions. Jane would announce, speaking of her husband, "If I used two prepositions in a row, Perkins would hit me with a stick." We wanted balance (Jane taught me, in gardening as well as writing, to have groups of three or five, not two or four) but not too much balance. Sometimes Jane reported that "Perkins" wanted her stanzas equal in length, and took some pleasure in defying him.

Mostly, though, when fooling around with words we were after freshness and strong feeling. We congratulated ourselves when we moved the most outrageous line in a poem or story to a more prominent position, or found a stronger, less predictable expression. Near the end of our years together, we talked about Jane's poem "The Way Things Are in Franklin." Jane had used the word "laconic" to describe the "wives/ of pipefitters and road agents," and Joyce suggested that word was, perhaps, too expected. Briskly Jane raised her pen: "Garrulous!"

Jane's most frequently repeated remarks, during workshop, were, "What clever friends I have. What <u>clever</u> friends I have" and, "The natural object is always the adequate symbol," which she found in Ezra Pound's *Make It New* and which was the closest thing we had to a group creed. We said it to one another when we'd just cut an explanation, a justification, or an abstract formulation of feeling or belief, clearing away clutter around an image. Jane trusted the natural world to provide all the meaning we needed, which doesn't mean that in her own work she always described what she experienced or had always experienced what she described. She looked for concrete, specific images, but became impatient with herself if she thought she was simply writing down what she saw. When "Three Songs at the End of Summer" was reprinted in *The Best American Poetry: 1989*, Jane provided a comment: "This poem is personal, and painful, and it is the kind of poetry I'd like to turn away from. There's very little invention in it. It is memory and reportage."

I have mixed feelings about that remark. I think Jane must have been depressed when she wrote it, or embarrassed because Donald Hall was the editor of the anthology. I'm also fascinated that she wrote not about what she'd done but what she planned to do next—and many of her subsequent poems are full of invention. On the publication of "Gettysburg: July 1, 1863," about the intimate thoughts of a dying Civil War soldier, someone wrote asking Jane whether she'd arrived at the poem through channeling. "What did you answer?" I said. We were walking in New Haven. "I said I used my imagination," said Jane firmly.

Jane used her imagination and her knowledge, changing details and inventing. Joyce and I had dogs before Jane did; early dogs in Jane's poems, like the one in "Parents' Weekend: Camp Kenwood" who "established her front feet/ on the fence and barked" or the one who stopped barking in "Campers Leaving: 1981" originated in what we called "dog envy." And of course, Jane's firm belief in concrete language, whether or not it described what she'd actually seen, didn't prevent her from writing beautiful and powerful abstract statements:

"But sometimes what looks like disaster/ *is* disaster." "God does not leave us/ comfortless." "You see, we have done harm." "It might have been otherwise."

"If you've got it, flaunt it," Jane used to say. As a workshop we pushed one another's writing as far as it would go, letting the folks on the page suffer and also allowing them joy. In our own lives, too, we encouraged one another to flaunt what we had and to want what we wanted. That first workshop meeting was not only good for my writing, it was one of the few times I'd talked honestly with other writers about success. We wanted it—publication, readers, and money—even though we'd already had a little. Jane used to say "The day after a banquet you're hungry again." I'd gotten into the bad habit of apologizing for ambition, saying hypocritically to people I knew, "Oh, I'm just grateful that somebody once printed something I wrote." As Jane's friend I learned to know, and to admit, that I wanted more.

For eleven years, until Jane became sick with leukemia a couple weeks before a scheduled workshop meeting, we met as a group three or four times a year. During Jane's illness we didn't stop critiquing one another's work; she never had a well day during those final fifteen months, but we exchanged suggestions for her poems and my stories by mail, on the phone, and in visits. The three of us were not together again, however, except for Jane's funeral.

I said earlier that Jane and Joyce and I were colleagues rather than competitors. I don't want to suggest that we were saints who felt nothing but pleasure at one another's successes, although certainly we felt a great deal of pleasure: we worked so hard on all our stuff that it would have been impossible not to feel triumphant when other people admired it. Still, I am sure there were times when each of us got something the others wanted, at a moment when one of the others could have used a little encouragement. I think Jane's honesty, there too, made things easier. "I can't die until I have a reputation, Alice," she wrote me on July 16, 1986. She used to say ruefully, "I want all the praise all the time." Writing to me in sympathy after one of my books received a mixed review, she said, "It simply kills me that not every human being on earth loves every word I have ever written!" (11/1/88) She recognized that at some level we are all insatiable; having acknowledged that, it was easier for all of us to start celebrating when one of the others had good fortune.

One terribly sad effect of Jane's depression, I think, was that it was hard for her to believe that her successes counted. Mention of publication or a prize came in a scrawl at the bottom of a letter, or not at all. Jane was modest and careful not to brag, but also, I'm afraid, she didn't get nearly as much of a lift from such occasions as she might have. She doubted them, as well. She once speculated that an editor had accepted a poem of hers only because he and Don had had lunch together thirteen years earlier. She worried that any success came only because she was Don's wife. On a bad day she could convince herself that almost nothing that had happened amounted to much, and I think occasionally her doubts led her to resent other writers' successes. When I began publishing fiction and acquired an agent, Jane let me know often how furious she was that agents scorned poetry because there was little money in it. Now her poems make plenty of money. Sometimes I think that happened because Jane dared to want it.

Jane was quick to dismiss other people's failures but temperamentally unable to put aside her own, whether because of depression, her dour, pious grandmother, or some other cause. If a magazine rejected my work, it was edited by idiots; if it rejected hers, maybe she wasn't any good. In March of 1985 Jane mailed me a rejection letter she'd received from a magazine editor to whom she'd sent her poem "Sun and Moon." She didn't send a copy; she sent the editor's actual letter, which reads,

Dear Jane,
    "Sun and Moon" moves peacefully to its conclusion, with some kind of pathetic left-over in nearly every stanza. It's a lovely piece of work. I only wish we had the space for it. I am sorry.

After some thought, I realized that by "pathetic left-over" the editor meant residual feeling. Pathetic as in pathetic fallacy. But of course his choice of words had a completely negative effect. Jane scribbled on the edge of the letter that this editor "always manages to insult one . . . I'd like to take the *pathetic left-over* and smear him with it." After that, Jane and I used the words "pathetic left-overs" when talking about cleaning out refrigerators, but also when talking about writing. I joked; she didn't quite joke. The unfortunate phrase hurt her more than it might have, I think, because it suggested a fault she worried about. She'd speak of "pathetic left-overs" when she felt her writing was tired and uninspired, when she thought she was re-writing poems she'd already written.

Our conversations, as friends and as workshop members, were of-ten about our habits as writers, the pace at which we wrote, how much writing was enough for people who considered themselves full-time professional writers, and whether there was such a thing as too much writing. I think Jane had different and contradictory feelings about these questions, as she did about many others; Jane was un-troubled by contradiction. (We once pointed out to each other as we walked down Ragged Mountain that below us the pond appeared to lie between us and the road, though we knew it didn't. I hung myself off the edge of a cliff to discern the road located where I knew it had to be, but Jane wasn't perturbed; she knew the road was between us and the pond, and also *not* between us and the pond.) About the pace of writing, I think Jane sometimes believed one thing and sometimes another.

None of the three of us held a full-time job. Joyce has always taught a good deal, and during the years we worked together she had a time-consuming baby. Though Jane once taught a class and for a long time wrote occasional essays for the *Concord Monitor*, on the whole she didn't work for money except as a poet. I have always taught, but Jane and I often needed to assure ourselves that writing was our job, and a real job. Jobs are done regularly, and as a fiction writer I did write more and more. Jane, however, didn't write when she was depressed, and that made her feel worse. Still (she'd point out to me, and I'd point out to her), when she wasn't depressed she mounted the stairs to her study every day and wrote steadily: a working person.

Yet I think at heart she had another view, and it was that for writing to be highly charged, to be worth reading, it had to come at the right time, and maybe after long silence. When Jane was writing steadily, she was often dissatisfied with what she wrote. In May, 1985, she wrote "I went to Ann Arbor, helped my mother put on a yard sale, came home and wrote a poem called 'Yard Sale.' Boredom!" In June, 1990, came a letter in which Jane said, "I've drafted three shallow poems in three days. Maybe I can make them thicker and more interesting as I work on them. They are 10¢ poems." At least she thought there was hope for those. On June 10, 1988,

> I'm slogging along on a poem about Charleston, S.C. and the Confederate Museum. I'm putting it together without excitement but I'm working. It seems to me that I never get as excited about starting poems as I used to. I used to feel a rush of physical excitement. I'd have to keep going downstairs to pee . . . I don't miss that exactly.

Or, on August 10, 1989, "My ear is not working, my poetry ear. I can't write a line that doesn't sound like pots and pans falling out of the cupboard."

The writing about which she spoke with pleasure often broke through a silence, then came easily. April 16, 1989:

> I have written something new, which I am very excited about. While I was in A[nn] A[rbor] I heard my mother say, 'Let evening come.' We were talking about getting depressed as the day goes on, and wanting bedtime to come so you can become oblivious. . . . I think Let Evening Come is going to be my title. I have written the poem very fast. Of course you will have to see it before I know whether it is any good.

I think she enclosed it, and it was almost exactly the poem we have now.

I believe that Jane went back and forth on the question of whether it's better to write steadily or to keep silent until one is truly ready: if she waited for inspiration and intensity, she wasn't working at her job; if she didn't, she produced pathetic left-overs. Waiting was hard. "I'm having a terrible time at my desk," she wrote on March 1, 1988, "(by which I think I mean I haven't started anything new for two months). I can't seem to start anything. I'm revising but I need to do both."

Because I've been most comfortable when I work most days, I was always advising Jane to do that too, to enjoy the daily work even if it wasn't always obviously first-rate. Her depression when she wasn't working was so terrible that I wanted her to work and escape it. And she'd try to comply: "I am upstairs on Monday morning, waiting for a delivery from United Aesthetic Service."

Or,

I listen to what you tell me about writing. I really do. The prose has been nice to work on. I actually took pleasure in it, the first thing in a long time. I do—you are correct about this—expect to wrench something out of my soul every time I start a poem. I can't go on thinking that way.

Of course she did go on thinking that way, as she had to. And I believe that she was proud of thinking that way, knowing how good her best work was and what she had to go through to produce it. She was quick to tell me when she thought my work was becoming forced; reading her comments on what I did, I can see that she worried that I wrote too much, that I wrote when I should have refrained from writing. On March 5, 1993, she wrote me a devastating letter in response to one in which I'd said impatiently that I might not wait for the workshop to meet before sending new work to an editor. "Dim your lights a little, pal," she wrote.

There really is such a thing as working too fast. I see Don do it, and I see the quality of his work suffer for it. You seem to be working tremendously out of your <u>will</u>. There is no floating in your mind or work now. I think you may be over-determining your fiction. I'm not asking you to apologize for your fecundity. I am suggesting that you continue to work with your friends. You seem to be hurtling off to the edges of the galaxy—it's cold and lonely out there.

Earlier, in response to stories, "The new story I feel ends will-fully" and, "The story feels <u>made</u> to me, not inevitable. It distresses me not to like it better than that." When I was at work on my first novel, which I admitted was a long piece of fiction but didn't *call* a novel for a long time, she counseled me to slow down, to let it come from the unconscious, unforced. In the same letter in which she claimed to be taking my advice about writing, she said, "Now I'm going to dispense advice—you don't have to hurry the Big One. The Big One will get more and more interesting over time. Let it grow in the dark like a mushroom. And don't pick it too soon."

Slowly I've learned to keep what I'm writing even from myself. I'll never be the kind of writer Jane was. I don't have the nerve to stop for months or even weeks; but at least I know about the darkness she spoke of. The more we worked together, the more I could keep what I wrote secret and unformed until the right time had come. We were writers together except when we were writers intensely apart.

We were also readers together. Letters of Jane's talk in detail about her reading of Proust, Tolstoy, E. M. Forster, and especially Keats. Jane told me once that it pleased her immeasurably that her pub-lisher, Graywolf, embossed her books with her initials, J. K., espe-cially because those were also Keats's initials. She lectured about Keats, Bishop, and Akhmatova at Bennington College just before she became ill with leukemia; people there reported that she asserted that Keats was a "fuck 'n' die" poet. She wrote me on December 22, 1993, as she was preparing for those lectures, "I think Nightingale is the greatest poem in the language. Everything he ever wrote prepared him to write it. He only had to live his way, inexorably, to the moment." And a month later, just eight days before she was diagnosed with leukemia, she wrote about Dickinson:

> I've been mining Dickinson. I've found out some things about her Structures—you probably knew them already. I can't wait to talk to you about it. I'm making diagrams on the poems, linking parallel syntactic structures. They take even more than I knew from hymn structure, and at this point in my life, knowing the gospels as I do, I can tell you that she knew her Bible, by gum. Her struggle with God is constant in the poems.

Of course I didn't know anything about what Jane had discovered, and I never found out.

The workshops, and our friendship, weren't always easy. I visited the farm in the winter of 1992, not long after Jane and Don's first trip to India, where they lectured and read on a state department tour. Jane's response to India was profound. She came home enthralled with Indian people, clothes, art, food, and religion. During my visit I watched her slides with pleasure, and loved the Indian meals she cooked, but I also felt uncomfortable. It seemed that she was suddenly rejecting everything in her life that had preceded the Indian trip, including her religion and the very way she thought. Much later I understood that she was troubled to discover that Indians seemed to have a religion that felt true; how then could her own, different, belief also be true? At the time, when she expressed doubts about subjects I knew had always been important to her, and doubts about her own life, I thought she was indulging in intense rejection of herself. She talked and talked about seeing a dead baby in the Ganges, and how a new Indian friend allayed her dismay by explaining what his religion and culture made of that baby. I was wildly jealous of this man, Rajiv. I suppose I thought she didn't love me anymore, and only wanted Indians for her friends. At one point in the visit she insisted I was angry with her. I was, but denied it. I said she was angry with me, and she denied that.

A month or so later, Jane brought a poem about the dead baby in the Ganges, and her crisis of faith, to a workshop at my house in New Haven. We argued. She didn't know what I meant and I didn't know what she meant. Joyce tried to be decent to everybody. Jane found me unkind, and I was burning with jealousy and rage that my Jane should be rejected and dismissed—by herself. I felt that the poem, "Woman, Why Are You Weeping?," was asking us to concur in her self-rejection. (Later, Jane made some clarifying changes and I saw that I had misunderstood what she had in mind. The poem was never quite finished, and was not included in *Otherwise;* it was included in *A Hundred White Daffodils.*) Another poem, about Connecticut, was, I felt, contemptuous. I was hurt at that, too; I thought she was expressing disdain for the (non-Indian) place where I lived. I happened to be tired and tense, and I expressed my anxieties much too harshly; Jane was hurt and angry.

Still, before she left she helped me make a list of what I needed so that I too could attempt Indian cooking. She wrote a long list of ingredients: cardamom, coriander, cumin. The list, in Jane's distinctive handwriting with a few additions in mine, now hangs framed in my kitchen, where I do sometimes cook Indian food, though more timidly than she did.

Jane went home and wrote me a letter in which she threatened that if I was as harsh as I'd been, I'd destroy our friendship. She included a sticker on which she'd typed "Be Kind," saying the phrase came from the Dalai Lama. She'd applied one like it to her refrigerator and proposed that I apply this one to mine. I felt terrible and guilty, but I couldn't put a sticker reading "Be Kind" on my refrigerator. I just couldn't. I still have it.

After about a week of unceasing misery, I phoned the farm. Jane was out. Don listened to my story, saying sympathetically, "I know, I know," whenever I paused. As we spoke, Jane came home and took the phone. She said it had been the worst week of her life. We cried. We calmed down. I had bought a cookbook and was preparing Indian food. Jane wanted to know what I had in the house. A cauliflower? Let's see, what could I do with it . . . did I have ginger?

During those years, Jane and I saw each other, in addition to workshop meetings, quite often for people who lived two hundred miles apart. I wrote to her at least once a week and she wrote back when she could. She was the colleague in the next office. A moment after typing the last sentence of the first draft of my first novel, I rolled a new sheet of paper into the typewriter, typed "I finished my novel," and mailed that news to Jane.

When we were together, Jane and I didn't talk about writing as much as about friends and families and husbands, though we talked plenty about the writing life, about how to find time to write despite the legitimate needs of others. We climbed Mt. Kearsarge several times, Mt. Cardigan once, and took many walks near Eagle Pond Farm and in New Haven. Jane taught me to garden and visited the soup kitchen where I volunteer; it made her cry. When I visited the farm, we often cooked. Once we picked rhubarb from the field across the road from the house and made a strawberry rhubarb pie. "Let's make a dessert every time you come," Jane said. She hated being what she called "Suzy Homemaker," but she was an excellent, imaginative cook, ferociously devoted to health. I remember only one meal she cooked that I didn't especially like; it seems to me it was almost entirely beets. I have a recipe Jane gave me for a Brown Soda Bread she served me, made with steel-cut oats and cracked wheat flour. I called it Leisurely Breakfast Bread because it took so much time to chew and swallow, and cheated when I baked it, adding raisins. At times Jane was strict with herself to an impossible degree; the only poem of hers I don't much like is "Potato," about feeling guilty because she'd thrown out a partly rotted potato.

Jane's capacity for guilt was legendary. She felt guilty that George Bush was the president of the United States, though she hadn't voted for him. She felt guilty that Gus the dog trusted her when she offered him a biscuit. Joyce and I teased her about the poem "Biscuit," in which Jane speculated that she might have offered him a stone. We pointed out that Gus liked chewing stones.

Conversation with Jane was freer than the talk I've had with anyone else. It wasn't so much that we told each other secrets, as that we didn't consider any topics off-limits. Jane seemed willing to say anything to anybody. She and Don read together at Yale in the summer of 1989, when I was teaching in the summer school there. I introduced them to the Deputy Director of the Summer School, who said politely to Jane, "How are you?" Jane replied, "Premenstrual."

During my visits, there wasn't too much evidence of depression; I know that's because when it was really bad, she didn't let me come—which hurt, though I knew it shouldn't. She did tire easily, and, like a nursery school teacher, was always sending me off to take a nap. And Jane had a deep pessimism interwoven with her unmistakable delight in life, a pessimism that I think was her birthright as a depressive. When one of my sons was going through a hard time, she and I sat in my backyard, listening as he played his guitar and sang, and I found myself able to hear with Jane's ears: to hear the pain in his voice I'd been missing.

Occasionally I thought she detected pain that wasn't there, or exaggerated bearable pain. Another son wouldn't do his homework and failed math. She agonized for him, because she couldn't do math when she went to school, and dismissed my assurances that he could perfectly well do it if he'd just bother. When I finished reading a new story to the workshop, Jane would murmur, "So much pain!" Usually I was glad she saw it that way; I'd been trying to write about something hard, and other people sometimes didn't notice. In her letters I heard a great deal about depression and sadness:

> To give you an idea how my mind works when I'm down:
> When the paper toweling runs low on the roll it makes me
> sad! Everything makes me sad. Birdsong makes me sad. Late
> summer flowers make me sad, phlox and asters.

In the workshop and in our friendship, Jane taught me that kindness matters more than success, that success can't help but matter, that the main thing is to write simply and clearly—and that the main thing is to tell the truth about feeling, no matter how hard that is. She taught me that if only we three could be writers together, then maybe we could be writers. When she was lying ill in Seattle, in terrible pain from the radiation that accompanied the bone marrow transplant that might have saved her, she told me on the phone that she felt as if she were someone new. I think she felt different because she'd gone through so much, but also because she now had somebody else's marrow in her bones. We had talked and joked in advance about taking in a stranger's bone marrow, fascinated to learn that recipients acquire the blood type of the donor, if it's different, and become immune to diseases the donor has had instead of their own diseases. So when Jane said she felt like someone else, I couldn't quite take her seriously, but I also did take her seriously. "Do you still believe in God?" I asked her.

"Yes."

"Do you still believe that the natural object is always the adequate symbol?"

"Passionately," said Jane.

She hadn't changed all that much, so I asked if she still loved me. That week, we thought she'd live.

JANE KENYON

Seven Letters to Alice Mattison

5.28.85

Dear Alice—

Have I missed the second story in <u>The New Yorker</u>? I look eagerly every time.

I've been overly busy and underly inspired. . . .

Still no word from Knopf. Still no book of translations. If being an adult means that one can postpone gratification, I must be very grownup by now. Is it wrong to want fame and fortune? Probably. Better just want to be <u>good</u>. But let's get paid, too.

I am so bored. . . . I went to Ann Arbor, helped my mother put on a yard sale, came home and wrote a poem called "Yard Sale."

Boredom!

Last time I knew, Joyce's parents were coming to visit her during the time we were going to meet. And Lucy is going to be here from June 7–17th. So what's to become of our schedule I don't know.

I <u>need</u> to get together. I'm feeling discouraged and dry.

You must be through at Albertus. I feel a certain glee about it, vengeful person that I am. . . .

The washer is broken, the Saab is overheating, there's a problem somewhere in the drainage field. The world is too much with us. It <u>glugs</u>.

A high school in Peterborough, N.H. wrote to me,

asking me to participate next spring in their Young Authors Program. The letter begins, "Dear Mrs. Hall. . . ." Shall I kill them or just say I'm busy?

It's hormones, Alice. I'm ready to burst.

Are you well? Working? Reasonably content?

I miss you—

Love,

J.

P.S. We have procured a kitten named Ada. She's a little dickens. Gus is forlorn. I try to make it up to him by kissing his nose. . . .

---

27 March 89

Very dear Alice,

I'm slow to answer your letter because I thought I would see you this week, but our monthly visit has been delayed by Gussie's wild spring diarrhea—a word I <u>always</u> have to look up in the dictionary. He goes through this (we do) every spring. I've changed his name to Mr. Soupy Poopie. So you can see that I'm operating on a very high intellectual level here.

We had a wonderful vacation—I read Maxwell's <u>The Folded Leaf</u>—magnificent—you <u>lucky person</u> to hear him read! When we came back, however, we came back to a terrible thing. Our minister's wife, a woman of 81, got lost in the woods and died of exposure. I'll tell you about it when I see you. We all loved her, and we're all undone.

I'm going to read at the Blacksmith on April 6, and that afternoon Don and I plan to go out to Lexington and meet baby Elizabeth. I can't wait.

Did you send off "Cake Night"? I can't wait to see the new story. I'm accumulating some things I'll need help with. Elegant locution! I hope by June or so Joyce can see her way to a workshop.

Surely by now your cold is absolutely gone. Mine lasted 2½ weeks.

I have a new hospice patient, but I don't think I'll have her for long.

On the way to Barbados I bought a <u>New Yorker</u> and I read "Bears" on the plane, feeling proud.

Alice, <u>get your book typed</u>. Save your eyes, and the aggravation. It would be money well-spent.

I have drafted a poem about Barbados that is really the equivalent of "My Trip to Barbados: A Slide Presentation, Suitable for Senior Citizen Dinners."

Sunday is the Library of Congress "do." I think I'll try to buy a decent raincoat up in New London—"our nearest town that you would call a town"—this afternoon.

It's to be 60 degrees here today. The crocuses are up. Alas, so are the daffs and tulips, and they're going to be sorry one of these mornings when it's -2 degrees.

I miss you! We're coming on the 7th and I'll call—

Much love,

J.

(on Barbizon Hotel stationery)

12/4? 5?/89

Dear Alice,

We're staying in a birdcage here at the Barbizon. I mean this room is <u>tiny</u>, but it's where Oxford is housing its Sales Reps. Perkins will entertain them tomorrow at lunch.

I waved going through New Haven. It's Monday. You will have been at the soup kitchen.

It's so cold! It would be so terrible to be homeless in this weather.

I'm full of electricity. My clothes are clinging to me and I feel like a country mouse.

Perkins just let himself in with his plastic card with little holes in it that serves as a key. The porter reprogrammed it as we came in. We don't have these appurtenances in Danbury, N.H., 03230.

I plan to spend most of my time at the Metropolitan museum. I was dragged through the Hermitage in 1 hour so I guess in two days I can begin to see the Met.

I believe I am two blocks from Bloomingdales. I'll look into that.

Sunday was funny up our way. Our (S. Danbury Church) furnace wouldn't go on, so we invited ourselves to the Wilmot Center service, which Jack does before he comes over the back road to us. Well . . . the Wilmot Church furnace wouldn't go on either, so both congregations met in the Wilmot Library. It was charming in a way—packed, the first Sunday of Advent and Communion Sunday to boot. We sang lustily without the organ. It was different . . . Ours is a moveable feast.

We've survived hunting season. Gus and I had our picture taken for the new book jacket.

I'm going to have to crank it up and do some Christmas shopping. It has no clear antecedent.

Did R.A. go for the story? I feel in my bones that he did.

In a little while we're going up to see Andrew and Natalie and Miss Emily, bearing gifts.

This hotel has busloads of people with Iowa accents so I guess I don't have to worry that it's too snooty. I hate over-fancy hotels. There is no need for such a thing.

I'm always so amazed that people live here, Alice. You'll laugh at me.

Well, I hope the mushroom has been growing. I've been working . . . I changed the end of the "C" poem so that we <u>both</u> cry, and got rid of that Mysterious Boarder.

> Lots of love,
> Janie

1/1/90

Very Dear Alice,

It's the first morning of the new year and I just felt like saying hello. . . .

I couldn't walk with Gus this morning—it was too icy. I slipped three times before I got to the end of the drive. Poor little doggie. He kept looking around at me in distress. I got as far as the foot of New Canada before I realized it was just impossible. So everything feels off this morning. I forgot my prayers and my vitamin pills. . . .

Today I'm going to pack up a big box of coats I have that I never wear, and tomorrow I'll mail them to Rosie's Place, a women's shelter in Boston. My mother made some of these coats, and I have never liked them, sorry to say. Maybe some-one else will like them, or at least can use them.

This had better be the year for Joyce's book, or else. There will be a Penguin for you (!), a Graywolf for me, and four books for Perkins, God help us—the Oxford book of artistic anecdotes, the collected poems, a book of essays about New Hampshire, and a new edition of <u>Remembering Poets</u>. I look at it this way: If Perkins didn't work so hard, I wouldn't have the luxury of writing only what I want to write. I can live on chocolate truffles.

Cousin Forrest just came and sanded the drive.

I'm back to reading Proust. He flew off on a military tangent last night, describing battle theory. I was tempted to skip, the way people are tempted to skip the battles in <u>War and Peace</u>, which, of course, would be a great mistake. I have developed a way of reading Proust. I read it all, but I pay close attention only in the parts that really interest me. On love and art he's terribly good. Others have noticed this before me.

We've really gone amok in Panama, haven't we . . . I am ashamed of my President. When are we going to learn that we cannot rule the world?

My cold is hanging on. Perkins has a cold too, but I don't think it's my cold.

I saw an incorrect use of the apostrophe in a headline on the front page of <u>The Globe</u> this morning! What is this world coming to?

You probably have Boys underfoot, or do they take themselves off for the day? Boys and dogs.

I think I need another cup of coffee. It's only 9 and I'm winding down.

Well, chum, let's do our work, and as Richard Nixon used to say, "Let the chips fall where they may."

Happy new year and lots of love,
Janie

Thursday, Jan. 20.[1994]

Well, my dear,

It is 36 degrees below zero. The mercury is nearly invisible. I have to say that it is frightening. We decided not to go to Boston for the BSO rehearsal.

I shopped yesterday for my mom, and for us, and so the thing to do is stay home, make sure the pipes don't freeze, and wait for this to be over.

I've been in my study since 7:30 reading Dickinson, poking at poems, and staying in the light of my light box. At this point, I have one powerful headache, and I'm about to go downstairs and crawl back in bed. We are closer to the bears than we like to think.

We took a birthday cake to Dick yesterday, and you would think we had taken—I don't know what. I made a pot of coffee, and Dick brought Nan into the sitting room, and we had a little party. Nanny just beamed. Then Perkins took Dick out for a haircut, and I did some surreptitious cleaning. We never spent a couple of hours better in our lives.

Perko keeps running out for things—gas, milk, going to the bank. I think he is just showing off because his car will start.

Poor Gussie can't understand why I don't put on my running clothes. I keep letting him out and standing by the door until he is ready to come back in—an average of 57 seconds. He settles down for a while, then wants to go running again.

As I was waking up this morning I had a dream-like conviction that Blake's strange engraved figures are humanoids from UFO's. Then I had some coffee and came around.

I'm just going to stagger downstairs with this and put a stamp on it.

All love, wish you were here,

Janie

———

March 14, 1994

Dear Heart,

This is my first hour in my study, and the first act which I have committed on my typewriter. I wanted it to go to you.

I feel very shakey and strange, but you cannot imagine the joy I feel in being up here.

It is Monday morning. You are writing to me.

This morning I dropped the little box in which I had gathered all the stuff I use to dress my Hickman wound. A lot of it fell under the bed. I felt like putting my hand through the window. I felt like sobbing for an hour.

> I have to go now.
> I love you,

---

15 June 1994

Dearest Chum,

I'm sorry you got depressed. Friday evening was so very happy for me, for us. I guess we were all bound to get let down after it was over. Perkins and I both woke up just <u>black</u> on Monday morning.

He's turned out to have quite a cold, and he has slept in the parlor for two nights so I won't get it. It could be serious for me, although my counts are up enough now that I would have something to fight with.

I am simply dreading my sojourn at the hospital. I think I cannot bear a week, and then I think of three months. . . .

I've been poking at the poems I sent you and Joyce. They are almost ready to go, I think. I plan to try <u>The Atlantic</u>, and <u>Poetry</u>.

The gardens are such a mess, but the peonies are blooming now, and they seem not to have suffered from not being fertilized this spring. They are so luxurious. I'm picking them, and since the ones in back come on later than the ones along the porch, we'll have them for almost a month.

It's been terribly hot, even up here. The animals seem to suffer. Ada is fairly stoic, but I think she's pretty uncomfortable. Gus pants a lot. I will wet them down if they seem to be in real trouble.

You'll get used to working in your new office. I think you did a very smart thing when you rented it. It's impossible not to be vaguely aware of the boys, and their comings and goings, when you're home. This way you are really off limits.

I'm about out of energy and attention for the morning. Something shy of an hour seems to be what I can manage. I've been up here the last three mornings.

Oh, my shirt! I just love it. I only take it off to wash it!

> Love and more love,
> Janie

GREGORY ORR

from

Our Lady of Sorrows

A reminiscence of the collaboration between Joyce Peseroff, Alice Mattison, and Jane awakened some of my deepest memories of arriving in Ann Arbor in the fall of 1972. Somewhere pretty early on, Donald and Jane and I began to get together on a regular basis to work on our poems: marathon workshops with a peculiarly affectionate and powerful dynamic, one that I've never found since. I believe my presence there was important for Jane because it was a way for her to listen to Don's comments on her poems without still being his student. I existed as a kind of third point on a triangle, a buffer between them. These workshops were wonderful: honest, clear, funny. Well, one of the things that turns up in Don's poem "Without" is Jane's way of repeating something twice, and one of the things that I always remember from the workshops was a certain point at which she would just sit back a little bit and say, "What fun we're having. What *fun* we're having." Apparently she never realized that she was saying these things twice, but they seem very much to me to be incantatory blessings, and I'll try to persuade you of the significance of incantation. But there's another thing about these repetitions that seems to reach to the very essence of Jane, and that is the ability she had to be both completely present and aware, and at the same time to be, in some sense, "detached." I think of her hero Chekhov and his double nature, his insistence that the writer needs compassion down to his fingertips, which is another signature of Jane's being. But Chekhov also had the clinical eye of a scientist, the enormous capacity for detachment of a doctor. And this simultaneous engagement and distance is very much present in Jane's work.

I want to draw back a little bit. I have a feeling that, besides being a major poet of the personal lyric, there is something else happening with Jane, which goes back to the Romantics. Since the first movements of Romanticism there have been certain poets in whom the life, the legend, and the work braid together to create a larger significance for the culture. There's something about the figure—and I think this is clearly going to be true about Jane Kenyon—that calls out to some deep longing for meaning, meaning that is embodied in peculiar ways in the life itself. Two figures who immediately come to mind are John Keats and Emily Dickinson. In quite a different vein, we have Hart Crane and Dylan Thomas. I think also of William Blake, though perhaps that's just a personal prejudice . . . also Sylvia Plath, who has not been mentioned often in this gathering. I think of these figures as almost secular saints. Blake says somewhere that "true religion is the worship of great men." Obviously I'll transfer this to great poets, and simply stop there.

If Sylvia Plath was Our Lady of the Rages, Jane was Our Lady of the Sorrows, Our Lady of Vulnerability. And I'd like to look at Jane's story in a larger context, one in which we can try to understand what the example of her life and work is about . . . I'll say her work, and I think we'll see the life through the work.

I'd like to propose that at the heart of what I'm saying is the issue of vulnerability of the self. And so I want to propose a few kinds of models of what it is like to be an individual self in the world. I've always felt it involved an enormous amount of terror. This comes out of my own life, but I'm grateful that it corresponds in some ways to things in Jane's life. Here is a self, an embodied self, bisected by the present moment. Here's how we exist in the world.

Everything that has happened to us has vanished, everything in the past moment is gone. All that we loved, all that we dreaded, all that we ate for breakfast have vanished forever. In front of us is the blank screen of the unknowable next moment; we exist in this world without knowing what's going to happen next. How can we know? It's not revealed to us. So here we are already poised between the vanished past, which has vanished even as I speak of it, and an unknowable next moment. Let's say I add another dollop of dread and within us we have what I would call the buried self, which is all of the things inside us: feelings, sensations, thoughts, images, memories, painful memories that have migrated out of the vanished past to take up residence inside us. And we have the voice inside us that will never shut up, at least I do; God help me if I'm speaking to an audience who doesn't know what I'm talking about. I like to think of it as "Radio Free Brain," this twenty-four-hour broadcasting station. And believe me, it's not like NPR, giving lucid essays and commentary; it's just chattering. It's both a running commentary on the chaos of what it is to be inside my head, and an aspect of that chaos itself.

This moves us to something that I would call a double awareness. To begin with, the role of disorder in our lives is enormous. It takes the form of randomness, accident, the unknowable. It takes the form of the chaos of feelings inside us. This disorder, by the way, is not a moral term. Passionate love and joy are as disordering as grief and despair. We all know that; I'll later propose that the reason we write love poems is to try to make order out of our chaos. This disorder exists both subjectively and objectively. It exists in war; it exists in weather. One thinks of addiction, dysfunctional families, the loss of a loved one—are these outside or inside events? The answer, of course, is that they exist in both places.

So what we have now is this enormous, almost overwhelming experience of disorder, and an equally strong human need for order, a human need to believe in some kind of coherence. In fact I think our minds function spontaneously with a kind of interplay between these two powers. All of us face the blank screen of the unknowable next moment. And our minds spontaneously respond to that disorder, that awareness of anxiety, with ordering powers. Every one of you knows this—you're walking into a situation in which you don't know what's going to happen, and your mind just spontaneously creates possible images and scenarios. We do this all the time; we don't necessarily focus on it, nor are we even always aware we're doing it. Sometimes the scenarios are terrible, sometimes they're glorious, but either way they serve to allay anxiety and dread; they're how we live. What's beautiful about poetry is its capacity to translate this human experience of disorder and the need for order into language; to translate it up out of the physical world into the world of language where the poem can be constructed as a replica, a drama of this interplay of disorder and order. It's not a translation of chaos into cosmos; I think poetry is far deeper than that. What it does is *mirror* the interplay; it proposes both disorderings and orderings. And this holds true all the way from an epic like the *Iliad* down to Issa's haiku about the death of his son.

I'd like to shift now to what I think Jane Kenyon writes, the personal lyric, which takes the story of the "I," the individual self. I think culture invented lyric poetry along with religion and philosophy to help people understand the world, and to discover ordering powers. But religion and philosophy are different in that they propose external ordering powers that exist outside the self, and that the self must align with. What's amazing about the personal lyric is that culture gives the individual self the tools to order and the self has to do the ordering itself. It's a personal struggle, a struggle to create what Robert Frost calls "a momentary stay against confusion." This is what the lyric poem is: a gift from culture to the self to deal with existential crises. What do I mean by existential crises? I mean all kinds of disorder, but especially the buried self, the world of feeling and subjectivity, what it means to be a self in the world. The personal lyric, in some ways, dominates Western poetry since the Romantics, for certain historical reasons having to do with the collapse of other cultural ordering powers, both political and religious. But what we really need to know about the personal lyric is that it has existed in *all* cultures at all times. The personal poem, with an "I" who speaks in an attempt to order its joy or grief, exists now in every culture on the planet, which is about 3,000 different cultures. It has existed in every culture we know about historically. There are incredibly sexy love poems from the New Kingdom, Egypt, 3,300 years ago that could pass for wonderfully contemporary erotic poems. There are poems of grieving and loss in the *Chinese Book of Odes,* again written 3,000 years ago. These are personal lyrics: the lament, the love poem. Love and death—the two major crises of the self.

Poetry offers us the formal ordering power of incantation, the repeated line. It offers us story, conflict moving toward some kind of resolution. Jane Kenyon is a great poet of story—to arrange, to relate a narrative with a beginning, a middle, and an end with proportionate parts, with details emphasized, noticed perfectly. Isak Dinesen once said, "Any sorrow can be borne if it can be made into a story, or if a story can be told about it." Certainly story is at the heart of Jane's poems. Incantation is also central to Jane's poems: the magical repetition of phrases like the rhythmic moans a grieving mother might make. The repetition of a phrase has survival power: "Let evening come. Let evening come." "It might have been otherwise. It might have been otherwise." These incantatory orderings are set against enormous possibilities of disorder. A third ordering power that is strongly present in Jane's work is the ability of the self to go out into the world, to become an "other," to feel what an "other" feels. It has to do with the self being permeable, something that opens itself to the world, as in Walt Whitman's poem, "There was a child went forth every day, and the first object he looked upon, that object he became,/ And that object became part of him..." There's this reciprocity between the self and the world which is deeply at work in Jane's poetry, and in the work of the self trying to survive. It's the force of eros, the force of connection with the world. We can see this in Wendell Berry's poetry, where the natural world is connected through eros, through wedding, through husbandry. The forces of eros that connect self to other self, self to world, are opposed by the forces of thanatos, of death, of isolation. Paul Breslin talked about what happens when the anti-urge, thanatos, overwhelms the self. The ability to notice, to see collapses; the self closes in and can no longer connect to the world as Jane so completely does in her moments of beatitude.

Maybe what I want to say is that this opening of the self to disorder seems to be the way the lyric teaches us to survive. The dominant ideology in our culture says the way to survive disorder is to put on armor and pick up a sword, to survive by the way of the warrior. You overwhelm; you control. The lyric poem proposes a different path. It says that the way to survive disorder is to become vulnerable to whatever the disorder is. We see this in D.H. Lawrence's poem "Song of a Man Who Has Come Through," written in 1914:

> Not I, not I, but the wind that blows through me!
> A fine wind is blowing the new direction of Time.
> If only I let it bear me, carry me, if only it carry me!
> If only I am sensitive, subtle, oh, delicate, a winged gift!
> If only, most lovely of all, I yield myself and am borrowed
> By the fine, fine wind that takes its course through
> the chaos of the world
> Like a fine, an exquisite chisel, a wedge-blade inserted;
> If only I am keen and hard like the sheer tip of a wedge
> Driven by invisible blows,
> The rock will split, we shall come at the wonder, we shall
> find the Hesperides.
>
> Oh, for the wonder that bubbles into my soul,
> I would be a good fountain, a good well-head,
> Would blur no whisper, spoil no expression.
>
> What is the knocking?
> What is the knocking at the door in the night?
> It is somebody wants to do us harm.
>
> No, no, it is the three strange angels.
> Admit them, admit them.

It's a weird poem, right? Don't ask me what it means, except that the "winged gift" seems to take a wrong turn in becoming this "wedge-blade inserted." The speaker picks up a sword and starts whacking away at the rock in an attempt to get to the water within. Good luck! It clearly doesn't work; he says, "What is the knocking?" and suddenly there's a sense of terror, of the self in jeopardy again. "What is the knocking at the door in the night? It is somebody wants to do us harm." This is the sense of self at risk, vulnerable, terrified. And then this other voice—where did this other voice come from? We haven't even been oriented in a landscape, but there we are in a house and someone's knocking at the door in the middle of the night, which to me is an image of terror. Even though we don't live in a police state, I'm still not happy when someone knocks on my door at night. "Somebody wants to do us harm," and then this other voice responds, "No, no, it is the three strange angels. Admit them, admit them." What are these angels? They're strange. They're not from God. We could make them Biblical if we wanted to, but I think they're weirder than that. They're strange angels. The answer lies not in what they are but what we do with them, which is admit them. Admit that they exist. Let them into the architecture of our security. Let them enter the self; let the self become vulnerable to them. This is what Keats calls negative capability—not negative in the sense of "anti-" anything, but rather a receptive passivity, an opening of the self to disorder without anxious reaching after fact and reason.

Jane's work is superbly exemplary of that path of vulnerability, that opening to the disorders of subjectivity. It could of course be said that she had no choice, that such things as depression are already inside the self, and announce themselves regardless. But that's beside the point. The point is not about whether disorder manifests itself in our lives, but what the act of admitting these angels can do, what the act of writing a poem can do. It seems to me that it does two things. First we have to allow ourselves to be open to this risk, to let angels in. It's like what Theodore Roethke says, "The edge is what I have." Why do we do this? Because we want to survive. How does a poet do this, how does Jane Kenyon do this? The poet survives by writing the poem. The act of writing is itself the struggle to survive, and it works. The proof is that the poem exists; it's that simple. The existence of a poem is proof that a suffering self survived whatever the disorder was by creating a symbolic drama of its struggle. In this light you can see that even Sylvia Plath's fiercest and most apocalyptic poems are poems of survival. Certainly Jane's poem "Having It Out with Melancholy" is an instance of somebody opening up to disorder and surviving through the ordering powers of imagination. Theodore Roethke says, "This shaking keeps me steady. I should know." The way of the lyric poem is a terrifying way; the order only lasts for that moment. As Frost warns us: it's only a *momentary* stay against confusion. This is how Sylvia Plath can write a poem of great, great rage and survive that rage, and then three months later commit suicide. Because unfortunately this is the problem with lyric poetry: it's only as good as the moment it helps you to survive. Every poet can tell you this. We can't write a poem of enormous desolation, survive that desolation, and then read it next week in order to be consoled; somehow it just doesn't work past the moment.

But there is more at stake than the survival of the poet. The second survival is the survival of the reader. The lyric poem reaches out and helps the reader to live by echoing or representing some kind of analogue to an experience he or she has had. In other words, the personal lyric extends an invitation by presenting an experience with which the reader can sympathetically identify. This is the invitation that Whitman extends at the very opening of his poem "Song of Myself": "What I assume, you shall assume, for every atom belonging to me as good belongs to you." It's an invitation we consider every time we pick up a poem, and the poems that we embrace, that enter our lives, are the poems that we identify with. If we don't identify with them, they're not interesting to us. But the poems that we take inside help us to live. They give us hope and courage, which are *terribly fundamental human gifts* from one self to another. Stanley Kunitz once said that the poem is "the voice of the solitary that makes others less alone."

Jane's poem "Man Waking" is one that seems to come out of the depths. *De Profundis* is the Latin opening to one of the psalms: "Out of the depths we call to Thee, oh Lord." This is song, a poem from the abyss. It's interesting that it's not in the first person, as "Having It Out with Melancholy" is; it's her entering another person's life, as she does in the Gettysburg poem. I wish I could read the Gettysburg poem; then I could say to you, "This is what Whitman does when he says, 'I do not ask the wounded person how he feels. I myself become the wounded person. My hurts turn livid upon me as I lean on a cane and observe.'" Keats calls it "the chameleon poet," which is a more raucous term for this kind of sympathetic identification, this ability to become an other. I would add that there's also something eerie in Whitman's assumption of stigmata: "My hurts turn livid upon me as I lean on a cane and observe." Here is this simultaneous involvement and detachment of Chekhov's work, of Jane's work. Here is Whitman's proclamation that "Agonies are one of my changes of garments." He both becomes that other suffering self, which is terrifying, and observes that self from a distance. Here is "Man Waking":

> The room was already light when
> he awoke, and his body curled
> like a grub suddenly exposed
> when something dislodges a stone.
> Work. He was more than an hour
> late. Let that pass, he thought.
> He pulled the covers over his head.
> The smell of his skin and hair
> offended him. Now he drew his legs
> up a little more, and sent
> his forehead down to meet his knees.
> His knees felt cool.
> A surprising amount of life
> came through the blanket. He could
> easily see his hand. Not dark enough,
> not the utter darkness he desired.

To me this is a poem of pure thanatos, of isolation, of retreat into depression and despair. The man doesn't even want to see his hand, an object that connects him to the world. But the amazing thing about a poem that comes of the depths, out of the abyss, is this: it tells us that the human spirit still exists even at these depths; that it can give shape and form, articulate expression, to its condition, and this gives us hope.

There's one last thing I want to say, which is that there seem to be certain poets who are not simply poets of survival, but poets of transformation. They've not just expressed and regulated their subjectivity, they've transformed it into values and principles that one can live by. These values are frighteningly contingent, but they *are* values, and they're different than the ones offered us by the dominant culture. I do want to say that Kenyon seems to me to be one of these poets whose work transforms subjectivity this way, and this is why her life, her work, and her legend have arrived at this power of healing, the way saints were imagined to be able to intercede for us. It is the power of innerness and passion to create meaning. There's a list of values that lyric poets have created beginning with Sappho, who said, "Whatever one loves most is beautiful." She also says, "I have a daughter Cleis, golden as a flower. To me she's worth more than all the gold in Lydia." This is tenderness, intimacy; it's another one of the lyric values that poets have created, and that exists wonderfully in Jane's work. In the poem "September Garden Party" she goes back inside the house and waits, imagining fingers coming up her thighs. This is the image the poem ends on: the mutuality of sex, sex as reciprocity of gift.

Wrath, I think, is also a lyric value. It's Blake's rage; the rage of "Howl"; the rage of Philip Levine's "They Feed the Lion." It's the political rage of Adrienne Rich; the intimate rage of Sylvia Plath's "Daddy" or "Lady Lazarus." The rage of the victim, which creates power out of powerlessness. It is, of course, linked to the Old Testament prophets. Also those twin pillars of Whitman's vision: pride and sympathy, sympathy above all—this is what Jane Kenyon does so completely. Charles Baudelaire says somewhere that there are certain states of being in which every-thing before your eyes—every object, every thing, every action that unfolds—is a perfect symbol; that all the poet has to do is record what's there. Jane Kenyon talked about reporting things, as if this was what she did in her darker moments; "I only report things." Elizabeth Bishop used to say, "I just write down what happens," which is, of course, to-tally absurd. What they both had was this power of locating moments that perfectly symbolize a state of being in which the self is seen in the world. Sometimes it takes focused moments. One thinks especially of flowers with Jane, the moment in "Peonies at Dusk" where she pulls the peony toward herself and examines it the way one would examine a beloved's face. One also thinks of Gus the dog, who is that joyous aspect of her being that most revels in the sensory world, the world of embodiment and incarnation where we live and suffer. Finally, I'd like to quote some lines from a beautiful poem of hers called "The Stroller," a section in which, again, you see this kind of reciprocity. She's look-ing at a drawing her father made of her childhood stroller, and says, "Looking at it/ is like looking into a mirror/ and seeing your own eyes and someone else's/ eyes as well . . ."

GALWAY KINNELL

How Could She Not

for Jane Kenyon (1947–1995)

It is a day after many days of storms.
Having been washed and washed, the air glitters;
small heaped cumuli are carried across the sky;
a brief shower, its parallel streaks
visible against the firs, douses the crocuses.
We knew it would happen one day this week.
Now, hearing that she has died, from the open door
I look across at New Hampshire. There, too, the sun
is bright and clouds are making their shadowy ways
along the horizon. How could it not have been today?
In another room, Kiri Te Kanawa is singing
the *Laudate Dominum* of Mozart—
as if deep in the past, her voice barely hearable
above the whisperings of rows of scythes
and the rattlings of horse-drawn mowing machines
drawing their cutter bar's little reciprocating
triangles through the timothy—to the stalks
being made to lie down in the sunshine.
In the dark of early this morning, did she wake
almost used up by this year of pain and despair
remitted briefly now and then by hope
that had the undertaste of lead? In first light,
did she glimpse the world as she had loved it,
and see that now it would not be wrong

for her to die and that she could leave
her beloved in a day like paradise?
At sunrise, did she loosen her hold a little?
Having these last days spoken her whole heart
to him, who spoke his whole heart to her,
might she have felt that now, in the silence,
he would not feel that any word was missing?
How could she not have slipped into a spell,
when full daylight came, with him next to her,
his arms holding her, as they had held her,
it may then have seemed, all her life?
How could her cheek not have pressed
itself a moment to his cheek, which presses
itself to hers from now on? How could she not
rise and go, with so much sunlight at the window,
loved arms around her, and the sound, fading,
deepening, hard to say, of a single-engine
plane in the distance no one else hears?

MAXINE KUMIN

Dinner at Jane and Don's

Dinner at Jane and Don's. I am unable to pinpoint the date but it must have taken place in the early 1980s. All four of us were still relative newcomers to New Hampshire. In 1975, after his grandmother's death at the age of ninety-seven, Jane and Don had come back from Michigan to Eagle Pond Farm. The plan was to spend a year there, but at some point the decision was taken to make this a permanent move. They went back to Ann Arbor to pack up the house and then returned to Don's grandparent's farmhouse for good.

In 1976, the last child gone, we had made the decision to move full-time to the ancient farmhouse we had bought on the cheap in 1963 and used carelessly as a summer camp and weekend retreat for thirteen years. Repairing roofs, dealing with recalcitrant plumbing, discovering gap-toothed hay rakes and broken bits of workhorse harness in old barns were endeavors we two couples had in common.

Before dinner, a tour of the Hall/Kenyon renovations. The old first-floor bathroom was no more. The bedroom had been reborn as a modern bath and laundry. A new bedroom extended from the back of the house. A sign over the bathroom door announced that this was the Caldecott Room, a nod to the children's book prize Don had won for *The Ox Cart Man* in 1980, which had made these renovations possible. The ell created by the addition allowed for a secret garden, its bricks laid by Jane, where she cultivated her lilies—lilies that toil not, nor do they spin—and labor-intensive peonies. It was high summer and I remember the peonies, both burgundy and white, were wide-open. Fulsome and fragrant flowers, they had been my mother's favorite, too. No wonder a frisson went through me.

I wish I could say I remember the menu, but I do not. Don's tall, red-headed son Andrew was there, newly graduated from the University of Wisconsin. There were candles and flowers on the table. A good wine went around. Jane served graciously amid the animated conversation. When the main course was completed, she announced that Perkins would clear and bring in dessert. This startled me; I had until then not been aware that someone else lurked in the kitchen, waiting to perform the homely chores of cleaning up. When Don rose and began to gather the plates, I finally caught on.

So much has been said and written about Perkins and Jane that I hesitate here. For more than twenty years we remained friends on our two farms on either side of Mt. Kearsarge. While I may never cultivate a peony, I always think of Jane when our lilies bud up in early summer.

WENDELL BERRY

Sweetness Preserved

I am going to talk about some poems—lyric poems—as the products of a story. Most poems, whether or not they tell or contain stories, come out of stories, and often they bear reference to the stories they come out of. For a couple of generations now, critics and teachers have not thought it wise to approach poems by way of stories. They have thought that poems should be read "as poems" or "as texts," as words written or printed on a page, ignoring the story the poems come out of.

I am willing to suppose (for the sake of thought) that such poems as I am going to talk about must finally shrug off their stories, and all else they do not explicitly contain, and stand before us on their own. I am aware that some poems stand before us on their own because they must; we do not know the stories they came out of. But in reading poems that are perfectly anonymous, we still know that there is more to them than the "text." We think of a poem and in the same thought think of what it is about, if it is about anything. Literature involves more than literature, or we would not be grateful for it.

Suppose we know not only a body of poetry but also the story that the poetry came out of. How then are we to help knowing what we know? How are we to help knowing, for instance, that some poets are pilgrims, and that their poems are not just *objets d'art,* but records, reports, road signs, or trail markers? By what curious privilege are we allowed to ignore what we know?

But I would like to go a little further still, and honor the possibility that the stories that poems come out of are valuable in themselves, so far as they are known. Those who are living and writing at a given time are not just isolated poetry dispensers more or less equivalent to soft-drink machines, awaiting the small change of critical approval. We are, figuratively at least, members of a community, joined together by our stories. We are inevitably collaborators. We are never in any simple sense the authors of our own work. The body of work we make for ourselves in our time is only remotely a matter of literary history, which we think too much about. The work we make is the work we are living by, and not in the hope of making literary history, but in the hope of using, correcting so far as we are able, and passing on the art of human life, of human flourishing, which includes the arts of reading and writing poetry.

There is a danger of presumption or imposition in what I am about to do, for I am not an authority on the story I am going to talk about. The complete story of a person's life cannot be entirely known or told. However, I do know unavoidably and unforgettably that Jane Kenyon's poems came out of a story. I know as well that Donald Hall's did. And I know that the poems of both poets came to a considerable extent out of the same story—or perhaps out of the intersection or overlapping of two stories; I want my language to be accurate and courteous, and am not confident of my ability to make it so.

The story of Donald Hall and Jane Kenyon is not my story. And yet their story is not absolutely distinct from mine, for their story is one I have depended on, and have spent a good deal of time telling over to myself and thinking about. And of course I have been attentive to the poems that came out of it. Their story and their poems have affected, instructed, troubled, consoled, and clarified my understanding of my own story.

Because I am a storyteller and was from childhood a hearer and reader (and believer) of stories, I have always known that people live in stories. And so it has been a little shocking to me to realize also that it is possible for people to wander outside their stories. When

Donald Hall and I first met, at a literary party in Manhattan in the winter of 1963, both of us were living outside our stories. I find it readily supposable that Don didn't know what to make of me, even if it is supposable that he tried to make anything of me at all. I certainly didn't know what to make of him, and the reason was that I didn't know what to make of anything. Later, when both of us were again living inside our stories, we would recognize each other and become friends. This happened, I think, because we both loved our grandparents and we both derived from childhood homeplaces that we did not like to forsake. We have corresponded in two ways.

At the time of the party in 1963, the two of us were in "exile." I give that word an emphasis because it was so important and applied so peculiarly to young writers in our generation. We came to our calling in the shadow (and the glamour) of eminent literary exiles: James, Pound, Eliot, Joyce, Stein, Hemingway, and others. Moreover, those in charge of our education tended to think that they were preparing us for careers, not for settling down anyplace. The question before us seemed to be, not how we might fit ourselves and our book knowledge into our home landscapes, but how we would fit into our careers, which is to say our exile.

This is confirmed by Donald Hall's early poem entitled "Exile." Looking back at that poem now, I find nothing in it that surprises me. It is a good poem. It is also an inevitable product of the poet's era and education; it had to be written by somebody. It states the case beautifully:

> Imagining, by exile kept from fact,
> We build of distance mental rock and tree,
> And make of memory creative act.

This is an exact enough description of the poet's job of work in Don's "Elegy for Wesley Wells," also an early poem. It too is a good poem—I don't mean at all to be denigrating this work of "exile." In the "Elegy," the poet mourns and celebrates his grandfather, Wesley

Wells, a New Hampshire farmer, a good one apparently, but one belonging to an age that, at the time of the poem, is "bygone." The poet (in the way of a young elegist, which I was once myself) is hoping to grant a measure of immortality to his grandfather by means of his poem. It is, to me, an extraordinarily moving poem. I have never read it without being moved by it, though by now I have lived beyond the notion that immortality can be conferred by a poem, and though by now my reading of the poem is influenced by my knowledge of a story that the poem, so to speak, does not know. When I read "Elegy for Wesley Wells" now, I feel a humorousness and a sadness that the poem did not anticipate.

In immortalizing his grandfather Wells, Donald Hall the young elegist is also immortalizing a part of his own life, which he now considers to be finished. That life, if it is to have a present life, must have the immortal life of art. Maybe you are outside your life when you think your past has ended. Maybe you are outside your life when you think you are outside it. I don't know what Donald Hall in later life would say. I know only what I in later life would say. I would say, partly from knowing the story I am talking about, that though you may get a new life, you can't get a new past. You don't get to leave your story. If you leave your story, then how you left your story *is* your story, and you had better not forget it.

Now I want to refer to another poem that is a landmark both in the story I am dealing with and in my own consciousness of poetry and of the world. This is the poem called "Maple Syrup," written about twenty-five years after "Elegy for Wesley Wells." The poem tells about an experience shared by a couple designated merely as "we." Since I am observing no critical conventions here, I will say that this "we" is comprised of the poet Donald Hall and the poet Jane Kenyon, who have returned to the house of Donald Hall's grandparents, Kate and Wesley Wells. The two poets, married to each other, will live their life together in this house on this farm, relinquished and immortalized in the "Elegy" so many years before. In the poem "Maple Syrup" they go through the house together, to "the back chamber" full of artifacts and relics, and then down into "the root cellar," where they find a quart of maple syrup left there by Wesley Wells. And here I must let the poem speak:

> Today
> we take my grandfather's last
> quart of syrup
> upstairs, holding it gingerly,
> and we wash off twenty-five years
> of dirt, and we pull
> and pry the lid up, cutting the stiff
> dried rubber gasket, and dip our fingers
> in, you and I both, and taste
> the sweetness, you for the first time,
> the sweetness preserved, of a dead man . . .

We (that is, now, the poet and his readers) have come a long way from "Elegy for Wesley Wells." We have left the immortality of art and have come, by way of a sort of mortalization, to a communion of lovers with each other and with the dead, which is to say that we have come to a marriage rite, joining two mortals to each other and to other mortals, bringing them perhaps within imaginable reach of a more authentic idea of immortality. Donald Hall, who in the "Elegy" is maybe a sort of bard, has now become, in the full and mysterious sense, a love poet. Or we might say that, having started out to be a professional, he has become an amateur, working (like the best kind of professional) for love. The sign of this is that the memory of Wesley Wells, once elegized into a mental landscape of the finished past, has become a living faculty of the poet's mind and imagination. The sweetness of the dead man, now, is not preserved in an artifact but in the lives of those who taste it.

One more thing. Because this rite of marriage occurs in this story, it does not give new life just to the couple, who now enter into its "one flesh"; it gives new life also to the dead and to an old house. It matters that this is an old house that is familiar to the bridegroom. If the house had been sold to strangers, according to the common destiny of old houses in our day, Wesley Wells's quart of syrup, if found, would have been thrown away. It would have seemed fearfully old and fearfully anonymous. To Don, and to Jane, trusting Don, it was mortal and everlasting, old and new, and sweet.

Having set up (so to speak) these two landmarks, an elegy and a celebration of marriage, I am much more moved than I would be by either of the poems alone, for I know the story that joins them. The two poems are joined by this story because the story of Donald Hall had become also (to the degree that separate stories do converge) the story of Jane Kenyon.

What had happened was that these two stories had converged in one of the stages of Donald Hall's exile, teaching at the University of Michigan, and their convergence had made him free to return to the family house in New Hampshire. The agent of this freedom was Jane Kenyon who said, according to her husband, "Why are we thinking of *here,* when there is New Hampshire?"

Not long after Don and Jane were settled at Eagle Pond, Don wrote to me, telling what they had done, and I wrote back some advice: don't take on too much farming too quickly. Don has pointed out the advice was wasted, since he did not intend to take on any farming at all—leaving me with the consolation that, anyhow, if he had needed it, it would have been good advice.

I am not sure when I met Jane, except that it was a good while ago, when she and Don were still heating their house with a very handsome wood-burning stove. I was on a speaking and reading trip in New England, and was able to stop by just for a short visit and lunch at a local eating place. I remember a tour of the house, but not much that was said. I remember being impressed by Jane's self-possession and dignity and quietness. These qualities continued to impress me after I knew her better. She was a writer, but she appeared to be watching "the literary world" without anxiety or great excitement.

Now the requirement of honesty is going to embarrass me, for I have to confess that I didn't read anything by Jane for a long time after I met her. For one reason, I felt a certain complicated sympathy for her—a poet who had set up shop smack in the middle of another poet's subject. The other poet's claim to this subject was well established; the other poet was her husband. It was easy to wish what she might have been, say, a painter. Another reason was that I liked her, and if she was a bad poet I did not want to know. (I'm hoping not to discover that such feelings are unique.)

And then Bert Hornback invited Don and Galway Kinnell and Seamus Heaney and me to give a reading at the University of Michigan in January of 1986. For this there was a reason and a real reason. The reason was the public reading on Friday night. The real reason was that Bert wanted his students to have a late breakfast and conversation with the visiting poets on Saturday. In this age of careerist "research professors," Bert is a real teacher who thinks nothing of the trouble it takes to capture poets alive to talk with his students.

The visitors gathered at Bert's house for supper before the reading. When I came into the kitchen as the mingling and talking began, Jane was standing by the refrigerator, watching the situation develop with the composure that I mentioned before. For the sake of political correctness I have been trying to avoid saying that Jane was beautiful, but of course she was, and of course I could see that she was. When we greeted each other, she said, "Wendell, I can't give you a hug. I have a bad cold." Baffled utterly by this generosity, I remember thinking that I had nothing better to do than catch a bad cold.

I have to go ahead and confess also that I do not greatly love literary occasions. The reading on Friday night was as readings are. The occasion beginning at breakfast on Saturday, however, was a literary occasion that surpassed itself. It was a *friendly* occasion, one of the loveliest that I have known. What I so liked about it was that everybody was talking for pleasure. There was no contention. Nobody defended a "position." There was much laughter. The students were hesitant to take part, but after a while they too entered into the conversation, and we had that additional pleasure.

Finally, late in the day, somebody—I don't remember who; it wasn't me—said, "Jane, why don't you read us a poem?" Jane, who had been sitting almost outside the room, saying little, perhaps nothing at all, during the conversation, fished up from somewhere a page that she had brought with her and spread it open to read. For me, this was the only uncomfortable moment of the day. I don't remember what I thought, but it would have been like me to have started trying to think of some ambiguous compliment to make in case I thought the poem was bad—something like "Well, Jane, you certainly do write poetry." And then that quiet woman read beautifully her poem "Twilight: After Haying":

> Yes, long shadows go out
> from the bales; and yes, the soul
> must part from the body:
> what else could it do?
>
> The men sprawl near the baler,
> too tired to leave the field.
> They talk and smoke,
> and the tips of their cigarettes
> blaze like small roses
> in the night air. (It arrived
> and settled among them
> before they were aware.)
>
> The moon comes
> to count the bales,
> and the dispossessed—
> *Whip-poor-will, Whip-poor-will*
> —sings from the dusty stubble.
>
> These things happen . . . the soul's bliss
> and suffering are bound together
> like the grasses. . . .

The last, sweet exhalations
of timothy and vetch
go out with the song of the bird;
the ravaged field
grows wet with dew.

I hope I have adequately prepared you to imagine my relief. Now I must ask you to imagine something else. However many poets there may be who know from experience the subject of this poem by Jane Kenyon, I surely am one of them. I have lived countless times through that moment at the end of a day's work when its difficulty and heat and weariness take on a kind of sublimity and you know that you are alive both in the world and in something greater, when it is time to go and yet you stay on, charmed. I had never tried to write a poem about it, and that day, when I had heard Jane read her poem, I knew that I would not need to write one; Jane had written better about it than I could. Sometimes I feel competitive or jealous when I *suspect* that somebody has written better than I can about something I know. When I am *certain* that somebody has done so, then I am relieved, and I feel happy. "Twilight: After Haying" made me happy that day in 1986, and it has made me happy every time I have read it since.

Wittgenstein said, "In art [and, I assume, in writing about art] it is hard to say anything as good as: saying nothing." I believe and honor that, and I keep it in mind. But also we obviously need to speak from time to time of the things that have moved us. We need to wonder, for instance, why we remember some things and forget others. I have remembered Jane's reading of her poem that day, I think, because it was impossible to mistake the revelation of the event: here was a poet present in her work with an authority virtually absolute. I don't mean that she is in the poem personally, but that all her gifts are in it: her quietness, gentleness, compassion, elegance, and clarity, her awareness of mystery, her almost severe good sense. This poem, like just about every one of her poems, is unconditional; it is poetry without

qualification. It has no irony, no cynicism, no self-conscious reference to literary history, no anxiety about its place in literary history,
no glance at the reader, no anticipation of the critic, no sensational-
ism, no self-apology or self-indulgence. How many poets of our time
have been so unarmed as to say, "The moon comes / to count the
bales . . ."? As she herself said (in the next poem of *The Boat of Quiet
Hours*):

> These lines are written
> by an animal, an angel,
> a stranger sitting in my chair;
> by someone who already knows
> how to live without trouble
> among books, and pots and pans. . . .

—which is to say that she was authentically a poet of inspiration.

And this, to return to the story, seems to have settled pretty
quickly the artistic problem of a shared life and subject. My wife
Tanya has pointed out to me, from her knowledge of her own story,
that Jane Kenyon had become, in fact, an exile in the very place that
her husband had once felt himself to be exiled from. For a while after
coming to Eagle Pond, she seems to have remembered "Ruth amid
the alien corn":

> I'm the one who worries
> if I fit in with the furniture
> and the landscape.

And:

> Maybe
> I don't belong here.
> Nothing tells me that I don't.

But such lines as these testify to a radically different approach to the problem of exile. The modern American version of exile is a rootless and wandering life in foreign lands or (amounting to about the same thing) in American universities. Jane Kenyon, like Ruth of old, understood her exile as resettlement. Very few American exiles, and not many American settlers, have asked "if I fit in with . . . the landscape" or worried about belonging to a place. And already one is aware of her originality, as one continues always to be aware of it. I mean "originality" in what I take to be the best sense: not the enactment of a certain kind of literary intention or ambition, but the grace to submit to influence—the influence of places, passages of scripture, works of art; the influence of all her subjects—and the grace and patience to find within herself the means to respond. Her contribution to this story is hers distinctly.

When I read a disparagement of the book *Otherwise* in the *Hudson Review,* I was offended, but also puzzled. How could anybody able to read fail to see the quality of that book? But after a while, I believe, I figured it out. Jane Kenyon's work, in fact, makes an unnegotiable demand upon a reader. It doesn't demand great intellect or learning or even sympathy; it demands quiet. It demands that in this age of political, economic, educational, and recreational pandemonium, and a concomitant rattling in the literary world, one must somehow become quiet enough to listen. Her poems raise unequivocally the issue of the quality of the poet's ear.

A true poem, we know, forms itself within hearing. It must live in the ear before it can live in the mind or the heart. The ear tells the poet when and how to break the silence, and when enough has been said. If one has no ear, then one has no art and is no poet. There is no appeal from this. If one has no ear, it does not matter what or how one writes. Without an ear, the traditional forms will not produce George Herbert, nor will "free verse" give us William Carlos Williams.

Jane Kenyon had a virtually faultless ear. She was an exquisite master of the art of poetry. Her voice always carries the tremor of feeling disciplined by art. This is what over and over again enabled her to take the risk of plainness, or of apparent plainness. Her ear controls rhythm and sound, and also tone. It is tone as much as anything that makes one able to say what is unusual or unexpected. It is because of her perfection of tone that Jane Kenyon is able to say, "The moon comes / to count the bales. . . ."

It is her perfection of tone that makes her poems able to accommodate sudden declarations of spiritual knowledge or religious faith, and that gives to so many of her poems the quality of prayer. It rules in her poems and passages of humor. It is the enabling principle in the political stroke of the poem entitled "Fat," and of the affirmation always present in her poems of sorrow. I am suggesting what I suppose cannot be demonstrated: there is a practical affinity between the life of her soul and the technique of her poems.

The poems assemble themselves with a seeming arbitrariness, which is perhaps a comment. The poet looks at her subjects and experiences as they come to her and sees that they are ordinary; they are the stuff of life in this world; they could have come to anybody, at any time, in any order. They are revelations of ordinary satisfactions, joys, sufferings, deliverances that, in being revealed, become somehow numinous and resonant—extraordinary. In seeing that the poems are revelations, you see that they are not arbitrary but inevitable; in the course of the poem, form has occurred.

Sometimes the poems are poems of suspense; everything waits for the final line, as in the poem called "Things":

> The hen flings a single pebble aside
> with her yellow, reptilian foot.
> Never in eternity the same sound—
> a small stone falling on a red leaf.
>
> The juncture of twig and branch,
> scarred with lichen, is a gate
> we might enter, singing.

The mouse pulls batting
from a hundred-year-old quilt.
She chewed a hole in a blue star
to get it, and now she thrives. . . .
Now is her time to thrive.

Things: simply lasting, then
failing to last: water, a blue heron's
eye, and the light passing
between them: into light all things
must fall, glad at last to have fallen.

The poem gathers itself as quietly as a snowy night, and then by the end a kind of dawn has come and everything is shining. That seems to be all there is to say. This poem confirms for me as well as any I have read what I think is the fundamental fact of poetry: if you can explain it, it is something else.

Nor am I able to say much more about this story that I have undertaken to talk about. It is, I think, a good and valuable story. Two poets entered into it together, consenting to its foretold cost, lived it out, met its occasions, and made, separately and together, a life and a body of work that, for some of us, the world is now unimaginable without. They tasted a sweetness stored up by others; they stored up sweetness to be tasted by others. And what are we friends and beneficiaries to say? Well, finally, maybe no more than "Thank you."

JEAN VALENTINE

Jane Kenyon, 1947–1995

Jane Kenyon was twenty-five or so when I first met her: she was sitting at a round white metal table out in the patio of a Florida hotel, in January, looking into an aviary full of monkeys playing in green Florida trees—writing a poem about them. She and Donald Hall were still living in Michigan then; he and I were there in Florida to read, etc., and then they were going on to visit some baseball team's winter training camp. Jane was writing the poems that would soon make up her first book, *From Room to Room.* She was a smart, warmhearted, lovable young woman, and I loved her right away. I remember she wrote me a few months later, and asked if she could put my name into her Florida poem, and I said, Please don't—I was so shy then of appearing or of receiving—how much now I wish I'd said yes, how much I wish my name appeared in one of her poems.

Some years later, after she and Don had settled in New Hampshire, they got me invited to read at Dartmouth, and I visited them at Eagle Pond Farm. She showed me her workroom, the spacious room under the eaves she went to every morning, its desk, its photo of Adrienne Rich over the desk. I remember Jane told me on that visit about the experience she wrote down later in "Having It Out with Melancholy."

But I don't think she told me then that Melancholy had come, like a crow; only the first part. Was she sparing me? I only remember our calm thrill, that she "saw" such things.

Once a little later I came close to getting to know her better: a neighbor of Jane and Don's was going to Australia for the summer, and I was going to house-sit. But the neighbor fell ill, didn't go, and I didn't go. How much I wish I had. Do we get to meet somewhere else? Does she get to write one more book?

In 1979 I saw Jane and Don at Elizabeth Bishop's memorial service, in Agassiz Hall at Radcliffe, Jane with tears running down her face. I asked her if she'd known Bishop well; not at all, Jane said, she had just loved her work so much: the poet sang Baptist hymns to a seal!

And here was Death like Melancholy, flying to pull out one of his dear ones.

Sometime in the late 1980s I wrote Jane and asked her if she had any publishing ideas for me—I was coming out of a five-year silence, working with alcoholism, not poetry. She wrote to her publisher for me, and she told me that those silent years had been years of "soul-making." Around that time we found out that in our childhoods we'd been called "Janie" and "Jeanie," and called each other by those names from then on.

Two more times only I saw her, in 1988 and 1989, both times when I was on January visits to MacDowell. Once she came over to Peter-borough, and we walked down the snowy path and had tea in my stu-dio. We sat and drank tea by the fire and read each other our poems. She had gotten thin—she had suffered a lot of death, physical illness, and depression in the 1980s.

The following year I went over to their place again, and again Jane and I sat down and read to each other awhile. I remember my joy when she said my poems were "wild"—

Her poems were wild, with spiritual longing. Soul-making.

In May of 1994 she was given the PEN Voelcker Award. Too sick to receive it herself, she asked me. "I wish I could be there to scoop up the treasure." Here is the note she asked me to read:

Unambiguous joy was my guest the whole afternoon
and evening after John Morrone's call telling me about
the Voelcker Award. In spite of being ill—or because I am
ill—I'm deeply happy about it.

Being confirmed in one's work encourages still more work, and this award makes me want to live a long time and write a great deal.

The award also reminds me that there really are people who read books, even my books! The judges are all poets whose work I respect enormously, and that adds to my delight.

My deepest thanks go to them, and to Alice Mattison, who nominated me, to PEN America, and to those responsible for the creation of this award.

Late in Jane's illness, Galway Kinnell asked her if he could read a poem of hers at a tribute to Jane Cooper, who named her as a beloved friend and influence; she chose a poem for Galway, and then she said, "But you're going to read this poem to Jane Cooper, and there's a lie in it! You must remember to change this line when you read it," and she instructed him what change to make.

Thinking of Jane Kenyon's poetry—*From Room to Room, Twenty Poems of Anna Akhmatova, The Boat of Quiet Hours, Let Evening Come, Constance,* and *Otherwise*—I think of the progress of wisdom; as Eudora Welty said, "The events in our lives happen in a sequence in time, but in their significance to ourselves, they find their own order . . . the continuous thread of revelation."

Elegy for Jane Kenyon

The rooks rise off the field in a black W
and break up, black Cassiopeia breaking up
at the hour of your death. Your music is broken
and eaten among the American poets

and you are gone,
angry wolf, sad swallow,
and you are gone.
Blest boat, blest water,
gone in the first hour
and gone in the second hour . . .

CAROLINE FINKELSTEIN

The Beacon

Jane Kenyon. How do I remember her? What do I write that is new, that is honest, that renders Jane as I perceived her? I wish I could call her up (she was terrific on the telephone) and ask her for help with this, but she is having lunch with Mary or her first cat, or she is a cat, or that mote that just flew past the salmon-colored begonia on the terrace. She would have loved that flower. She was very definite about flowers. I remember a polite argument about anchusa, which is a blue plant—good if you want blue in the garden—but hairy. She didn't mind the texture of the anchusa's stalk. I hated it. Everyone knows Jane had a beautiful garden but I don't really remember Jane in her garden although I do remember her digging one more bed on the right side of her driveway. She was wearing jeans and works shoes. I don't remember if this was to be another flower garden or a place for vegetables. Probably another flower garden. But then she got sick and that new bed was shortly covered over with weeds.

Jane Kenyon wrote a poem for me. It was inspired by a visit we made to the Museum of Fine Arts in Boston. We were there to see some Dutch paintings. I don't remember whether they were landscapes, or those flowery *Vanitas* paintings the Dutch were so fond of. Those paintings usually depict flowers overflowing their vases, flowers with a bit of rotting here and there in the bouquet, some leaves destroyed by insects. The insects are perfectly recognizable. Everything is. On the table that holds the vases there are often clocks to show the passage of time and sometimes a skull just to make sure one gets the point of the clock. These are gorgeous but scary paintings. The flowers in the vases, like the flowers in French and Italian medieval tapestries, hold blossoms that grow at *every* season, impossibly collected. Surreal.

These Dutch paintings are still lifes, grisly metaphors that catch you unaware. Death seems far away when you look at the perfect replication of a carnation. I don't know how long it was after the museum that Jane contracted leukemia.

We met on a weekday. Jane took the bus in from Concord, and I drove in from the country in southeastern Massachusetts. It seemed easy then, parking at the museum parking lot, walking across the street to the big lobby with the glass doors, then waiting for someone you loved. It is harder to drive in Boston now. There is more traffic and it is more aggressive. Friends I had in Boston have moved away.

We ate lunch in the Members Dining Room. I think I drank some wine. Jane had no wine. She unwrapped tiny pills she had in a handkerchief and took them, one by one, with water. Jane had bipolar disorder. Those pills were for that. I don't remember anything we talked about but I do remember Jane beginning to cry in the middle of lunch. Why was she crying? Was it something I said? I completely forgot that she had just swallowed pills because she cried for "nothing" in the middle of lunch. It was hard for me to remember Jane suffered from depression. To me, she always seemed totally witty and totally kind. The times she hid away, the days and months she turned her face to the wall, I didn't know about that, I *couldn't* know. It scared me.

When is it we learn to jettison some of our selves, to become less intrusive in the story? Isn't it then that we pay true homage to another? I am writing an essay about Jane Kenyon yet I am constantly in the essay. How do I take myself out? How do I present JANE to this paper, or simply, Jane one day in a museum having lunch with a friend, then looking at Dutch pictures?

She wasn't very tall but her carriage was so straight that she gave the appearance of being tall. She had wild, dark brown hair. Her cheekbones were wide. When she stopped wearing her glasses and got contacts, "Caroline," she said to me, "I'm coming out!" She had great jewelry, earrings always, and a very particular style. I never saw her be anything but herself.

When we finished lunch, and coffee, and our chatter (the pills had worked), we went to the exhibition.

Here's the magic of the story. Here's why the intrusive "I" of memory isn't consigned wholly to selfishness. Jane was a beacon. She illumined every picture with her eyes, and her mind's eye. Things I would never have noticed, she made brilliant. Subtleties were pointed out. Concepts were understood. We walked from room to room, Jane always gentle, always excited, purposeful, funny. I had never observed paintings with so much care—with so much *looking*. It was the art itself, not the artist, or the history of the picture, or where it belonged in the long history of pictures, that she made me see. It was the poem itself on the page, regardless of what had made the poem, or the social constructs behind the poem, or even the language or syntax—but the very thing itself. Something whole. Something *made*. The thing *being*. I saw art through the vision of another artist. It moved me.

The poem that Jane wrote about that day recalls some of the sixteenth-century Dutch objects we saw on those old canvases: bread and cheese on a plate, a "gleaming pewter beaker of beer," a woman making lace with "a moist-eyed spaniel lying/ at her small shapely feet"—actual objects we noted and put in our heads. But then the poem does a mysterious turn and the last stanza, four lines, is not about anything we saw that day. It is Vermeer's "The Letter" Jane writes of:

> And the merchant's wife, still
> in her yellow dressing gown
> at noon, dips her quill into India ink
> with an air of cautious pleasure.

How constant the artist is! How inextricably wedded to inspiration! Although we saw no Vermeers, the paintings we saw were, in a sense, *all* Vermeers: Dutch, of things interior, houses, windows, plates, rugs, chambermaids, beer, and, perhaps, a little middle-class adultery. Jane called the poem "Dutch Interiors." By putting in the Vermeer we did not witness that day, she played with *interiors*. She presented not only the artifacts we *did* see, but also imagined an action prompted by a woman's heart. A woman of imagination imagined the behavior of the woman of a portrait.

The Jane of that day was a like a white peach, beautiful, a little out of the ordinary, sweet, smooth, endangered. How long was it before I heard on the phone about "too many nosebleeds" and the next day heard "leukemia"? Who remembers? Who remembers when, after the first round of chemotherapy, she was home from the hospital and seeming chipper. She lifted up her shirt to show me her Hickman— an IV device inserted directly into her chest to make an infusion of intravenous medicines easier. I was so shocked I pulled up my own shirt, which made her laugh like the "naughty, red-cheeked girl" of her poem.

People die. "Die soon or die later," my son quotes his Zen master. I can imagine telling this to Jane. I can imagine her immediate, ironic laughter. *Her* death was enormous. It took her much too long to die—her suffering served no one, no thing; it enlightened none of us who watched her body fail. That she was "cut down in her prime," and suffered so grievously—the Zen master would say his phrase, and I have to make do with it. But I am no Buddhist.

When she was sick I would ask her on the telephone how she was doing. "I'm doing," she'd say. Then she wasn't. Writing this on an early August morning, I can look up and see my neighbor's mimosa in bloom, pink, flat flowers surrounded by leaves like feathers, flowers and leaves stirring in a soft wind. There is no Jane. There are her books of poems, her poetry beloved everywhere by friends, and by strangers. The poems are straight and clear. That she herself was an intensely complicated human being, wildly strong, incredibly gifted, and mortally sick, does it matter to the work? We sat in chairs at the table. There was ice water, and polished cutlery and the white tablecloth. There was the hankie holding the little pills. There were her little sips from the water glass. And then there was the art. Room after room of painted canvases in gilded frames. Pictures of hams, of cheese, of flowers. Perhaps a stalk of mimosa in one of those incredible bouquets. Her velvet jacket. Her hands. That ring. The way Vermeer painted her in her New Hampshire kitchen, pouring juice from a jug.

ROBERT BLY

A Few Lines about Jane

I loved Jane's presence in her house, her laughter over onions, the way she called Don "Perkins" so he wouldn't get too uppity, her deep affection for him that one could feel had lengthened into a permanent loyalty, as if the wildebeest's tail had stretched out and become as long as the plain he galloped over; and I loved the way she would say to Don, if he had unwittingly put a phrase of hers into one of his own poems, "Watch your ass." And I loved the sober, precise, elegant, quiet way she would read a poem. Being pulled up from such depths, the water was always refreshing.

But I loved most walking with her in the woods. Then she would speak of her spiritual longing; we know that only a fraction of that longing appeared in her poems, but that portion was enough so that we knew we were looking at the poems of a genuinely spiritual poet.

> I am water rushing to the wellhead
> filling the pitcher until it spills. . . .
>
> I am the patient gardener
> of the dry and weedy garden. . . .

Her garden was often dry and weedy. It was sometimes depressed and empty. Or it was desperate and stagnant. But those who dig patiently in such gardens may find one day they are also water rushing to the wellhead and falling out into the sunlight.

I loved the way she would imitate Vera Dunham. "You vant to

translate Anna Akhatova? It ees impossible! Don't even try it! It's too great! Ze passion, divine, impossible! Ze form, impossible in English! It's hopeless. Don't even try. All right, let's begin." She loved Vera, and she loved Akhmatova, and some of her thousand-year-old so-berness of the Russian Orthodox liturgy somehow slipped into her New Hampshire poems. I loved her sauciness, her calm ambition on which no flies ever settled, her admiration of her women friends, the way she carried jokes and grief up into her attic study like a Russian servant carrying a glass of water.

—•—

The other day, when I was weeping with some people over the turns and sorrows of a Russian fairy tale, turns that we never would have chosen, flights into the unknown that seemed to come from some culture five thousand years older than ours, I didn't know what to say. So I read them a poem of Jane's:

> Let the light of late afternoon
> shine through chinks in the barn, moving
> up the bales as the sun moves down.

Where else can one see that except in a barn? Boards always shrink; that's the way life is. So sun goes through between the boards and hits those chunky, gorgeous bales on the other wall. Then that ecstatic light gradually hits bale after bale moving upward as the sun itself, some gloomy creature in the west, moves down. She takes up that un-American idea again: let the cricket do what it wants to do, let the toes of the shoe curl, let the thumb and the forefinger caress each other:

> Let the cricket take up chafing
> as a woman takes up her needles
> and her yarn. Let evening come.

So in this descent, the woman with her college education and her novels of Jane Ausen is not that different from the cricket. The chafing and the sewing will all happen. She gives permission to evening.

> Let dew collect on the hoe abandoned
> in long grass. Let the stars appear
> and the moon disclose her silver horn.

I love this repeating of the word "let." I can't tell you what joy I feel reading it, as if some sane person had finally seen the beauty of time, had seen how gorgeous it is that the horse's hooves gradually grow longer, that even hoes grow old. Probably the hoe doesn't want to be abandoned any more than we do. But the grass is long, what can you say? The stars are sober types; they don't exaggerate much. But the moon has always heard a lot of Russian stories in her youth. If you want to deal with her, you'll have to deal with the silver horn as well.

> Let the fox go back to its sandy den.
> Let the wind die down. Let the shed
> go black inside. Let evening come.

Now she goes into *n*'s, the beauty of that sound of *n*, "sandy den." It seems to us that all those sandy dens of the gopher, the coyote, and the fox, all those places are made out of *n*'s. The fox goes into that place just as Yeats goes into one of his own poems full of *n*'s, and *o*'s. At the end of the poem the wind dies down. The shed of our mind goes black inside. All of this seems so brilliant I am stunned. It's all right for evening to come.

> To the bottle in the ditch, to the scoop
> in the oats, to air in the lung
> let evening come.

She is not forgetting our greeds for whiskey, for Coca-Cola, for a little bit of cough medicine. All of those creaturely enclosures are just as good as a scoop lying in the oats. To pick up one of those metal moon-shaped scoops and fill it full of oats, what a joy. Let's do it while our lungs still agree to take in air, which is oats to them, and the hysterical earth agrees to take in evening. Have I said I love this poem?

> Let it come, as it will, and don't
> be afraid. God does not leave us
> comfortless, so let evening come.

How beautiful it is that the word "it" has finally appeared. We know when we are asleep that it runs everything, including our dreams, and I suppose we've learned in the last forty years not to be afraid of our dreams. At the end of the dream some detail will occur like those small boys who run laughing among the gravestones in the old alchemy story. God does not leave us comfortless, so let evening come.

The Yellow Dot

In memory of Jane Kenyon

God does what She wants. She has very large
Tractors. She lives at night in the sewing room
Doing stitchery. Then chunks of land at mid-
Sea disappear. The husband knows that his wife
Is still breathing. God has arranged the open
Grave. That grave is not what we want,
But to God it's a tiny hole, and he has
The needle, draws thread through it, and soon
A nice pattern appears. The husband cries,
"Don't let her die!" But God says, "I
Need a yellow dot here, near the mailbox."

The husband is angry. But the turbulent ocean
Is like a chicken scratching for seeds. It doesn't
Mean anything, and the chicken's claws will tear
A Rembrandt drawing if you put it down.

LIAM RECTOR

Remembering Jane Kenyon

I once made a pilgrimage to Eagle Pond Farm in New Hampshire, which from Donald Hall's memoirs and poems I imagined to be some kind of Valhalla, to be Home Itself. As Don did in New Hampshire, I grew up staying most summers at my grandparents' farm in Virginia, which was Home Itself to me. We both mightily loved our grandparents and loved old-time things and places as part of that. When I took the bus to Eagle Pond I thought of New England as a fairly old-time thing, a region of what Lenin called "plain living and high thinking," and I was going through an enchantment with the Yankee part of the country Up There. The bus took me to a small general store and in a light snow Don was there in his car.

Where Don and Jane lived was a house right off a huge gash of rural highway, not nearly as idyllic as the Virginia farm where I partly grew up. But it was night and when I got inside the house I could see and feel the enchantment and see and feel that Don and Jane had made quite an ancestral home of it all. Compared to me, a manic talker, Jane was silence itself. Jane struck me as the sort who didn't say much and then meant what she said, a kind of female Gary Cooper. She was kind and welcoming, and she let the boys alone to have their yak.

Jane was one of those women who become ferociously beautiful in middle age. I love the beauty of older women and especially women who age naturally, as many do in Cambridge, where I eventually made my home in the 1990s amidst the most beautiful aging women on earth. Jane's older beauty took place wildly in her hair, which grew to be a lioness's mane. (When chemotherapy took her hair from her she once donned a Rastafarian wig, and we all laughed at the hair-gone-by and her gameness in donning such an unlikely wig.) Her eyes had also become more beautiful, her body more beautiful, and her maturity and sympathy for all that lived had become painfully beautiful, startling, ennobling. She had the sense of *pietà* we find in Rilke.

I found Jane's first book of poems, *From Room to Room,* unremarkable. To my taste, the poems there are more a description of experience rather than an experience unto themselves. It is always something of a problem when you like the poems of friends but not those of their spouses.

But by her second book Jane had, through translation, taken on the influence of Anna Akhmatova and created in her own poetry the "luminous particular" Don has written so well about, a luminous particular where T. S. Eliot's objective correlative meets James Wright's deep image and imagines, notates, and produces an experience in and of itself, and I began to love Jane's poetry too.

"We write, in mania, about depression," Don once wrote, and Jane could sometimes sink into a depression I was sure I had never visited. For me, I was certain suicide would come long before I reached that point, but Jane somehow managed to persevere. Perhaps it was her religious faith that sustained her. Jane would seem to be stolen away by complete despair and was unreachable, unavailable, and would sit there like a ghost of herself, not able to speak at all. It seemed to me not that she was choosing not to speak, but was literally *unable* to speak. Visits were sometimes cancelled at a moment's notice when this happened, and her friends came to accept this.

At one point I fell in love with Tree Swenson, co-founder of Copper Canyon Press and book designer for all of Jane's books with Graywolf

Press. Soon Tree and I were visiting Jane and Don at Eagle Pond, where we discovered a newfound symmetry as literary couples. Tree and I were married in the back garden of Don and Jane's home in the spring of 1993. The marriage was presided over by a woman who was a Unitarian minister, and Don and Jane and Tree and I all read from Eliot's "Four Quartets," a solemn but wise and truthful poem for a wedding. Only my daughter, Virginia, and a friend of Tree's, the artist Anne Hirondelle, were otherwise there. Jane and Virginia took a bunch of flowers from Jane's garden and made a scarecrow that presided over the ceremony as a kind of beneficent spirit.

The dates and timing are to some extent mixed up in me now (illness is a miasma), but at some point in all this Don contracted colon cancer. Soon that cancer metastasized to his liver, and a large portion of his liver was removed. We didn't think he had long to live. I orchestrated a tribute to Don's work at Old Dominion University in Virginia. Because we thought Don was soon to be a goner, there was something of a memorial service in this, while Don was still alive. Don accepted all this cheerfully (if a bit ruefully), gratefully, and great swarms of his many friends came to speak. There were other tributes, in different places. But, as fate would have it, Don recovered; Don endured.

There then came years of triumph in Jane and Don's life. They were featured in a Bill Moyers documentary called *A Life Together: Donald Hall and Jane Kenyon,* which was awarded an Emmy because of the articulateness of its subjects and because of an artful style of simplicity in the form of the film itself that was regenerating and heartbreaking. Jane and Don read at the Dodge Festival in New Jersey and were wildly received there, and a video record was made of that. Jane by then rightly felt she had come into her majority as a poet and, rather than staying behind and not having much to do with what Don could do for and with her publicly, she began to give readings with Don. They even took up the stage role of lovers in A. R. Gurney's play *Love Letters*. Things were rolling. Don had published his master-work, *The One Day*, and Jane's poems were at their height with books such as *Let Evening Come* and *Constance* acquiring reviews, recognition, and her own growing readership. Articles and interviews about the two of them and their lives together appeared in the *Boston Globe* and the *AWP Newsletter*, and everything seemed on the side of life going forward. They were invited to tour India together by the State Department and theirs seemed the best of marriages. Jane took to cooking a lot of Indian food.

I founded the graduate Writing Seminars at Bennington College in the winter of 1994. Don and Jane signed on as associate faculty, faculty there not to conduct workshops, as the core faculty did, but to lecture on literature and inaugurate our program as a center focused as much on reading as on writing. The main vortex of the program, as I envisioned it, was formed around Don and Jane—Don the dynamo of the person of letters upon which we based the ethos of the new program, and Jane the pure poet who kept to her images and their ever-encompassing verities and worlds. We also had as associate faculty Sven Birkerts reading early chapters of what became his seminal book, *The Gutenberg Elegies: The Fate of Reading in an Electronic Age*. It was a poignant time. We had three feet of snow, icicles everywhere on trees and buildings, and we skittered from fire to fire, knowing we were in the midst of something historic in literature.

Jane was not a teacher in any professional sense. She had not constructed a persona in which and through which to teach, and she was not a natural teacher. Teaching, I think, frightened her. That's one way of putting it. Another way of putting it is that it absolutely terrified her. She was not an essayist, an assayist, or a village explainer. But when she sat down in a small room with our initial twenty-four students and did readings and talks on Bishop, Akhmatova, and Keats, there was not a dry eye in the place. She simply read the poems beautifully, slowly, and talked about what they meant to her. She was especially good on what she called "the fuck and die" poems of Keats, and students took the point when she told them how much her work had changed when she took on the translation of Akhmatova and found her master there. Students often balk at the idea of a "master." They assume one must be a slave, in response. But the role of master to apprentice has been an old and venerable one in literature, and it has been a passage through which most of the strong poets I know have passed many times, with many masters, as a kind of variant of serial monogamy.

Many teachers ask questions of their students, but not many teachers are able to withstand and indeed modulate a silence when no answer from students is immediately forthcoming. Jane as a teacher knew how to make silence speak, and she drew her students into the questions she proposed, rather than rushing to answer the question herself. She was a walking Quaker meeting, and in establishing a rapport with Jane one learned much about what Rilke called "the need to speak" and what might create anyone's consequent need to listen, which puts us to the arc, the communion between writer and reader.

Jane loved coming to the readings we held every night at the residency. In fact, at her Bennington reading, the last reading she ever gave in public, she said that she could get used to this, this "getting read to" every night. She also said she was tired. In the utter retreat and down-periscope immersiveness of Bennington residencies, we all practice exhaustion as something of a pedagogy, taking Galway Kinnell's lines from a poem called "Wait": "You're tired. But everyone's tired./ But no one is tired enough" as a kind of credo to breaking through to the openness where we might actually be educated. Now when I listen to the tape of that final reading of Jane's I can never hear her "I am tired" remark without hearing also the cold she felt she had when she left Bennington, the flu she thought the cold had turned into when she got home, and the leukemia she discovered she had from a nosebleed that commenced soon after she was home.

If someone wrote a story about a comparatively young woman contracting leukemia after her older husband has gone through cancer and survived, I'm not sure anyone would really believe it. Readers might balk at feeling emotionally manipulated, as some did, for instance, in Larry McMurtry's novel *Terms of Endearment.* But there it was. An old man who had just bested cancer was left to care for a younger wife who had leukemia and was too soon in for the fight of her life.

For fifteen months Jane and Don fought that fight, in interludes of great terror and greater hope. Tree and I visited them in Seattle, where Jane underwent a bone marrow transplant, one of the most painful bouts in the cancer world. We visited them in a fairly antiseptic apartment near the hospital where Jane, after the bone marrow transplant, was slumped over in a set of sweatclothes and could barely talk. She looked mashed. She listened to us talk for a while and then retreated to their bedroom, where she said the chatter of us outside gave her real comfort.

Soon Jane was home from Seattle and we all had great hopes that she would survive and completely recover, but this was not to be. Shortly before she died, Don called us in Boston and said it was time to get up there and see Jane. Jane and Tree went over Jane's selection of a painting Jane wanted to see on her volume of selected poems, *Otherwise,* which she and Don had so carefully put together. There and then Jane and Tree had their last conference together as poet and book designer. Tree and I also brought along a Yorkshire terrier who was then only a few weeks old, whom we had named Kenyon. Things were very solemn; things were very sweet and tender. We left thinking we might never see Jane again, and we never did. Tree went home and worked feverishly to get a proof of the book's cover off to

Jane and in fact sent the proof off by overnight mail just hours before the call from Don came, the call where Don recounted the process of Jane's breathing moving through her last hours, eventually becoming no breathing at all.

At Jane's funeral I read one of her poems, "Let Evening Come," and I, along with one of Jane's best friends, Alice Mattison, was among the pallbearers. (All caskets are truly heavier than you expect them to be, even with the considerably lightened weight of Jane Kenyon inside.) Robert Bly led us in singing "Amazing Grace" at Jane's gravesite, which was later marked by a marble tombstone that bore Don's name and the date of his birth, as well as Jane's name and two dates. We had to keep Gus, their beloved dog who took so many walks with Jane in her life and in her poems, at home. He was wild with grief and confusion.

Stratis Haviaras, the poet who directed the Poetry Room at Harvard, and I then organized a memorial to Jane in which Robert Bly, Don, Marie Howe, Alice Mattison, Joyce Peseroff, Tree, Geoffrey Hill, and I read from Jane's poems and talked about her life. The 500-seat room filled so quickly that we decided to do a second memorial right on the spot, and the 300 outside were soon spirited into another Harvard room that Stratis quickly arranged. On the rostrum in the first room, we would have our say and then hurry to the second room, where we would do it all over again to an audience that deeply appreciated our coming to them. This was the first inkling I had of the larger audience for Jane's work that was to come. I put together another memorial service at an Associated Writing Programs conference in Washington, D.C., and the outpouring was still gathering momentum. It fell to me to announce too at that gathering that Allen Ginsberg had died just the night before.

We then all just settled into bleak New England mourning. For my part, I spent a raging few years questioning how any god could let this happen, which drove me from a skeptical and buoyant agnosticism into a virulent atheism. Others took up different ways of absorbing all that had occurred. For many months I wondered if I could in fact go on with the Bennington program. A part of its foundation was missing.

Otherwise: New & Selected Poems went on to sell 50,000 copies and is still going strong, keeping Jane alive in all of us. Jane has become, as Auden once intoned about Yeats, her admirers. We were all heartened to see Alice and Joyce and Don put together *A Hundred White Daffodils,* a collection of prose and one poem by Jane, for which Tree designed her final cover for Jane.

Jane's poems now endure throughout the world. People arrive from all over the country at Don's door and ask if it's all right if they walk some of the walks Jane took in her poems. Her luminous particulars have been inscaped by her readers and are now part of how they put one foot in front of the other, in what dancers call "muscle memory."

Gus lived on, lonely, and died not so long ago. All of Don's friends had to attend to the grieving wild-animal-widower Don has written about so well in his poems to and about Jane, and Don has continued to teach at Bennington and gone on to be the very signature of the program. Robert Bly has joined him as a writer-in-residence at the Writing Seminars, and they give talks about poets such as James Wright, which make students glad to be alive and glad to be there. The students know they are in and inheriting a large time and movement of poets.

There are poems Jane wrote that will be, as Frost said, hard to get rid of, poems such as "Let Evening Come," "Happiness," "Having It Out with Melancholy," "Not Writing," and "Otherwise." They will survive in the memories (and memorizations) of readers as long as important, lasting poetry is carried forth. At our most recent tenth-year residency in January of 2004 we showed the Moyers documentary, *A Life Together,* one more time. There she was: Jane Kenyon, with a twelve-foot head and her glorious hair up there on the screen. When I first saw the documentary I thought that Jane was not going to be able to speak to Moyers because of her depression. She seemed gone to that dark, unspeakable spot. But then she rallied and gave one of the most articulate characterizations of depression it has ever been my privilege to hear. Jane was like that. Depressed and despairing sometimes in a manner where no one and nothing could reach her—rallying and laughing at salacious jokes and dark, sexual humor after that. Tending her flowers, her animals, her life with Don, her friends, and her home. Jane took on a master and reorchestrated Akhmatova's power of imagery and tone, and out of that emerged a raw and refined experience for the reader as the reader takes in Jane's utterly individuated voices. Jane had lust and she had a large prayer in her heart. She prayed it out loud for us to read and sort out for ourselves. She was quiet and beautiful there toward her end, and she wrote the pure poems.

DONALD HALL

Ghost in the House

For twenty-three years, until she died of leukemia in 1995, I was married to the poet Jane Kenyon. When I first met her, Jane was moody. Laughing extravagantly with other student poets, she was funny, outrageous, and smart. Then she would go silent, withdraw, her mouth curved down, her forehead knotted. Most of the time when she felt low, she kept to herself. She consulted a university doctor who prescribed a drug that appeared to deepen her depression. When we were first married, she spent two years in psychoanalytical therapy, which did not cure depression but which helped her to interpret feelings, to avoid the emotional erratum slips that most of us should wear on our foreheads: "For 'compassion' read 'anger' throughout."

Three years after we married, Jane and I moved to the isolation of a New Hampshire farmhouse, largely at Jane's urging. For twenty years we lived in the same house, inhabiting a double solitude. We thrived in cohabitation and in boundaries. Each leaving her/his separate hive of writing, we could meet in the kitchen for another coffee, midmorning, without speaking; we would pat each other's bottoms. In our silence, we were utterly aware of each other's presence. In our devotion to poetry and to each other, our marriage was intimate and content.

And nothing is simple. By temperament, I was impatient, always eager, as Jane said, for "the next thing, the next thing." Often she sank into speechless discontent while I remained energetic. Then in her poems I encountered depression that was more than moodiness.

An old harness in the barn suggested itself a noose. There were poems of blankness and lethargy:

> I had to ask two times
> before my hand would scratch my ear.

In another she wrote:

> . . . The days are bright
> and free, bright and free.
>
> Then why did I cry today
> for an hour, with my whole
> body, the way babies cry?

Eleven years after we married, Jane was diagnosed with bipolar mood disorder.

> . . . the soul's bliss
> and suffering are bound together
> like the grasses . . .

She was never delusional; her mania was notable but God never telephoned her. On the other hand, her depression ranged from deep sadness to agony, and Jane was more frequently depressed than manic.

Psychiatrists have documented the high incidence of bipolarity among artists. Writers are the most bipolar—and among writers, poets. See "Manic-Depressive Illness and Creativity" by Kay Redfield Jamison in *Scientific American,* February 1995. One percent "of the general population suffer from manic-depression." Jamison cites figures for mood disorder in artists, depending on different models of sampling, that go upward from 38 percent.

No one can induce bipolarity in order to make poems. Does the *practice* of the art exacerbate a tendency? Surely for the artist the disorder is creative in its manic form—excitement, confidence, the rush of energy and invention. Maybe DNA perpetuates bipolarity because mania or hypomania benefits the whole tribe, inventing the wheel and Balzac's *Cousine Bette,* while depression harms only the depressive and those close to the depressive.

Ten years after we married, I watched Jane lower into the blackest place. She had been a principal caregiver for her father, and she was with him when he died. She stayed up all night with him when morphine confused him, and with her mother tended him twenty-four hours a day. The cancer that wasted him, his collapse in mind and tissue, commanded her asleep or awake. In 1982, six months after the death, we drank a beer one night in the small town of Bristol. As we drove back, Jane sank under a torment and torrent of wild crying. At home she curled on the sofa in the fetal position and wept for three days. I wanted to hold and comfort her, as I had earlier done when she was low, but now I could not touch her. If I touched her, she would want to scream.

She spoke little, in gasps, but she told me that she was not angry at me, that she loved me, that her despair had nothing to do with me. It was heartbreaking not to touch her, not to be able to give comfort. Doubtless my anxious presence across the room was another burden. I understood and believed that I was not responsible for her melancholia. In later returns of her sickness, she continued to worry that I would misinterpret her feelings. She persuaded two doctors to tell me that her depression was caused by the chemistry of her brain, that it was endogenous and unrelated to our life together.

That first black time, she gradually stopped weeping and her mood rose slightly. She saw our internist, who recognized clinical depression and prescribed drugs; I'm not sure which drug he began with but it must have been tricyclic. The Prozac class of drugs (which didn't help Jane) was not yet available. For advice on treatment, our doctor spoke with Dr. Charles Solow, head of psychiatry at Dartmouth-Hitchcock Hospital. Later, Jane visited Dr. Solow regularly, and relied on him for treatment until she died. He prescribed a variety of drugs, and talked with her continually—kind, supportive, sympathetic. Jane was medicated most of the rest of her life. She kept wanting to survive without pharmaceutical help, and in 1992 tried the experiment of going naked. A precipitate plunge returned her to medication.

In "Having It Out with Melancholy," she makes a stanza:

> Elavil, Ludiomil, Doxepin,
> Norpramin, Prozac, Lithium, Xanax,
> Wellbutrin, Parnate, Nardil, Zoloft.
> The coated ones smell sweet or have
> no smell; the powdery ones smell
> like the chemistry lab at school
> that made me hold my breath.

The tricyclic Doxepin helped her for three years, the longest stretch without a deep trough. During these years she had her ups and downs, she was sad and she was gay, but Doxepin appeared to prevent deep depression. As she inhabited a fragile comfort, she could work on her poems. Then her body learned how to metabolize the drug and she needed larger doses, until it was no longer safe to increase the dose.

This drug, like others, gave her a dry mouth, but the side effects were not miserable. Some drugs did nothing for her, or reduced the intensity of orgasm, or included side effects nasty enough to disqualify them. When she was manic in 1984, she took Lithium, which she hated. Lithium is known to suppress creativity. After that year, she was never manic for long episodes. Often she dosed daily on a combination of drugs—Wellbutrin maybe, a tricyclic or two, a trace of Lithium. Another drug that helped was an old MOA-inhibitor, Nardil, which kept her from depression for almost a year, but limited her sleep so much that she became exhausted and had to stop taking it. Despite her energy and relief from dolor, I didn't like some side effects of Nardil, nor did her closest friends. She seemed much as she seemed in mania: dogmatic, combative, sometimes querulous, abrasive sometimes—without her characteristic alertness to the feelings of others. But Nardil held depression off. She described herself in a section of "Having It Out with Melancholy":

9 Wood Thrush

High on Nardil and June light
I wake at four,
waiting greedily for the first
notes of the wood thrush. Easeful air
presses through the screen
with the wild, complex song
of the bird, and I am overcome

by ordinary contentment.
What hurt me so terribly
all my life until this moment?
How I love the small, swiftly
beating heart of the bird
singing through the great maples;
its bright, unequivocal eye.

With Dr. Solow's help, Jane avoided deepest depression much of the time, but its misery lurked at the edges of her daily life, and sometimes sprang from the shadows. I remember Jane on the bathroom floor banging her head against toilet and pipes. Another time she arrived trembling after driving back from Concord: she had fought all the way the impulse or desire to drive off the road into a boulder or a stone wall. And I remember a terrible Christmas Day, when I gave her as usual too many presents, each of which depressed her further. Someone who is stupid, bad, ugly, fat, and hateful does not deserve presents; gifts mocked her. After this bout lapsed, the presents I had given her always retained a tint of misery. The counterpart can be true: recollections of a manic experience may cheer you up, even though you know that the joy was endogenous and ended in depression.

Despite her thoughts about hanging herself with a horse's harness, despite her fear of driving into walls, I did not think that Jane would kill herself. Maybe her treatment kept her from the extremes that lead to suicide. Surely her Christianity helped: she knew that self-destruction would be an insult to God. There was also her sensitivity to pain and her fear of it. This woman, who dreaded pain so much, suffered fifteen months of physical agony in her attempt to survive leukemia. Her desire to live, when she knew that her chances were poor, astonished her. Only at one moment during her illness did she seem depressed in the old way (she was *not* cheerful about leukemia) and it was while her mother lay dying three thousand miles away—the daughter unable to nurse, herself requiring intense care. The hospital psychiatrist in Seattle noted "suicidal ideation without intent," which may well describe her earlier thoughts and images of self-destruction.

Much of that time, during her last twelve years of physical health, Jane dropped low, she suffered, but she functioned; she wrote poems especially as she climbed out of depression. Her most direct account is "Having It Out with Melancholy." It pained her to write this poem. It pained her to expose herself. But writing the poem also helped her to set depression out, as she knew it, depression and its joyful tentative departure. She wanted the poem to help others who were afflicted. The first time she read it aloud, in 1991 at the Frost Place in Franconia, she paused during her reading, resisting tears. When she ended, a line of people waited to talk with her: depressives, people from the families of depressives.

When Jane was mildly depressed, medium-depressed, supported by drugs but weary and fatigued and without serenity, she found a way to raise her spirits and energy for a few hours. In her worst blackness, I could not touch her, but in grayness an orgasm would make her happy and eager to work. She leapt out of bed to write or garden.

Therefore, we made love whether we felt like it or not. Endorphins restored, for a moment, energy and the desire to work. Sometimes her climax was merely distant thunder. Such a side effect banished Paxil to the wastebasket.

Mania became obvious first in 1984, but looking back I can recall earlier moments, including a prolonged mystical experience in 1980. She felt the presence of the Holy Ghost, and felt that the spirit was female. The presence passed but its memory remained. Mystics are bipolar: Gerard Manley Hopkins wrote sonnets of ecstasy and sonnets of despair; St. John of the Cross described the dark night of the soul. If God enters the human spirit, why should he not use the brain's wiring?

Of her 1984 mania I remember most clearly two or three months, spring and summer of that year. During this first extended elation, I did not know what I confronted. I thought: I must learn to live with an entirely changed woman; I am married to someone I don't know. Frugal Jane *had* to buy a peridot ring; indecisive Jane, who always asked me to make choices—what restaurant to go to, which night to see the play, what book to read aloud—knew *exactly* what we should do, when and where. In her superabundant energy she was bossy: before, she had hidden in my shadow; now she charged forward as bright as the sun of June. She was consumed by desire; on her thirty-seventh birthday we seemed to make love all day long.

The radical change confused and upset me. When Jane went manic I fell into depression. She soared up and I plunged down—a moody seesaw. I felt "suicidal ideation without intent." Then I understood, with shame, that for years I had used her depression to think well of myself: I was the rock, unchanging in all weathers; I was the protector. Now her manic elation and her certainty cast me down. After this first episode of her mania and my response, I put away my complacent self-congratulation.

She fell into depression after mania ceased. Six months later she turned manic again, weeks not months, and spoke carelessly, hurtfully, without malicious intent—in ways she would not have done without mania. By this time I knew what was happening. Thereafter, mania was brief.

Her friends sympathized entirely with her depression but also suffered. Although we were relatively reclusive, we had friends at our church, poet friends who came for weekends, old friends from Ann Arbor, our families. Jane, when she was well, spent more time in company than I did, lunching with women friends in New London twelve miles away. Her closest friends were two other writers, Alice Mattison and Joyce Peseroff. They saw each other when they could, and workshopped together several times a year. The excitement of their meetings exhausted and elevated Jane. Depression never canceled a workshop, but once she asked Alice not to come calling from a summer place in Vermont. Every month Jane and I drove to Connecticut to see my mother, in her eighties, to shop for her and to visit. Several times, when she was depressed, I had to drive down alone. Sometimes I put visitors off at Jane's urging. I telephoned a dying friend to tell him he could not visit. I canceled a skiing visit from my son and friends because Jane could not see anyone. Every summer Jane's brother, sister-in-law, and niece visited from Ann Arbor. Once I had to telephone and ask them not to come. It was generally I who telephoned, at Jane's request, because she could not herself make the call. On occasion when acquaintances made briefer visits, Jane remained in the bedroom with the door closed while I sat talking with them elsewhere.

One of the hardest things, if you are depressed, is to try to hold yourself up in the presence of others, especially others whom you love. I remember a birthday for granddaughters at my daughter's house. Jane stood looking on, wretched, hardly able to speak. She was quiet, there were many people, and she practiced invisibility. My daughter looked at her and said, "You're *miserable,* aren't you?" When Jane nodded, Philippa spoke with sympathy and left her alone. You do not try to cheer up depressives; the worst thing you can do is to count their blessings for them.

Depression was a third party in our marriage. There were many happy third parties: poetry, lovemaking, the church, reading Henry James aloud, watching baseball, afternoons spent swimming and sunbathing by Eagle Pond. There were evenings of raucous laughter with friends, not mania but gaiety. Yet depression's ghost was omnipresent for both of us, in dread if not in actuality. She was obdurate in the face of it, trying to be well, writing out of depression to exorcise the illness for her own sake and for the sake of others. Then listlessness and sorrow and self-loathing would overcome her again; then with new medication she would return again to her daily life.

Back

We try a new drug, a new combination
of drugs, and suddenly
I fall into my life again

like a vole picked up by a storm
then dropped three valleys
and two mountains away from home.

I can find my way back. I know
I will recognize the store
where I used to buy milk and gas.

I remember the house and barn,
the rake, the blue cups and plates,
the Russian novels I loved so much,

and the black silk nightgown
that he once thrust
into the toe of my Christmas stocking.

Jane always understood that her melancholia was inherited, present from birth, but she did not go on medication until after her father's death. Maybe long-term caregivers are more prone to subsequent depression, or to exacerbation of depression—even more prone than people shocked by a sudden unexpected death, who grieve for words unspoken. (With a long illness, everything can be said—if anything can be said.) Trauma affects the chemistry of the brain. The death of the cared-for one—as well as the desperate prolonged caregiving itself, which failed in its purpose—may make changes in the brain like the changes of post-traumatic stress syndrome. For fifteen months I sat by Jane's side, obsessed by her leukemia and her suffering. In the hospital I fetched warm blankets and made lists of questions for our hematologist. At home I saw to her pills and infused her with food and drink and chemicals. I helped her walk and cleaned up after her.

After she died, I was miserable in my grief. I screamed, I spoke to her pictures and at her grave, I wrote her letters in verse. I dreamed that she had run off with another man; I could not sleep because I dreaded dreaming. But I was not depressed in the way that Jane had been depressed.

It has been observed that the survivor often takes on characteristics of the dead. To embody them? To fill the vacancy? Six months after Jane's death I found myself standing near the birdfeeder with Peterson's *Guide* in my hand. The birds had been Jane's preserve for twenty years at the farm. I thought birds were just fine, I loved their song, but I didn't know one from another. With Jane gone I was taking her place.

Jane was affected by the growing darkness of October, November, December, along with her other symptoms. I had always enjoyed the short days: They felt cozy. Late autumn in the year of her death, something like Seasonal Affective Disorder overcame me. I brought her light box from her study to the top of my desk. Then, thirteen months after her death, I became manic for three months: I lost twenty pounds, slept two or three hours a night, and pursued women boldly. Perhaps my sexual need was a response to nightmares of Jane's adulterous abandonment. Perhaps it was eros doing combat with thanatos. (I think of how lovemaking lifted Jane for a moment from gray depression.) Perhaps it was only the familiar symptom of mania. Amazed at my elderly energy, I never considered that I was manic or hypomanic until I crashed into despair and murderous rage, rapidly cycling. (I sought help, and have been helped.) Maybe I perpetuated Jane by imitating her. Maybe inherent bipolarity became activated, the brain altered because of caregiving, failure, and loss.

Jane concluded a poem, begun after her father died, "Oh, when am I going to own my mind again."

MIKE PRIDE

Still Present

On a humid June day more than a year after Jane Kenyon died, I spent twenty minutes in the room where she wrote her poems. Jane's husband, Donald Hall, had left the room pretty much as it was. An exception was a sampler on the north wall. Alice Mattison, Jane's close friend, had stitched it. "You're going to live," it read. It had hung in Jane's bedroom downstairs until she died. Don moved it up to the study because it bothered him to have it around.

I am a relentless if somewhat arbitrary chronicler. I walked around Jane's study scribbling notes about what I saw. In my journal that night, I even drew a crude diagram of the room, indicating where the furniture stood. Jane could look out the south window over her desk to Mt. Kearsarge, the natural landmark around which life in northern Merrimack County revolves. I could not see the mountain on this June day because the sugar maple out front was in full summer dress, but the view must have inspired Jane, especially in winter. I had asked her once if it wasn't difficult to be the second poet in a farmhouse that had been in Don's family for a century and a quarter. She was fierce in reply: "That mountain treats everybody the same."

The single door to Jane's study opened from a storeroom that she and Don called the Back Chamber. It was one floor above the kitchen, two above the root cellar. The room itself was about ten feet by ten feet with a ceiling perhaps eight feet high, though, as a corner room on the second floor, with the roof slanting above, its shape was irregular. The walls were pale yellow, making the study seem bright. A small, low second window let in light at the southwest corner. Diagonally across from this window, near the door, there sat a silver-gray Cottage No. 3 woodstove. Jane and Don had found it in the house and had it restored. Jane lit it most mornings, even in summer, and a pail of kindling and an empty ash pitcher stood ready beside it.

This was a writer's study. Shelves lined most of the walls. Through the books and mementos she had placed on them, Jane had painted a self-portrait. There was a picture of Anna Akhmatova, the Russian poet whom she had translated and borrowed ideas from. There were books by other writers who had influenced her: Chekhov, Keats, Elizabeth Bishop. "One can't be a poet by force," Chekhov said, and Jane had copied the admonition by hand and hung it on her wall. There were many photographs of Don, including one with his friend Daniel Ellsberg. "When I married Don, I married poetry," Jane once told me. Her parents were present in the study, too, her mother in a black-and-white studio portrait, her father through his framed drawing of a stroller. She had also framed a letter rejecting the only prose piece she had ever submitted to the *New Yorker*. The letter was a model of editorial kid gloves: "Since Katherine White died, we haven't run anything about gardens here, and Bob isn't really keen to do so. Good luck placing this lovely piece."

As I walked about Jane's writing room cataloging these things, I felt like a voyeur. True, this was not her closet or her underwear drawer, but her death had invested these objects with poignancy and intimacy. The Jane of this room seemed so present. She might walk in here any morning to write notes and postcards in her cursive hand, which unfurled like ribbon across the page, or to type the second draft of a poem on her IBM Selectric. Although I was nearly certain that in life she would have allowed me to prowl around her study, on that day part of me fretted that she might catch me doing it. This was fourteen months after her death, and Don had begun to let her go. He was winding down a series of postmortem poems in which he let Jane know all that she was missing on Eagle Pond. "She's too far away now," he told me that day. "I don't mean we're estranged, but the time is over when I didn't think or dream about anything else. But things happen—you know, the necessity to stay alive. I say that with some sadness and some guilt, but I also know it is inevitable and right." Still, her study remained alive with her. It was not a place that had been left for good, but neither did it need a "Be right back" sign. This room was expecting her as much as she had wanted to return to it.

But Jane's study was also a finished thing. Through a writer's life there flows a torrent of books, drafts, manuscripts, correspondence, periodicals. If you're not careful about what you keep and how you keep it, before you know it the piles of paper will get the better of your space. Jane was careful. Her study was now a museum of what had meant most to her in life. When she wrote, it helped to have certain literary works at hand. Within easy eyeshot she wanted reminders of family, of friendships, of the humility that turns out to be a writer's friend. You can't force poetry, but the temptation to do so is not unique to you. You reject my work? I'll show you. Jane was dead, but through the walls of her study she whispered. To us modern rationalists, the Spiritualism that enthralled the Victorians seems quaint, but I felt its draft that day.

Probably I make too much of this. The composed, orderly Jane of the study was far from being all of her. As a poet, she wanted to be transparent, to divulge and illuminate, not to conceal, but this did not mean she put everything on the surface. Early in her career, those who compared her poems with Don's often called them simple, meaning simpleminded. I never asked her how she felt about this, but Don knew, and he shared her fury. "There would be people who would say how nice it was that I was all full of big ideas and that she was so sweet and simple," he told me. "She'd want to break their jaws. She did affect simplicity, but she wasn't simple. Her style was a glass of water—a hundred-proof glass of water."

Jane's leukemia seemed doubly cruel because it came just as she had achieved national renown as a poet. Not two months before she was diagnosed, Bill Moyers's documentary on the two poets of Eagle Pond aired on PBS nationwide. Jane and Don had begun reading publicly together, and the belittling comparisons had ended. People came to hear her as much as they came to hear him. By this time Jane had perfected a short lyric poem in which she invested objects and actions with emotions, and her readers made and cherished the connections. She wrote bold incantations—"Let Evening Come," "Briefly It Enters, and Briefly Speaks"—with rhythms and images certain to comfort and inspirit. For *Constance,* her last book, she wrote a long poem about her manic depression. After she read it aloud, listeners flocked to her like disciples.

Jane was grateful for her success but suspicious of it, too. She was in a groove as a poet, but she knew a groove could become a rut. She was in her forties, and she lived with a poet in his sixties who was still experimenting. She was anxious and ambitious about her poetry. It was important for her to keep moving. During an interview just after *Let Evening Come* was published, she told me she was already restless to push beyond the poems that now seemed to come to her so easily. "I need to be working on a kind of frontier where I don't know myself what's going to happen next," she said.

It was in the same spirit that Jane had overcome her reluctance to write prose. As I was leaving her study, I noticed an Amnesty International calendar for 1994 on a wall near the door. Two years old now, it was open to March, the month after leukemia took over her life. In the calendar's square for March 28, Jane had written, "Monitor piece due." I am the editor of the *Concord Monitor,* Jane's hometown newspaper, and I had recruited her to write occasional columns on local life for the paper. Don had often urged her to try her hand at prose, but she resisted. She was uncertain of her skills and afraid of failure. But she had broken through those fears to write for the *Monitor,* just as I am sure she would have risen to new challenges as a poet.

She did not make her March 28 *Monitor* deadline. Less than a month after that date had passed, she wrote me a short note in response to my invitation to her to remain on our board of local contributors. She wasn't quitting, just taking a leave of absence. "I find myself so disabled that I really can't be sure of my ability to write any-thing," she wrote, underlining the "anything." And, in a kind after-word: "You're the person who got me writing prose, and I'm always grateful for it."

I remember only the context of how this came to pass. In 1986, stealing an idea from another newspaper editor, I wrote a column for the *Monitor* inviting local residents to try out as columnists for the paper. My thought was that there were all kinds of expertise in the community that ought to be reflected on the paper's editorial and op-ed pages. After soliciting tryout columns to make sure applicants could write for a general audience, I selected a board of contribu-tors that year to write one column each every two or three months. The first group included a pastor, a professor, an environmentalist, a lawyer, a farmer, a historian, and a teacher. The next year we added a neurosurgeon, a full-time mother, a feminist witch, a quadriplegic activist for the handicapped, and a lifer at the state prison. In the spring of 1989, I invited Jane to join the board of contributors. I be-lieve she had declined my request the year before, but this time she accepted.

I was not looking for a poet to write about poetry, although I knew Jane's vocation would make it into some of her columns. My hope was that she would help us expand our reach into the commu-nity. I wanted her to write about life in Wilmot, where she lived, and the towns around it. And that is what she did. For all her problems with manic depression and her need for solitude to write poetry, she thrived on country life. She volunteered for the local hospice pro-gram, became a connoisseur of the last of the local five-and-dimes, brought two Estonians to town in an exchange program as the Cold War gasped toward its end. She was the longtime treasurer of the South Danbury Church. In short, she embraced her community, and all these sides of her made it into columns. She wrote about her gar-den, the honey wagon that came to clean out the septic system, the agony of waiting for acceptance or rejection notices to show up in her mailbox. She described how the cherubic faces of Mary and Joseph changed through the years in the church's annual Christmas pageant. With telling vignettes and personal reflections she introduced *Monitor* readers to the people who made the community go. Edna Powers, Jane wrote, "was a Democrat—an endangered species up this way—and not shy about it either. You never had to guess how she felt about anything." When Jack Jensen, her spiritual mentor, died, Jane shared what he had given to her: "Over the years my poetry changed to reflect my awakening. Life changed profoundly. I began to be grateful for things that I had always taken for granted."

Until she became too ill to write, Jane cheerfully signed up each year to remain on the board of contributors. What she gained from writing these columns, over and above the princely thirty-five dollars we paid for each of them, I can only speculate. She found, I think, that the columns were another connection to the community she had adopted and come to love. Anyone who has written for a local paper knows how gratifying it is to be approached at the grocery store or at church by neighbors eager to comment on those writings. It is the great and sustaining joy of community journalism. On another level, I think Jane learned quickly that writing columns about the community was not intimidating. It was not, in fact, all that different from writing poetry. You write about people. You look for the detail that shows what you mean. You seek the universal in the particular. You go for the concrete, avoid the abstract. The purpose of the enterprise is to draw out what matters in life: change, loss, love, hope, humanity.

The poet I encountered in Jane's study after she died was the same Jane who was an occasional columnist for the *Concord Monitor.* Shortly after I heard her read her poem "Having It Out with Melancholy" and saw how people afterward rushed up to share their own experiences with depression, I asked her to write a column on the subject for the *Monitor.* She said yes, but she wanted time to think about it first. Leukemia intervened, and she never wrote that column. Had she done so, she would have found within the looser bonds of prose new ways to express her feelings and thoughts about the illness to an audience that might never read a poem. I had seen it before. In those columns, as in her poetry, Jane wrote about what she knew. And sometimes, as in a 1989 column on gardening, her prose soared. "We are in fact like the grass that flourishes and withers, just as the psalmist says," she wrote. "Gardening teaches this lesson over and over, but some of us are slow to learn. We can only acknowledge the mystery, and go on planting burgundy lilies." There are few metaphors as familiar as this one, which holds up the laws of nature to our species' folly in resisting them. Yet from her chair with a view of Mt. Kearsarge, and from her experience in her country garden and her community church, Jane Kenyon found the power to make the metaphor her own. She was of this place, and it should have been no surprise to me when I entered her study that something of her beyond her worldly things should still abide there.

A Conversation with Jane Kenyon

Did your early life prepare you in any way for life in rural New Hampshire?

I was born and grew up in Ann Arbor. I went to a one-room school through the fourth grade. When I later went to city schools, I was terribly ashamed. I tried to pass as an urbanite. As a child, I lived across the street from a working farm. Ann Arbor is prone to urban sprawl—it was becoming a megalopolis. Moving here for me was getting back something that I had loved and lost.

Could you tell me about your beginnings as a poet— your first inklings that you might want to be one?

In the ninth grade my English teacher gave the assignment of writing a poem—something I'd never thought of doing. And I found that I loved it. I was a typical adolescent bursting with emotion that I didn't know what to do with.

I never stopped. In my childhood from the time I first remember I had an urge to make things. I put that urge to make things together with this love of language and emotional life, which is really what poetry is about—emotion. I grew up in an artistic household—both my parents were jazz musicians—and writing seemed to be my territory.

I was not a voracious reader until I was almost thirty. I was a good English student, and I got a good education at Ann Arbor High School. It was full of university kids. But I was not an enthusiastic student. I think I was probably quite a melancholy kid, quite a depressed kid. I knew I had an inner life, and I knew that was what really interested me. And I fed it as I could.

At the University of Michigan, I found a community of poets, and there were readings. I found my little corner of that huge university. My poet friends were then and still are very important to me.

How much do you lean on others to help you with your poetry now?

Don reads everything of mine and I read everything of his, and I listen to everything he tells me carefully. Also, I show everything to Alice Mattison and Joyce Peseroff. I never consider anything finished until I've taken it through my committee.

How do you work, and how long does it take you to write a poem?

I work every morning. I almost never finish anything in less than six months. I begin a poem and within a week I have a dozen drafts. I keep poking at it. I put it away and take it out. I start with a longhand version and go through maybe eight or nine typed revisions. When I reach a point where I can't do any more with it, I take it to Alice and Joyce. Then I revise it in light of what they've told me.

**You and Don are both poets working in the same terrain—
dominated by the same mountain. Doesn't that present
some problems for you?**

That mountain treats everybody the same. I do actually have a new
poem about climbing the mountain that I've written since this book.
The poem likens the mountain to a mother's body, to this great healing, embracing being.

Don's experience of coming here and my experience of coming
here were different. He had a past here, and I had no past here. I found
in coming here so much to remark upon. It was as if I had finally
found my subject. The sheer physical beauty of this place is like food
to me. I can't tell you how it nourishes my soul.

One of the great gifts of coming here was to come into a community. I never felt a sense of community in Ann Arbor. Here I felt it
immediately, and it's such a great joy to me, such a great comfort.

How does that sense of community influence your poetry?

It makes one less self-obsessed and more concerned about the needs
of others. It gives you a feeling that you are part of the great stream.
You're not alone.

**You wrote translations of Anna Akhmatova.
What did you take from her work?**

She's the master of the short intense love lyric. To me, that's it. Poetry
doesn't get better than that. What I've taken from her work is the
absolute conviction that the natural object will embody any emotion
you want it to embody. "The natural object is always the adequate
symbol."

In one poem, for example, Keats's anger is rising as his health
is ebbing, and he throws the food out the window that has been
brought to him. You don't have to say that he was angry—all you
have to say is he threw the food out the window.

There's a famous image in Akhmatova, where she has a woman

who's just had a sort of equivocal meeting with her lover. She's in such a state of confusion that she starts to put the wrong glove on the wrong hand. Now everything you see in that gesture—all of her discomfiture, all of her confusion—all Akhmatova says is the glove that belongs on the right hand I put on my left hand.

The title poem of your latest book, *Let Evening Come,* **seems different from the others. What can you tell me about it?**

I had virtually all the poems in that book written, but I felt that it just lacked one thing to pull them together. It was pretty dark. When I read from this book, people get very sober. There's not very much that's funny in this book. It's pretty somber, and I knew I wanted something redeeming, I wanted something—well, there's a wonderful quote from John's gospel: "The light shines in the darkness, and the darkness has not overcome it." That's what I set out to say by writing that poem.

There have been several poems given to me, as it were. I struggled with the end of it, but for the most part that poem was easy to write, and I just feel that poem was given to me. That's the only way I can talk about it.

Why? What do you mean?

I don't know. It seemed to come either from some very secret place— some place I hardly know myself—or else from somewhere else. It came through me. I didn't struggle with it. I didn't think, "Well now, what do I say next?" It just fell out.

How is that different from the way other poems come to you?

There's always great excitement in beginning a poem—even mania, if you will—but you have to use your critical faculties to finish a poem. You have to be patient if you're going to do this job, and you have to work long enough on a thing so that the critical faculties at some point come to bear. You know, being a poet is the funniest combination of being loose and being disciplined. It's a very funny combination: to be floating, to be listening, to be passive, and to be editorial.

Have you always been able to see life that way—as a poet?

(Facetiously) Yeah, I came out of my mother's womb that way.

You know, it isn't something I would choose for myself. There's a price. There's a price.

What's the price?

I really think that poets feel things more deeply than other people do. Our emotional lives are very rich and very complex, and sometimes quite overwhelming. This is not something I would choose. I'd rather be a landscape architect.

Are you serious?

I'm a passionate gardener.

How would you compare these two passions— for poetry and for gardening?

You know, they're not unalike. They both teach us about death and resurrection. They teach us patience, humility. There's always something going wrong in a garden that you wouldn't anticipate—some ghastly creature is eating the boltonia and ruining the leaves, a black spot is on the delphinium. It teaches humility. There is the joy of creation in the garden, the joy of shape and color and orchestrating the seasons of bloom, the heights.

I really think they're remarkably alike. The love of beauty is in both. The obedience to the laws of the universe is in both, the obedience to birth and flowering and death. One must be obedient to this. One is subject to this always.

**I notice a religious aspect in many of your poems.
Isn't that a rare thing in modern poetry?**

I've become more overt about my spiritual life. My spiritual life is so much a part of my intellectual life and my feeling life that it's really become impossible for me to keep it out of my work.

At first when I began to write about religious matters, I felt embarrassment, and I still feel a certain reluctance to talk about these very private matters in a public way. There are some things that go on in your spiritual life that must go on in secret. They cannot be talked about. They must not be talked about. They're between you and God only, and they're not to be talked about.

How have people reacted to that element of your poetry?

I have encountered astonishment. "You're religious!" one woman said to me after a reading at Erie College. And I said, "Yeah." But I think she found that the poems were religious in a way that did not alienate her, and this is what surprised her.

It's a very tricky business talking about personal matters, and yet it seems that my spiritual life has become something that I cannot suppress. It's so much a part of me. The danger, of course, is that one might brag spiritually. There might be bragging in these poems. This is something that I worry about a lot. And yet I take chances. I also open myself to ridicule by thoroughly secular intellectuals. But that doesn't bother me as much as the potential for spiritual pride.

I have had many mystical experiences, and these have been the most joyous moments of my life, the most illuminating, the most peacemaking moments of my life. Shall I not share these with people? People tell me that my poems are common to them.

The writing of "Let Evening Come" was a mystical experience. I felt calm, energetic, and lucid, and these words came to me. I knew in some way more than I know.

**Now that this book is out, do you see
a new direction for yourself?**

I'm not that organized. I don't choose a path. I'm just writing poems one at a time. What I try to do is just do my work every day. I try to do the best I can do every day. Every couple of years, I pick up my head and look around and see what I've got, then I put my head back down and I start culling again. I don't think in terms of books—I think in terms of the thing at hand. This is the only way I can work. Otherwise I would create so much pressure for myself that I would become quite incapacitated.

Is there anything that troubles you in your career right now?

There's a certain kind of poem I know how to write. I can write 'em, I can sell 'em to magazines, I can get 'em published. I can read them from the podium, and people say they love them. And yet I have produced them fairly automatically and fairly much out of the will. I need to be working on a kind of frontier where I don't know myself what's going to happen next. And I haven't felt I was working in that way for some time. So sometimes this feeling—almost a feeling of boredom with what you're able to do.

But if you're going to be an artist you have to be perpetually dissatisfied. Otherwise why would you get up in the morning? Why would you try again? You would think to yourself, "I've done it!"

I think I'm getting ready to write something that I don't know anything about yet. Writing these prose pieces (for the *Concord Monitor*) is shaking something loose. I have sudden access to more verbiage than I've ever had. It's as if I have discovered my new vein of verbal energy. I find that I have more to say than I thought.

How are the prose pieces different from the poetry for you?

They're more outward, less meditative, and more communal.

Do you see yourself as a feminist?

I'm not an overtly political person, but I am deeply concerned with recording women's existence. What is it like to be a woman living in New Hampshire in 1990? It's as if someone had asked me that. I am deeply concerned that women's experience be articulated and valued.

How did your relationship with Donald Hall come about?

Now I don't want people speculating about whether I busted up his marriage. I didn't. He was divorced when I got to know him. I don't want people speculating.

I was thinking about your poetry rather than your private life.

I first took a course from him when I was an undergraduate: Introduction to Poetry. It was a huge course, intended for non-English majors. It was the most wonderful course. The poets all flocked to it. That's where I met my group of peers. What Don did was instill an appreciation of poetry, line by line, word by word.

And later?

We were married in 1972. When I married Don, I married poetry. We moved here in 1975. The move meant I had twenty-four hours a day in which to do anything I wanted. I suddenly had all this time on my hands. It was after we moved here that I began to work every day. I began to read more, work more, because I had a lot of hours to fill. I had a lot of solitude. That's what it takes. I'm blessed.

Moving here has meant so much to me personally and professionally. I know that without the solitude and the kind of floating time I have here, without that suspension of time that I can achieve here by taking the phone off the hook and not answering the door—that solitude is critical to my work. For me, poetry comes out of silence, and I can have silence here.

The beauty of this place is just so nourishing to me. I just can't find words for how much I love these hills and trees and rocks and stone walls and old houses and people's asparagus beds. I just can't tell you how much I love what I see when I drive down Route 4 or walk in the woods with the dog.

Listening to you, I'm reminded of Dickinson and Thoreau.

I could very easily be a monk. It would suit me fine—if I could go to museums and concerts once in a while. When Don's away, I can go for days at a time without speaking. And I love it. If I need to talk to somebody, I talk to the dog and the cat.

I love solitude. Don and I allow each other to be solitary in the house. We respect each other's working time. We respect each other's concentration. If I see that he's thinking about something, I don't talk to him about when we're going to get the car stickered. And he does the same for me.

We have solitude here, and we also have communion. The business of writing is a very lonely occupation. Nobody does it for you. It's just you and the thought.

As for Dickinson, I haven't made her mine the way I've made Keats mine—line by line, I've made him mine. I admire her enormously. I find her extremely difficult. She rewards any work that you do to understand her. But Keats, Elizabeth Bishop, and Akhmatova, I've taken those poems apart the way you take a watch apart—to see how they work and how they go back together again.

Does it bother you to be the junior poet in this household?

Of course, the danger is that Don is at the point in his career where he's getting to be thought of as quite a statesman of poetry, someone with a lot of answers. And he is someone with a lot of answers. He knows things nobody else knows. But I also know things nobody else knows. It's funny how everything in your life, every experience, everything in your reading, everything in your thinking, in your spiritual life—you bring it all to your work when you sit down to write. And he knows what he knows and I know what I know.

I have had to develop over the years the conviction that I must be where I am in my work and in my human understanding. I can only be where I am. I can obviously not be in a place where a man who's nineteen years older than I am is—not professionally, not experimentally, not in any way. My women friends in particular give me the courage I need to just be who I am.

Don has enough energy for about three human beings. This year he's doing about five books. I do a book of poems, one slim volume, about every five years. Now if we're talking about weight, if we're talking pages, I'd have to think of myself as a pretty poor specimen. But I think to myself: I'm forty-three years old, I publish in good places, I'm doing okay. I just have to honor my own speed of work, my own way of working, my own vision. And I'm getting better and better at doing that.

It's like driving on Storrow Drive (a busy Boston thoroughfare). People might do their crazy shit all around you. They're just crazy, they're weaving in and out, they're doing everything but going over you. Your job is to stay on the road and not run into the person in front of you. That's all you're supposed to do. You just have to be where you are.

Critical Essays

LABAN HILL

Jane Kenyon

At a gravesite in the Proctor Graveyard in Andover, New Hampshire, stands a gravestone with the lines "I BELIEVE IN THE MIRACLES OF ART BUT WHAT / PRODIGY WILL KEEP YOU SAFE BE-SIDE ME." These lines are from Jane Kenyon's poem "Afternoon at MacDowell" and were written by Kenyon with her husband, poet Donald Hall, in mind. At the time Kenyon wrote the poem, Hall had cancer and was "supposed to die." The sad irony here is that Jane Kenyon died first of leukemia on April 22, 1995. The lines now stand in testimony to Kenyon, and they look, mistakenly, like the words were written for her. Consequently, both the "I" and the "you" in the epitaph refer to Kenyon herself and provide an odd, but telling, testament to her identity as a poet. Throughout her life Kenyon's work explored the difficulty of locating herself in the world, in a sense, "inhabiting a home." Her poems and prose repeatedly articulated the region of her senses: what she saw, what she heard, what she touched, what she smelled, and what she tasted. Her evocatively descriptive language attempted to map her relationship to her surroundings. In her poem "From Room to Room" she writes:

> I move from room to room,
> a little dazed, like the fly. I watch it
> bump against each window.
>
> I am clumsy here. . . .

Critics have described Kenyon's work as exploring the inner psyche, especially in relation to her own battles with depression. Essayist Gary Roberts noted in *Contemporary Women Poets* that her poetry was "acutely faithful to the familiarities and mysteries of home life, and it is distinguished by intense calmness in the face of routine disappointments and tragedies." Although accurate, these characterizations only partially encompass Kenyon's work, which should be remembered as much more courageous, passionate, and unblinking in the belief that people can find comfort and understanding in their immediate world.

Kenyon's Background

Jane Kenyon was born on May 23, 1947, in Ann Arbor, Michigan. The second of two children, her family lived in an area that is now within the city of Ann Arbor, but then was merely part of the township and was primarily populated by small farms and orchards not far from the Huron River. Her father was a musician who also taught music while her mother stayed home to raise the children. Her father suffered throughout his life from clinical depression. The family was staunchly Methodist and had several Methodist ministers on both sides. This doctrinal influence had a powerful effect on forming Kenyon's sense of herself in the world. She and her brother Reuel stayed often at her paternal grandmother's big house on State Street in Ann Arbor where her grandmother took in University of Michigan students as boarders. Her grandmother, Dora Baldwin Kenyon, had a strong influence on Kenyon as a child because of her dark obsessions with Christ's Second Coming and the end of the world as we know it. In an unfinished essay titled "Childhood, When You Are in It . . . ," collected with all of her prose in *A Hundred White Daffodils: Essays, the Akhmatova Translations, Newspaper Columns, Notes, Interviews, and One Poem* (1999), Kenyon described a defining experience: "I might have been seven or eight when my grandmother first said to me, opening her eyes wide, and then wider. 'The body is the temple of the Holy Ghost.' We were sitting in the dark living room, dark because the shades were kept half-drawn, and the sheer curtains were never pulled back. . . . I know that grandmother had said something solemn, and I knew that somehow *my* body was under discussion."

It was hard for Kenyon to fall asleep at the house on State Street because there was always a lingering sense that "Jesus would come in the night to judge [her] life." Like her grandmother's favorite hymn, "Onward Christian Soldiers, Marching As to War," Dora Baldwin Kenyon instilled in Kenyon a sense that life was indeed a battle for salvation in the eyes of the Lord. These doctrinal conditions helped underscore a deep sense of discomfort in both her body and her environment. Objects contained an aura or power beyond their material manifestations. These feelings of presence in things would come to influence her belief in the evocative nature of images.

By the age of nine or ten, Kenyon began to resent the dominance that her religious fear held over her. Out of this resentment grew a germ of distrust for the overwhelming responsibility of being judged by Christ. Concurrently, she became aware of the surprising absence of moral authority in the natural world. In her 1993 interview with David Bradt, collected in *A Hundred White Daffodils,* Kenyon described this time: "I spent long hours playing at the stream that ran through my family's property. We lived on a dirt road near the Huron River, across from a working farm. I fell in love with the natural world." She wrote about this time years later in the poem "In the Grove: The Poet at Ten," collected in *Let Evening Come* (1990), describing how "She lay on her back in the timothy" and "Nothing would rouse her then / from that joy so violent." These newfound feelings of comfort led her to denounce her Methodist heritage that promoted the notion that she was sinful by nature and to embrace a belief system akin to Jean Jacques Rousseau's noble savage. In her essay "Childhood, When You Are in It . . ." she wrote, "I announced to my parents that one could not be a Christian and an intellectual, and that I would no longer attend church. . . . Nature will be my god, and I'll be a good person simply because it is the right thing to do." Her grandmother's notions of a world threatening her salvation were transformed into a belief that it was exactly her grandmother's dangerous world that eventually would redeem her.

While she nurtured this safe haven in nature, other areas of her life underscored what little affinity she experienced elsewhere. In addition to her discomfort at home and at her grandmother's, she never fit in at school. At her one-room elementary school, Foster School No.16 Fractional, it was obvious to Kenyon that her teacher, Mrs. Irwin, did not like her, and Kenyon returned the favor. This mutual disregard made it difficult for Kenyon to enjoy school. Instead, much like her home and her grandmother's house, it became a place of dread. In her essay "Dreams of Math," collected in *A Hundred White Daffodils,* she writes, "I had math anxiety, as it's come to be called. Letters, reading, spelling made sense to me, but numbers had such strange proclivities. That zero times four was zero, canceling out the existence of the four, seemed dubious at best." She no longer accepted authority's interpretation. No one could ever say, "because that's the way it is." She learned that she must come to the knowledge on her own through an examination of the evidence before her. From her previous experiences she had learned to rely on her senses to lead her to the truth. It was this almost doctrinaire reliance on the inductive process that seemed to open her to the power of metaphor and poetry. To support these feelings about self-reliance, nothing in her junior high and high school years that followed fostered a sense of belonging to a community. Instead, she felt even more lost among the 900 students.

Several thematic concerns that appear in Kenyon's later work seem to have evolved from the conflict of childhood experiences. In *A Hundred White Daffodils* Kenyon has characterized this time as one in which she discovered that she "had neither the courage to rebel, nor an obedient heart." This skepticism and mistrust played a significant role in the poetic project of attempting to articulate a physical, emotional, and spiritual relation to the world that is uniquely authentic. In her early poems she had almost a rigid adherence to the transcendent power of the image, so that her poems were more like observations absent of a discriminating eye. In her notes for a lecture given at a literary conference in Enfield, New Hampshire, and collected in *A Hundred White Daffodils,* she said, "We celebrate the world by writing about it, we observe it more closely, with more love. We are more fully alive and aware because of our efforts."

Years at the University of Michigan

On graduation from high school, Kenyon attended the University of Michigan at Ann Arbor where she received a bachelor's degree in 1970 and a master's degree in 1972. It was there that she met her husband, the poet Donald Hall. In the spring of 1969 Hall led a class of more than 100 students. Jane Kenyon was among those students, but it was not until the following fall semester that they finally met when she was admitted to his poetry workshop. In an interview with Jeffrey Cramer published by the *Massachusetts Review* Hall describes how they met, "I remember one particular poem. . . . 'The Needle'. . . . I think maybe that poem got her in the class. Thank God." Along with ten or eleven other students, Kenyon met with Hall once a week for several hours in his living room. Nineteen years her senior, Hall led this workshop for two and a half years. Over this time Kenyon and Hall developed a friendship. Even though the relationship was initially a student-to-teacher one, over time there grew a deeper, more intense connection that led to marriage in April 1972.

Clearly, this relationship defined Kenyon's development as a poet. A tenured professor at the University of Michigan, recently divorced, and father of two when they met, Donald Hall was a mature poet in his forties. In contrast, Kenyon was a graduate student who was not altogether clear that poetry would be her life's work. As the two describe the development of their relationship, it was an attraction that both resisted at first, but somehow the inevitability of it was impossible to avoid. In the beginning, the imbalance of power with Hall having been her teacher was difficult. In an interview with Marian

Blue, collected in *A Hundred White Daffodils,* Hall described the difficulty of their change in relationship from student and teacher to lovers, "When we were first married, we had to cope with that earlier relationship. I couldn't criticize her poems, because then I became her teacher. It was physically confusing: her husband suddenly turns into Professor Hall." To resolve this dilemma, Hall and Kenyon invited a third person, their friend and poet Gregory Orr, to their home. This made all the difference. "When Gregory Orr would join us, then I could say anything about Jane's poems and she could say everything about mine. Greg's presence made it a workshop in which we were equals," Hall said. They adhered to this formula for the first two and a half years of their marriage. Orr then moved to Virginia, and Kenyon and Hall relocated to New Hampshire.

Kenyon described the differences between Hall and herself in the same interview with Marian Blue, "I think our visions are very different. Don has been writing a long time, and he has passed through many shapes and sizes, if you will, for his poems. He is writing large, ambitious, loose-limbed poems these days, poems in which all his wisdom appears. I am working at one thing—the short lyric. It is all I want, at this point: to write short, intense, musical cries of the spirit. I am a miniaturist and he is painting Diego Rivera murals. I'm not being modest about trying to write short lyrics in the tradition of Sappho, Keats, and Akhmatova." Kenyon's comparison of Hall to the famous Mexican painter Diego Rivera seems an unconscious acknowledgment of Hall's towering aesthetic presence in her life. To complete this allusion by then comparing Kenyon to the artist Frida Kahlo, Rivera's wife, might be considered a stretch, but the effort does hold a grain of truth in that Kahlo's canvases were much more contained and psychically pained than Rivera's, just as Kenyon's poems map a difficult psychic landscape that is much more personal and inward-looking than Hall's.

Eagle Pond

This towering presence did not diminish, however, when they moved in 1975 from Ann Arbor to Eagle Pond, Hall's family farm in Wilmot, New Hampshire, for Hall's year-long sabbatical from the University of Michigan. The farm had been settled by Hall's great-grandfather in 1865. In the *Life at Eagle Pond: The Poetry of Jane Kenyon and Donald Hall* web site, Hall, who spent his childhood summers and wrote his first poems there, described this return as both a coming home and a "coming home to the place of language." For Kenyon, the farm was an environment that was similar to the rural landscape of her childhood where she first discovered herself. This return to nature was essential to her beginning to write seriously for the first time. Within the woods and rolling hills populated with small farms, she rediscovered the subject that nurtured her own inner journey toward self-discovery. As Charles Simic observed on the web site, "Kenyon's country is both our rural New Hampshire and her inwardness in which we all recognize ourselves."

Before her arrival at Eagle Pond, Kenyon's commitment to writing was haphazard and undisciplined. In her interview with Bill Moyers, collected in *A Hundred White Daffodils,* she described this time, "I really didn't get going in my work until we came here (Eagle Pond). I have all the time in the world here. I had to do something to fill those hours, so I began to work more. I used to work only when the spirit moved, but when we came here I began to write every day . . . [and was] getting serious about this poetry business." The shape of her and Hall's days centered around a morning of writing in their own offices.

At the end of Hall's sabbatical year, they decided that Eagle Pond was where they would make their home. Hall resigned his professorship at the University of Michigan and embarked on a career as a freelance writer. By the late 1990s he was the author of thirteen volumes of verse, and author or editor of nineteen anthologies and books of prose. Over the years, it was primarily his work that provided the income that sustained him and Kenyon on the farm. While Hall continued mining the aesthetic veins that he had been working for years, Kenyon embarked upon a two-year immersion into the poetry of John Keats. Although she wrote very little about other poets, it is clear that Keats's sense of the lyric as meditation on one's relationship to the physical world influenced Kenyon's work. In her first book *From Room to Room,* published in 1978, most of the poems are anchored in observation, rather than engagement, of the world.

From Room to Room

All but two of the forty-three poems, "The Needle" and another unnamed poem, from her first book *From Room to Room* were written at Eagle Pond. Though beautiful, the strategies of "The Needle" are not quite consistent with the rest of the poems from the collection and do not bear the stamp of Keats's influence. Instead, the poem seems more consistent with her later work. The poem begins with a comparison: "Grandmother, you are as pale / as Christ's hands on the wall above you." Kenyon's early poems are typically absent of such figures of speech, particularly in the first few lines, as well as direct Christian references. Instead her poems arrive at the connotative much more timidly. She relies on her eye to describe and allows the image to evoke its own aura. The first poem in the collection is "For the Night." It is on the surface a series of descriptions:

> The mare kicks
> in her darkening stall, knocks
> over a bucket.
>
> The goose . . .
>
> The cow keeps a peaceful brain . . .

Reminiscent of early twentieth-century Imagism, the inflection in the poem arises ever so quietly in line five with the adjective "peaceful." Surprisingly, the entire poem rests on this adjective while what follows describes rather neutrally the way light moves and a bat flies. Its delicacy and spare lines appear anachronistic and somewhat derivative of William Carlos Williams's poems like "The Red Wheel Barrel" or "This Is Just To Say" in the way that Williams sometimes placed inordinate emotional weight on isolated parts of speech. The odd thing in "For the Night," however, is the speaker's absence. It is almost as if such a serene environment can only be observed from the outside, not from within. This void of presence leaves the reader wondering if the speaker's location, in contrast to this peace, is some kind of discomfort. As a first poem in a collection, "For the Night" is a strong statement of Kenyon's aesthetic and spiritual principles that nature holds the key to finding acceptance.

It is ironic that *From Room to Room* begins with such a strong description of a safe haven because much of the book examines moving from one place to another and the difficulty of giving up one home to find another. The second poem in the book is even titled as such, "Leaving Town." It again is primarily a description except for one simile at the end. "I felt like a hand without an arm." In the poem the speaker tracks the giving away of plants, the loading of the truck, the journey out of town, and the increasingly fainter radio signal of a Tigers game. The images play on the reader's sympathy for the painful experience of separation. "Friends handed us the cats through the half-closed windows." The last separation with the past is made through a window that is already "half-closed," not half-open, as if leaving can only be seen in the pessimistic terms of closure. This gesture of faithfulness to the past and to established relationships stands as a beacon for the difficulty she has discovering her place in her new home. The poems that follow in the book explore this conflict of making a context in a place where she had no context before and where there existed a rich context already without her.

Kenyon first catalogs experiences that set her apart from her new home. There's a strange absence and powerlessness in these poems in which the world that surrounds her has much more weight and presence than she has herself. One poem is titled "Here," but the lines describe a place in which the speaker is struggling to find a "here" for herself. Even though there is an epigraph from *The Book of Common Prayer,* which is supposed to emphasize her acceptance of her new place in New Hampshire, the actual poem contradicts this quotation by underscoring a sense of frailty, impermanence, and vulnerability because the speaker compares her connection to her home to a cutting just rooting in a glass of water.

> I feel my life start up again,
> like a cutting when it grows
> the first pale and tentative
> root hair in a glass of water.

Other poems, such as "From Room to Room," "The Presence of Others," and "The Cold," seem to highlight the permanence of what is already there in contrast to her own unrootedness. On the whole these poems are creating a vivid sensory experience of this conflict, except in a poem such as "This Morning," in which the speaker's presence is so absent that the reader has no voice or identity on which to anchor himself or herself. The pronoun "I" appears subordinated and located in the past.

> A nuthatch drops
> to the ground, feeding
> on the sunflower seed and bits of bread
> I scattered on the snow.

In contrast, everything else in the poem is so present that even the noise of the plow passing on the road draws the attention of the cats and makes "the house / tremble as it passes." This attendance by the world, however, does not add up to much, and this reflects so poorly on the "I" of the poem that the speaker has no real value and, thus, is not worth listening to. At times the humility in Kenyon's poems can devolve too dangerously into an expression of no self-worth. These tendencies seem like a foreshadowing of the clinical depression that she wrote about later on.

Nevertheless, the tenuousness of the speaker's presence provides some of the most lyrical moments in the collection. In "The Thimble," her discovery of this object leads her not only to feelings of connection to the past, but also to her community and, ultimately, to God. Not surprisingly, the connection to her new home is found through objects left behind by women who once lived there—the gray hair, the thimble. She finds a kinship with these women that culminates in "Hanging Pictures in Nanny's Room," in which Kenyon imagines the mentality and daily rituals of an ancestor in a parlor photograph. This finally leads to a sequence in the second part of the book where she finds a link to her past and to her mother and grandmother. From this axis that connects her legacy to her future, Kenyon is able to construct an environment in which she belongs. In this book it becomes clear how important women are to her sense of place. As a child her grandmother and teacher were key to her dislocation within her community. Now, it is the artifacts of long-dead women who help her find a home, and later in *From Room to Room,* it is the poetry of the Russian poet Anna Akhmatova that informs her poetry.

In the next-to-last section of *From Room to Room,* the speaker tentatively discovers happiness, but the journey is strange in that the speaker seems not to have an active role in the arrival of this emotion. Instead, she is merely a recipient. Critics have commented on Kenyon's work as being eerily calm and egoless, but this absence of self has deeper implications in its relation to how she defines herself. In "The Suitor" the speaker personifies happiness as someone who pursues her. This is further explicated in the next poem "American Triptych," where her only sense of being an active force in her happiness is as a member of a community.

> The store is a bandstand. All our voices
> sound from it, making the same motley
> American music Ives heard . . .

The poem's three parts feature the country store where "Cousins arrive like themes and variations;" kids playing baseball in a hayfield, beyond "deaths or separations," and a potluck supper at the Baptist church whose wholesomeness restores a sense of personal and national innocence:

> On the way home we pass the white clapboard faces of the library and town hall, luminous in the moonlight, and I remember the first time I ever voted—in a township hall in Michigan.

> That same wonderful smell of coffee was in the air, and I found myself among people trying to live ordered lives. . . . And again I am struck with love for the Republic.

From here, Kenyon is able to arrive at the final poem of the section, "Now That We Live." This poem celebrates the natural world around her with playful descriptions of a "Fat spider" and a "Brow of hayfield." Her use of adjectives has changed from the ponderous inflections of the poems early in the volume to an expressiveness that underscores a feeling that she is at last at home: "I belong to the Queen of Heaven!"

Translating Anna Akhmatova

The journey explored in *From Room to Room* is not limited, however, to the author's efforts at finding a place of comfort, but also is an expedition into Kenyon's identity as a poet. Kenyon in a sense moves "from room to room" trying on styles like prose poems and compressed imagist poems to find a poetic structure that she can inhabit. This journey concludes with translations of six early poems by Akhmatova, whose imagist techniques provided a model for the poetic sensibility that coalesces in *From Room to Room* and matures in Kenyon's later work. In his introductory essay to *A Hundred White Daffodils,* Hall described how crucial Akhmatova was to Kenyon's development: "[A]s she worked with Akhmatova's early lyrics, condensations of strong feeling into compact images both visual and aural, she practiced making the kind of poetry she admired most— an art that embodied powerful emotion by means of the luminous particular."

It was poet and translator Robert Bly who first suggested Kenyon study Akhmatova, and who, along with poet Louis Simpson, directed her to Vera Sandomirsky Dunham, a professor of Russian literature at the State University of New York at Stonybrook, in 1977. For the next eight years Kenyon immersed herself in Akhmatova's pre-revolutionary poems. In 1985, she published *Twenty Poems of Anna Akhmatova,* a small book of translations that is now collected in *A Hundred White Daffodils.* While Kenyon was working on the translations, Dunham apparently pressed her to render the poems in meter and rhyme to reflect the formal aspects of the Russian originals. Kenyon resisted, however. In her introduction, which was her only essay in literary criticism, Kenyon wrote, "Because it is impossible to translate with fidelity to form and to image, I have sacrificed form for image. Image embodies feeling, and this embodiment is perhaps the greatest treasure of lyric poetry. In translating, I mean to place the integrity of the image over all other considerations." This adherence to the primacy of image not only fit neatly into Kenyon's own poetics, but was also based in the poetics of the group of poets Akhmatova belonged to before the 1917 revolution. Kenyon wrote, "Acmeism held that a rose is beautiful in itself, not because it stands for something. . . . clarity, concision, and perfection of form. They summed up their goals in two words: 'beautiful clarity.'" These words could function as Kenyon's own aesthetic principles, just as the poems she selected to translate speak directly to her own poems.

In the first translation in the collection, "The memory of sun weakens my heart," the lines evoke an elegance that Kenyon aspired to in *From Room to Room*. Readers can hear echoes of Akhmatova's lines, such as "Against the empty sky the willow opens / a transparent fan. / Maybe it's a good thing I'm not / your wife," in "Now That We Live" and other poems in Kenyon's first book. The difference, however, is that Akhmatova's voice has the confidence and power that is lacking in *From Room to Room*. Even though Kenyon's efforts to master the pre-revolutionary poetic concerns of Akhmatova was her way of constructing a poetics of her own, there is a troubling thought that arises when considering, what she ignored: Akhmatova's later more epic and political work, including "Requiem" and "Song Without a Hero," two poems considered her greatest and most ambitious achievements. Nevertheless, this choice is typical of Kenyon who seemed to refuse to look where others have already gazed.

Religious Awakening

While immersed in the translations, Kenyon was clearly aware of the irony that both she and Akhmatova considered their marriages to be the beginning of their lives. For Kenyon, this was not simply because her adult life began at the same time as her marriage to Hall. The life at Eagle Pond and the surrounding community that she discovered through Hall's roots gave Kenyon a surge of power and clarity that led to the resolution of the spiritual emptiness she experienced as a child. Her spiritual journey began as simply and prosaically as an image in one of her poems. One Sunday, Hall suggested they go to church. At first it was more of a social act than a spiritual one, but soon the experience became "luminous." She started to take comfort from prayer and the assurance of pardon for sins. The sense of relief that came from this acceptance coincided with her realization that she couldn't avoid those human qualities, like selfishness and irritability, which she had hoped she would transcend. Prayer offered her a chance to acknowledge her own failings and start over.

At the suggestion of her pastor at South Danbury Church, Kenyon began to read the New Testament. She started with Mark's Gospel with Barclay's commentary, and went on to read the other gospels as well as the Acts of the Apostles, the Epistles, the Prophets, and the Psalms. In her essay "Gabriel's Truth," collected in *A Hundred White Daffodils,* she wrote, "Mary teaches us to trust God always, to live in hope, to respond with love to whatever happens, to give and not count the cost, to be faithful in the worst circumstances. She teaches us, men and women, not to insist on ourselves, on our own comforts and satisfactions. And she shows us, finally, that her strenuous love was able to defeat death." Not surprisingly, this passage encompasses many of the concerns Kenyon had had since childhood. It also accentuated another connection of hers. Once again, Kenyon finds truth and meaning through the words, actions, and legacy of a woman.

In most of her prose and interviews Kenyon refers to a turning point in her life. In 1980 she had a vision that deepened her faith and clarified her understanding of her place in the world. "It was like a waking dream. My eyes were open and I saw these rooms, this house, but in my mind's eye, or whatever language you can find to say these things, I also saw a great ribbon of light and every human life was suspended. There was no struggle. There was only this buoyant shimmering, undulating stream of light. I took my place in the stream and after that my life changed fundamentally. I relaxed into existence in a way that I never had before," Kenyon described in an interview with Bill Moyers, collected in *A Hundred White Daffodils.* After this experience, her poetry changed profoundly. It became more assertive and more clearly spiritual, which particularly becomes clear in *Otherwise: New and Selected Poems* (1996). In her short essay "Thoughts on the Gifts of Art" from *A Hundred White Daffodils,* Kenyon described her belief that every poem is "a state-of-the-soul address" and expanded on this with the statement, "Artists report on the inner life, and the inner life distinguishes us from centipedes, although I may underestimate centipedes."

The Boat of Quiet Hours

Kenyon's next collection of poems, *The Boat of Quiet Hours,* was published the year following her translations and contains sixty-two poems. In this collection, a New England stoicism arises that cannot help, with its reference to John Keats's *Endymion, Book I* in the title, to be perceived as a contemporary permutation of Kenyon's beloved poet Keats's concept of negative capability. In these portraits of domestic and rural life in northern New England there exists a selfless receptivity to the subject. In a review of *The Boat of Quiet Hours* poet and critic Carol Muske wrote in the *New York Times,* "These poems surprise beauty at every turn and capture truth at its familiar New England slant. Here, in Keats's terms, is a capable poet." The book opens with "Evening at a Country Inn" where the dramatic situation is the speaker empathizing with her companion's mourning. The poem is striking for its active energy, which is expressed in lines such as that describing a red cloud as "impaled on the Town Hall weather vane." This kind of verb signals a definite change for Kenyon from the tentativeness of the speaker in *From Room to Room.* A few lines later she writes, "Red-faced skiers stamp past you . . . their hunger is Homeric." The hyperbolic looseness reminds the reader that the process of dying happens in the midst of living. The wrenching tenderness of the last lines of the poem are particularly Keatsian in their attempt to redeem her lingering on death with a kind of gusto for life. The lines look for comfort in the quiet reduction of self's presence through its identification with the inanimate:

> I know you are thinking of the accident—
> of picking the slivered glass from his hair.
> Just now a truck loaded with hay
> stopped at the village store to get gas.
> I wish you would look at the hay—
> the beautiful sane and solid bales of hay.

These last lines of the first poem in the book could easily be taken as a statement of her poetics: what you see will redeem you. In this vein, the collection is then arranged into four seasons as if to track how life follows the cycles of nature, but there is a difference. Kenyon subtracts autumn and inserts what all New Englanders consider the fifth season, mud season. The first section, "Walking Alone in Late Winter," contains poems about death and loss. "At the Town Dump" echoes Theodore Roethke's poem "Root Cellar" in the belief in the value of even the most useless trash. "I offer it to oblivion / with the rest of what was mine." Not only what you see, but also what you leave behind, will redeem you. In "Killing the Plants" she takes this position a step too far by comparing her neglect of her plants to Hamlet's rehearsal of murdering Claudius. Clearly, the plants cannot be as guilty or deserving of revenge as Claudius. The extremely tenuous connection of this hyperbole to the scene described in the poem cannot sustain the exaggeration.

Section Two, "Mud Season," has a kind of Frostean edge in that the poems examine transitional spaces. Just as spring is a season that has the characteristics of both winter and summer, the poems in this section exhibit an occlusion that explores the difficulty of making clear distinctions in life. "The Pond at Dusk" looks at that time of day that is neither day nor night, when it is most difficult to see: ". . . what looks like smoke/ floating over the neighbor's barn/ is only apple blossoms." The speaker's descriptions seem contradictory because nothing can be made out in this light: "A fly wounds the water but the wound/ soon heals" and "The green haze on the trees changes/ into leaves." The titles of poems like "Evening Sun," "Sun and Moon," and "Frost Flowers" embody these confusions, while the poem "Photograph of a Child on a Vermont Hillside" explores how a photograph, which is a representation of someone, cannot really know that person. The photograph, like a poem, can contain an image but its meaning will always be elusive.

The third section, "The Boat of Quiet Hours," takes its inspiration from the lines in Keats's poem *Endymion, Book I:* "And, as the year/ Grows lush in juicy stalks, I'll smoothly steer/ My little boat, for many quiet hours. . . ." Consequently, the poems offer images that are finely observed.

> Now all the doors and windows
> are open, and we move so easily
> through the rooms. Cats roll
> on the sunny rugs, and a clumsy wasp
> climbs the pane, pausing
> to rub a leg over her head.

This first stanza of "Philosophy in Warm Weather" celebrates how in spring "All around physical life reconvenes." Kenyon explains her premise a few lines down: "Heat, Horatio, *heat* makes them / put this antic disposition on!" And again she references Shakespeare's *Hamlet.* This time, however, it works because she is not only taking on Hamlet's identity, but is also explaining what makes the world seem so crazy. There is no stretch in the playfulness of her reference the way the hyperbole failed in "Killing the Plants." Her feelings about being as alive as everything is in spring are brought into focus in "Camp Evergreen." The optimistic slant of the title cues the audience even before they encounter the mischievous images of "boats like huge bright birds" and "a fish astonishes the air, falls back/ into its element." All she really does in this poem is luxuriate in the sunlight, but still she knows that this ecstasy cannot be sustained.

> Now it is high summer: the solstice:
> longed-for, possessed, luxurious, and sad.

This quiet turn toward darkness resonates in this section because Kenyon can never seem to fully release herself into rapture. She tries, however, in poems such as "The Bat," which describes a moment when the speaker is suddenly confronted with a bat in her room. The poem explores how inspiration occurs without explanation and uses a startling comparison to illustrate the violence of this experience.

> At every turn [the bat] evaded us
>
> like the identity of the third person
> in the Trinity: the one
> who spoke through the prophets,
> the one who astounded Mary
> by suddenly coming near.

In her interview with Bill Moyers, Kenyon explained "The Bat": "What I had in mind was being broken in upon, the way Mary was broken in upon by Gabriel. You think you're alone and suddenly there's this thing coming near you, so near that you can feel the wind from the brushing of the wings." At least there is the possibility of exultation in the notion that a bat's sudden appearance can be similar to the experience of the Holy Ghost. Just this kind of contingency represents how Kenyon's poems move toward a resolution, but never quite arrive. In an interview with David Bradt, Kenyon had talked about the importance of Anton Chekhov to her work. In her poems this resistance on her part to closure, as well as her absence of moral judgment, seem directly influenced by Chekhov and stories like "Misery" and "Lady with the Pet Dog." In a letter to Aleksey S. Suvorin in *Letters on the Short Story, the Drama, and Other Literary Topics by Anton Chekhov,* Chekhov insisted on the importance of "objectivity. . . . The artist is not meant to be a judge . . . his only job is to be an impartial witness." Because of her own history of coming in conflict with others' truths, Kenyon would never insist on a particular way.

The Boat of Quiet Hours ends on an optimistic note in the season of summer. Section IV, "Things," starts with a song that reaches past Kenyon's strict adherence to T. S. Eliot's notion of the objective correlative. Instead, the speaker of "Song" attempts to say that there are times when even an external equivalent cannot stand for the internal state of mind that she feels right now.

> . . . But even this
> is not the joy that trembles
> under every leaf and tongue.

The statement is remarkable for its implications of an abundance that extends beyond the limits of summer's verdant tangle. In Kenyon's attempt to map out this unmarked territory in some of the poems that follow, the reader discovers that this outer region actually is the beyond. First, "The Visit" acts like a familiar landmark by occupying that transition space of dusk between life and death, while suggesting a presence of what is beyond the known.

> . . . but now I am aware
> of the silence, and your affection,
> and the delicate sadness of dusk.

This anchor in the darkness leads the reader through a series of poems that follow the dying of Kenyon's father. The series begins with "Parents' Weekend: Camp Kenwood," which contrasts the parents visiting across the pond to the freedom that she has in her own world. This is followed by several poems that directly address her father dying, "Reading Late of the Death of Keats," "Inpatient," "Campers Leaving: Summer 1981," "Travel: After a Death," and "Yard Sale." The pages end with the title poem of the section "Things." This is a poem of acceptance.

> Things: simply lasting, then
> failing to last: water, a blue heron's
> eye, and the light passing
> between them: into light all things
> must fall, glad at last to have fallen.

These last lines in the poem offer comfort by reminding the reader that things change. After summer, autumn arrives. The leaves fall. This ending is the beginning.

Let Evening Come

Like *The Boat of Quiet Hours,* Kenyon's third volume of poetry, *Let Evening Come* (1990), explores nature's cycles, but these five dozen first-person lyrics take "a darker turn." Published four years after her previous collection, this book picks up where *The Boat* left off by leaving that in-between space of dusk and entering evening, as well as by beginning with a poem that marks the end of summer. "Three Songs at the End of Summer" offers a shift in tone from one of rapture and hopefulness to sadness. The first song speaks of campers no longer having the time to learn to water-ski, while the second song pushes beyond simply time running out to a sadness that is unhinged outside any seemingly causal chain.

> Then why did I cry today
> for an hour, with my whole
> body, the way babies cry?

The last song in the series suggests a deep change in Kenyon's countenance by discarding her faith in the redeeming potential of the image with the line, "A white, indifferent morning sky." The song goes on to describe a state in which she "did not/ comprehend" and closes with words of deep hopelessness: "It was the only life I had."

The surprise about this change in demeanor is that *Let Evening Come* is clearly the work of a mature poet and exhibits this maturity in the cohesiveness of the collection. Unlike those in Kenyon's earlier books, the poems here are not divided into sections. Poet and critic Alfred Corn observed this harmony in his *New York Times* review, "This 'sunset' collection is unified around themes of nightfall, the sense of endings, the death of family and friends and, implicitly, the maturing of a poetic talent." Kenyon locates herself in and around the countryside near her home, but in this territory she is plainly at loose ends as the last lines of "After Working Long on One Thing" express.

> The sky won't darken in the west
> until ten. Where shall I turn
> this light and tired mind?

As in this poem, the lines turn from certainty to uncertainty. The use of questions and ellipses multiplies in relation to earlier collections. It is as if she has found the place, both emotionally and aesthetically, she so desperately searched for, and has discovered that the arrival did not supply the answer. Consequently, she wanders with her dog in a landscape that cannot console her.

In "Catching Frogs" the speaker waits for the right moment to scoop up the creature that never seems to come. Instead, "It grew dark." The poem ends with a meditation about the sense of absence after her father's death.

> I came into the warm, bright room
> where father held aloft the evening
> paper, and there was talk, and maybe
> laughter, though I don't remember laughter.

For Kenyon in these times, the evening can no longer be held "aloft" or at bay. She must "let evening come" just as she says in her title poem, and have courage in the face of its darkness.

> Let the cricket take up chafing
> as a woman takes up her needles
> and her yarn. Let evening come.

In this poem, a series of details are presented in a declining light in order to offer a prayer at the end of day: "God does not leave us/ comfortless, so let evening come." At this moment of impending darkness and desolation the speaker turns to prayer, because as Kenyon had discovered a decade earlier and had written about in "Childhood, When You Are in It . . . ," people can take "comfort from the prayer of confession and the assurance of pardon." From this point of expectancy Kenyon makes it possible for the reader to turn to the last poem in the book, "With the Dog at Sunrise." Like the setting's time of day this poem offers rejuvenation of a kind. The drama of the lyric is situated around a meditation on what to say to a friend who is widowed at the age of thirty-one. This thematic dilemma is reflective of the struggles explored in the previous poems in the book, but suddenly there is a change in energy. Her eye notices "that the poplars/ growing along the ravine/ shine pink in the light of winter dawn." With the first lines the redemptive power of the image has returned. Kenyon has restored her faith in the "luminous image." Consequently, as she ranges the countryside she affirms that "Searching for God is the first thing and the last,/ but in between such trouble, and such pain." This collection represents a turning toward the trouble and pain, and then finally a gazing toward God.

From this anchor Kenyon was able to examine a thematic concern that has lurked in all her poems but that until *Constance* (1993) was not directly addressed. Kenyon's work has been compared to Sylvia Plath in this respect, but there are, however, important differences in their treatment of depression as a theme. While Plath's poems can be overwrought, self-absorbed, and self-dramatizing, Kenyon's work contains a New England reserve that makes her poems much quieter and absent of histrionics. Also, Plath was obviously consumed by her depression. In contrast, Kenyon never gives up the fight. When discussing her depression with Bill Moyers, she explained why she would never commit suicide: "My belief in God, such as it is, especially the idea that the believer is part of the body of Christ, has kept me from harming myself. . . . I've thought to myself, 'If you injure yourself you're injuring the body of Christ, and Christ has been injured enough.'"

Constance

No matter how emotionally exhausted Kenyon became, her faith pulled her through. This is evident in *Constance,* in which she dips to the depths but then finds a way to break through the melancholy. This "was lost, but now found" theme is apparent in earlier poems in *The Boat of Quiet Hours.* In "February: Thinking of Flowers" Kenyon writes, "A single green sprouting thing/ would restore me." In *Constance* she has learned to call out more vigorously. The poem "Peonies at Dusk" focuses on the glory of the lifting, rather than the pale hope of a sprout.

> White peonies blooming along the porch
> send out light
> while the rest of the yard grows dim.
> . . . .
> I draw a blossom near, and bending close
> search it as a woman searches
> a loved one's face.

Her lover is joy, not depression. This is perhaps why *Constance* begins with a long portion of Psalm 139 as an epigraph. This psalm describes the presence of God everywhere, even in darkness: "Yea, the darkness hideth not from thee;/ but the night shineth as the day." Without this faith, it is clear Kenyon would not have been able to battle depression to a draw most times, and sometimes win. "Having It Out with Melancholy" is her longest poem and rightfully so since it is here that she illustrates that confrontation. The poem begins with an epigraph from Chekhov that sounds a note of hopelessness: "If many remedies are prescribed for an illness, you may be certain that the illness has no cure." The poem itself is divided into nine parts and covers one hundred lines. For a poet who describes herself as dedicated to the lyric, this poem extends to the outer boundaries of its possibility, but because of the divisions, the poem reads more as a series of nine lyric poems. Section 1, *From the Nursery,* is an indictment of melancholy's persistence. Framed in a series of second-person accusations, the speaker catalogs how melancholy wronged her and concludes with an apostrophe calling the disease "the mutilator of souls."

As a counterpoint, section2, *Bottles,* describes medications used to cope with depression.

> Elavil, Ludiomil, Doxepin,
> Norpramin, Prozac, Lithium, Xanax,
> Wellbutrin, Parnate, Nardil, Zoloft.

Section 3, *Suggestion from a Friend,* records the pain of others not understanding, while Part Four, "Often," chronicles how she copes with depression by going "to bed as soon after dinner/ as seems adult." Until this point the poem is more like a report than a poem, as if the world of melancholy was prosaic, not poetic. The next section, *Once There Was Light,* gives an account of the transforming vision she had in her early thirties, but this reprieve is not long lasting.

> Like a crow who smells hot blood
> you came flying to pull me out
> of the glowing stream.

The unrelenting presence of depression becomes a battle that has only small victories, such as the comfort of her dog's companionship and the sudden effectiveness of "monoamine / oxidase inhibitors."

> I come back to marriage and friends,
> to pink fringed hollyhocks; come back
> to my desk, books, and chair.

Surprisingly, Kenyon calls her personified depression the "Unholy ghost." This characterization seems to represent the depths that it can take her, since repeatedly in the past Kenyon has spoken about the redemptive power of the Holy Ghost. Fortunately, the poem turns optimistic in section 9, *Wood Thrush*. This section echoes Frost's poem "Come In," in which the song of a thrush draws his attention away from the coming darkness and from thoughts of suicide. The speaker in section 9 finds peace of mind while "waiting greedily for the first/ note of the wood thrush." At this moment, her anticipation leads her to a feeling of being "overcome// by ordinary contentment." The word "overcome" emphasizes the degree of melancholy she has reached because it implies a depression so deep that achieving ordinariness is an extraordinary feat. There is an underlying sadness that reverberates in her final celebration of the thrush.

> How I love the small, swiftly
> beating heart of the bird
> singing in the great maples;
> its bright, unequivocal eye.

The superlatives in these lines feel desperate in their overreaching descriptiveness.

Melancholy, however, is not the only kind of suffering *Constance* records. In "Pharaoh" the reader learns that the speaker's husband, like her father a number of years before, has been diagnosed with cancer. The poem first delves into how life changes after the news.

> Things are off: Touch rankles, food
> is not good. Even the kindness of friends
> turns burdensome. . . .

But the last stanza reminds the reader that her husband's potential death is what the speaker really must confront. To do so, she attempts

to ennoble him and his life by comparing him to an Egyptian pharaoh, saying:

> The things you might need in the next
> life surround you—your comb and glasses,
> water, a book and a pen.

One of the powers of this book lies in the ability of the speaker to
transcend self-pity. This trait manifests itself most sharply in poems
like "Coats," "Sleepers in Jaipur," and "Gettysburg: July 1, 1863," in
which the speaker can separate from herself and appreciate the grief
and emotional pain of others. Nevertheless, this unsparing eye can
be directed at herself as well. The poem "Otherwise" deals with the
troubles she had to overcome, not just her depression and her husband's cancer, but her own bout with a cancerous salivary gland in
the late 1980s. The poem is structured in a kind of call-and-response
arrangement where the speaker makes a rather mundane statement
about the day and follows it with a response of "It might/ have been
otherwise." The poem's last lines contain what can be considered the
final call-and-response.

> I slept in a bed
> in a room with paintings
> on the walls, and
> planned another day
> just like this day.
> But one day, I know,
> it will be otherwise.

Otherwise: New & Selected Poems

In *Constance* Kenyon draws on her deep belief that there is a regen-
erative force operating in the world. This belief was what sustained
her as more tragedy entered her life. Though her husband Donald

Hall survived two bouts with cancer, Kenyon contracted fatal leukemia. Her book, *Otherwise: New & Selected Poems* (1996), was published posthumously and provides a remarkable document of her life's work. One hundred and fifty-five poems came from her first four books, while twenty poems were previously unpublished; the last poem in the collection, "The Sick Wife," was the last poem that she worked on. The lack of a thematic cohesiveness to the new poems gives them an unfinished feeling in comparison to the polished and considered arrangement of her poems in previous books. In this vein the lead poem seems appropriate. "Happiness" observes how the emotion arrives suddenly "like a prodigal/ who comes back" and visits so randomly that,

> It even comes to the boulder
> in the perpetual shade of pine barrens,
> to rain falling on the open sea,
> to the wineglass, weary of holding wine.

In the end, the poem appears sadly ironic because the apparent subject of happiness is undermined by an undercurrent of helplessness and lack of control. Happiness comes without reason, and by extension everything else arrives by similar means. This submerged desperation breaks out in the next poem, "Mosaic of the Nativity: Serbia, Winter 1993," where God bemoans His inability to control what He has created.

> On the domed ceiling God
> is thinking:
> I made them my joy,
> . . . .
> But see what they do!

"Mosaic" is perhaps Kenyon's most non-Kenyonian poem. Located far from her home in New Hampshire, the poem contains an explicit political message framed in religious terms.

The poems that follow exhibit a quiet withdrawal by the speaker to a stance of observation, but this position is different from earlier work in that her eye reveals a world predicated on suffering. In "Man Eating" the speaker focuses on what the food is not ("caused no animal/ to suffer") and ends with an inorganic image that is clearly not life affirming ("he is eating/ with a pearl-white plastic spoon"). The speaker asks what has happened to her gardens and the countryside she has spent her life ranging.

This dislocation manifests more plainly in "Cesarean," a poem in which the speaker imagines herself at birth being delivered by C-section. Aside from the unnatural violence of the procedure, the poem is equally disturbing in its improbability. The baby, the speaker of the poem, observes, ". . . The clatter,/ the white light, the vast freedom/ were terrible." Kenyon is no longer simply facing the darkness; she is being consumed by it. The poem "Surprise" exhibits a similar turn. The speaker finds betrayal, rather than the delight she has expressed in so many earlier poems. In a surprise party:

> . . . The gathering
> itself is not what astounds her, but the casual
> accomplishment with which he has lied.

Other poems journey far from home into the past, the funeral home, the doctor's office, the nursing home, the New Hampshire MacDowell artists' colony and the town of Franklin, Dutch design, and finally her father's bedside. What is striking is how displaced from the cycles of nature these poems are. The only poem really inhabiting the natural world is a spare seven-line, thirty-five-word poem called "Spring Evening." The poem is remarkable in its utter absence of a self. It is as if the speaker does not exist within this province where images of abundance are observed.

> Again the thrush affirms
> both dusk and dawn. . . .

Frost's thrush returns, but its song is not special. The bird merely sings as it has seemingly done a hundred times before, the "again" underscoring the notion that the image cannot resonate.

The final poem in *Otherwise,* perhaps unfinished, is "The Sick Wife." This poem aches with just the kind of self-pity that Kenyon was able to avoid in the face of her depression, but cannot do so when confronting her mortality. She has earned this self-indulgence, however, because she is dealing with a fatal illness. She should be bitter and angry as well, but she is not. Instead she is simply overwhelmed with a sense of sadness.

> The windows began to steam up.
> The cars on either side of her
> pulled away so briskly
> that it made her sick at heart.

The occlusion and abandonment described in these lines offers enough of a glimpse at her suffering for the reader to understand the magnitude of knowing you are about to die. This is intensified by Kenyon's understatement. She does not list all the people she loves whom she will leave behind. Instead, she merely hints at the immensity of that loss by describing the sense of separation she feels sitting alone in a car. This lack of explicitness makes these lines all the more powerful and attests to Kenyon's enormous poetic gifts.

Other Posthumous Works

Just before her death, Pulitzer Prize–winning composer William Bolcom contacted Kenyon to put a selection of her poems to music. In her last months she and Bolcom worked together to select the texts. The result was a carefully planned sequence called *Briefly It Enters: A Cycle of Songs from Poems of Jane Kenyon: For Voice and Piano 1994–1996.* This work takes a listener progressively deeper into a sense of Kenyon's life, beginning with "Who," which imagines Kenyon's poetry emerging from some source beyond herself, "The Clearing," "Otherwise," "The Sick Wife," and concluding with "Briefly It Enters, and Briefly Speaks." This delicate, nuanced composition with discreetly melodic turns flirts with sentimentality, but just as Kenyon's poems resist melodrama so does Bolcom's piece. A year after her death, composer J. Mark Scearce put three of Kenyon's poems to music in a piece called *American Triptych: For Soprano, Flute, Clarinet/ Bass Clarinet, Violin, Cello, Piano, and Percussion: On Three Poems by Jane Kenyon.*

Another book of Kenyon's work, published in 1999, was *A Hundred White Daffodils.* This book essentially assembles in one volume everything but her poetry. Though Kenyon did not write much prose, in the early 1990s she did write a column for her local newspaper, the *Concord Monitor.* These pieces celebrate in prose the world she loved so deeply—her garden, friends, and activities. Each of these columns could stand in some sense as a statement on her art. In the column "The Five-and-Dime" she writes "half the fun of real dime stores, aside from their dedicated *thinginess,* is that the stuff is really cheap." Kenyon's appreciation for dime stores seems so appropriate since in her own way she was dedicated to *thinginess.*

The only poem collected in *A Hundred White Daffodils,* "Woman, Why Are You Weeping?" is one that Kenyon did not want included in her selected poems. It is a poem she did not feel was finished and so was reluctant to publish. Hall, rightfully so, includes this powerful and ambitious work. "Woman, Why Are You Weeping?" points to a complexity and depth that Kenyon might have turned to if she had lived. Deeply and explicitly religious, it compares her loss of faith to the disappearance of Christ from his grave after his crucifixion. The speaker feels forsaken by all gods.

> The fire cares nothing for my illness,
> nor does Brahma, the creator, nor Shiva who sees
> evil with his terrible third eye; Vishnu,
> the protector, does not protect me.

The utter despair in this poem is unrelenting. The only response for the reader is to mourn. The speaker asks "'What shall we do about this?'" but offers no answer other than pain and indifference.

> . . . The reply
> was scorching wind, lapping of water, pull
> of the black oarsmen on the oars. . . .

The weather, trees, animals, tender companionship, home, and work where she found joy, healing, and answers to significant questions are now absent. A terrible truth about the world has descended upon her, and the tools Kenyon had spent a lifetime honing fail her. A reader cannot help but be deeply saddened by the loss of this profound talent.

JOHN H. TIMMERMAN

from

The Poet at Work

When Jane Kenyon told Bill Moyers that "Let Evening Come" was "given" to her by "the muse, the Holy Ghost," she was not suggesting that the poem derived from some rhapsodic inspiration and that she was a mere vessel through which the words flowed. It is true that Kenyon herself was surprised at how "rapidly" the poem came, a word she used to describe its process to Donald Hall. From the start it held a conceptual wholeness and tonal unity that guided the stages of drafting and revision. Nonetheless, Kenyon still invested the full resources of her poetic craft in that drafting and revision. Writing poetry demanded hard and routine labor on a regular basis. It meant that she gave herself up to her tools—perception and language—for the sake of the reader.

In his scrambled religious state, Robert Frost wondered several times if poetry would be a sufficient offering on the altar to get him into heaven. He feared that even his "best offering may not prove acceptable in his sight." T. S. Eliot had similarly lofty—albeit more humanly directed—goals for the poet's task. The "familiar compound ghost" of *Little Gidding* asserts,

> Since our concern was speech, and speech impelled us
> To purify the dialect of the tribe
> And urge the mind to aftersight and foresight.

For Eliot, each word encapsulated truth; the poet erected the structure of words in such an architecture that, as the reader examined it, he or she grew mindful of the truths the poet had discovered.

Perhaps Kenyon's goals were less loftily stated. She did not see her poetry as a divine act—an offering unto God. Nor did she see her poetry as a conveyor of truth to the general mind (that is, a didactic tool). She sought above all penetrating lyrics of passionate beauty, words that the poem could not live without, imagery so crystalline that the reader could trace his or her own life in it. Above all, she cherished honesty. These goals informed her labor. Nevertheless, in interviews, addresses, and letters she did construct specific principles and guidelines for that labor. Before engaging those principles, however, it may be best to examine Kenyon's craft, considering her use of imagery, literary devices, melody, and language.

Kenyon's imagery may well be described as elemental. Although her poems often trip the reader into speculation, the imagery itself roots solidly in the material things of this earth. This pattern is well demonstrated in the volume *Let Evening Come,* which moves through the seasonal cycles of life at Eagle Pond Farm. Since the experience of seasons belongs to all of us, we as readers find the poems very accessible. Through them we experience what is intuitively felt to be true because the imagery is grounded in the world we know. Once homed in such familiar patterns, we more willingly assent to where the poems lead.

Precisely at this point the "luminous particular" that Kenyon sought comes into play, for by it Kenyon locates the reader in this world with meticulous particularity. Kenyon used the term to describe Anna Akhmatova's poetic art and its startling ability to capture the reader by means of a sharply defined image or metaphor. The "luminosity" is that casting off of light through the concrete, that illumination of the reader's mind.

Early in the writing process, Kenyon added words and images and tried out options in margins, providing the fullest portrait possible. In the later stages of revision, the process dramatically reversed.

Kenyon crossed out words, details, and entire lines as she narrowed the focus to the essential. She polished the work of all rough edges, focusing particularly on the precision of the imagery.

The fundamental attitude of nearly all poets toward imagery is encapsulated in the caveat "Show, don't tell." Instead of naming emotions, incarnate them in things or events. Often, however, this attitude toward imagery is simply accepted without demonstrable reason. Why has this opinion become a fundamental article of faith among modern poets? And how did it shape Kenyon's craft? The answer may be found a century earlier among the American Fireside Poets.

For nearly a full century, these poets—William Cullen Bryant (1794–1878), Henry Wadsworth Longfellow (1807–1882), John Greenleaf Whittier (1807–1892), and Oliver Wendell Holmes (1809–1894)—held sway over the American literary scene. They were the Literary Men of Importance, the Czars of Culture. Their tasks were to entertain and to instruct. Because they held the prominent chairs by the fireside for almost a century, there was little room for dissenting voices. Dissent to what, though? First, to the loose and sprawling narrative, often driven by the chugging engine of strict metrics and rhyme patterns. And second, to their frequent use of didacticism (reducing reality to simple nuggets of moralizing) and sentimentality: using feeling and emotions in the work for their own sake—putting them on display, if you will.

Precisely such issues fueled the turn-of-the-century American Modernists—T. S. Eliot, E. A. Robinson, Ezra Pound, and, arguably, Robert Frost. Each wanted to return the work to reality. Not surprisingly, Kenyon herself cites Eliot as a model: "Almost always if I search I can find something in the natural world—an objective correlative in Eliot's phrase—that embodies what I'm feeling at the moment. That's when a poem really takes off." But the issue requires qualification in Kenyon's case, for she realized that employing sentimentality was a far different thing than expressing sentiments—one's beliefs, disquietude, joy, sorrow. In fact, the ever-increasing readership of Kenyon's work is due in part to the way she admits readers to the emotional experiences and beliefs of her world. Rather than throwing sentiments at the reader Kenyon asks, "Do you see anything of yourself in here?"

Concerned about avoiding sentimentality, Kenyon was adamant that the emotion be embodied in the particular. Donald Hall observed that this belief solidified during Kenyon's work translating the great Russian poet Anna Akhmatova: "As she worked with Akhmatova's early lyrics, condensations of strong feeling into compact images both visual and aural, she practiced making the kind of poetry she admired most—an art that embodied powerful emotion by means of the luminous particular."

In "The Suitor" Kenyon uses simile not simply for poetic effect but also to direct the action of the poem itself. The poem opens with two people lying in bed in early morning light. At the open windows, curtains "lift and fall,/ like the chest of someone sleeping." In this sentence (three lines) the simile directs the poem just slightly outward to the windows, but sleep is still heavy in the room. In the next sentence (four lines), the narrator's vision moves beyond the immediate and concrete visual setting of the bedroom to an imaginative vision beyond the window. In fact, the very wind that lifts the curtains becomes her guide, drawing her out. Beyond the window the wind moves the leaves of the box elder:

> they show their light undersides,
> turning all at once
> like a school of fish.

The simile itself is light and delicate, like the wind. Then the wind, in the final four lines, blows lightly back upon the narrator, who seems of a piece with the airy imagery. "Suddenly I understand that I am happy," she announces. The emotion of happiness has already been the subject of the poem through its descriptive imagery. The narrator's statement simply confirms that for the reader. More significant, however, is her complete surprise at the emotion, evident in the way Kenyon shapes the final simile:

> For months this feeling
> has been coming closer, stopping
> for short visits, like a timid suitor.

This is not a poem of ecstatic release of emotion; rather, it reveals the delightful discovery of happiness through the unveiling power of the similes. That crafting permits the reader to say, "Yes. I see. This is what it is like for me also."

Kenyon employs the metaphor as artfully as the simile. Indeed, she will use a metaphor of such intensity that it nearly captures the entire poem in one breathless moment. In "Cesarean" she writes,

> The surgeon with his unapologetic
> blade parted darkness, revealing
> day.

Here the act of the cesarean is concentrated in three quick lines, but the suggestiveness of the metaphor carries the rest of the poem. The surgeon's parting of darkness and day is a God-like act. The blade is "unapologetic" because the surgeon-God has no need to apologize for bringing forth the gift of life. And as the poet's "small clay" is lifted from her mother's "large clay," the microcosmic world of the operating room erupts into white light and shouting. Kenyon wisely leaves it unstated, but at this point the reader senses an angelic choir heralding the new light of this life.

Because Kenyon concentrated on the lyric form in her poetry, a variety of sound patterns also appear in her work. One of Kenyon's favorite technical devices is enjambment. It permits a line to stop both meaningfully and syntactically, then surprises the reader by carrying both meaning and syntax into the next line, effectively making the lines work double-time—as a whole moment and as an ongoing

movement. The technique, very likely influenced by Kenyon's training in music, often opens a whole new way of seeing the situation she
is describing or provides a clever response to the presumed situation
of the prior line.

In "Three Songs at the End of Summer" we find these lines:

> The cicada's dry monotony breaks
> over me.

Read as a complete unit, the first line merely suggests that the cicada's
monotonous noise finally ends. But the enjambment into the second
line changes the meaning entirely. It places the poet directly on the
scene, where the monotony breaks over her like a cloud of sound.
Similarly, Kenyon will use enjambment to extend an image. In the
first stanza of "February: Thinking of Flowers," she describes the
windswept, snowy fields. In the second stanza she then moves from a
rather abstract declaration to a specific picture, then to a metaphor:

> Nothing but white—the air, the light;
> only one brown milkweed pod
> bobbing in the gully, smallest
> brown boat on the immense tide.

Here the enjambment of the third line startlingly turns the reader's
expectations. "Smallest" seems at first reflexive to the milkweed pod.
And it is—but it also turns into the adjective for the concluding
metaphor.

Also clearly observable in Kenyon's poetry is the musical lyricism
that creates moods ranging from the intense and rhapsodic to the
quietly pastoral. Several things contribute to this lyricism. Most important, of course, is Kenyon's own acute sensitivity to sound. She
liked to work with assonance and consonance. From "No" we have
these lines:

and it was time to turn away
from the casket, poised on its silver
scaffolding over the open hole
that smelled like a harrowed field.

The lines are quiet, yet the agony of grief infiltrates them as the casket is about to be lowered into the ground. The major pattern is the *s* sound in many of the words chosen: *was, casket, poised, its, silver, scaffolding, smelled.* With the exception of *casket* and *scaffolding,* where the *s* is hardened by the following *k* sound, all the sounds are soft and comforting. A tension works within this predominant pattern, however, through the harder *r* sound in *turn, silver, over,* and *harrowed. Silver* is something of an anomaly, since it starts soft and ends hard, but the other words are all suggestive of threat. To "turn away" is to suggest that something is over. The simile of the harrowed field is rough and disturbing. Most powerful, however, is the strategic third line, when the casket is about to be lowered into the ground. Here Kenyon employs the sinking, long *o* four times, dropping mercilessly into the "hole." Here is the unavoidable reality, conveyed as much by the sounds of the words as by their meaning.

Kenyon also employs both interior melodies and strategic repetition as musical devices. Seldom does she use end rhyme. When she does, it sometimes seems almost coincidental, as if she is rounding off a pattern established interiorly. At other times, the end rhyme repeats a word in a prior stanza to provide response or closure to the previous idea. Most frequently, the melody of the poem is carried by variations of vowel sounds.

In *From Room to Room* the poem "In Several Colors" exemplifies many of Kenyon's familiar devices, already well in evidence early in her career:

Every morning, cup of coffee
in hand, I look out at the mountain.

> Ordinarily, it's blue, but today
> it's the color of an eggplant.
>
> And the sky turns
> from gray to pale apricot
> as the sun rolls up
> Main Street in Andover.
>
> I study the cat's face
> and find a trace of white
> around each eye, as if
> he made himself up today
> for a part in the opera.

One immediately notices her characteristic use of enjambment in the first two lines. End-stopping the first line suggests a self-defining event. Every morning *is* a cup of coffee. The second line, however, broadens the portrait to include the narrator, holding her cup of coffee in the morning, looking out at the mountain. With the lines pushing one's reading of the poem through enjambment, one hardly recognizes the skillful evocation of mood through interior melody.

The predominant vowel sounds in the first stanza are *o* and *u*. Nearly all are short or attenuated sounds, and they are strongly varied by consonant placement. Such variation makes the one consistent interior rhyme, which is only a variation on the same syllable, all the more pronounced: *morning/ordinary/color*. Each instance also occurs early in the line like a major note, with the variations following in quick succession to the end of the line.

The second stanza continues the same vowel variation: *turns/apricot/sun rolls up/Andover*. In the third stanza, however, the musical variations on a single theme suddenly tighten to a finale with a playful and explosive series of perfect rhymes interwoven: *I/face/trace/white/eye*. For the first time Kenyon works the long vowel sounds. Then the last two lines carry this playful poem to its con-

Certainly story is at the heart of Jane's poems. Incantation is also central to Jane's poems: the magical repetition of phrases like the rhythmic moans a grieving mother might make. The repetition of a phrase has survival power. "Let evening come. Let evening come." "It might have been otherwise. It might have been otherwise." These incantatory orderings are set against enormous possibilities of disorder.

Perceiving the possibilities of disorder not only in the story of the larger culture but also in the story of her own life renders Kenyon highly vulnerable. Survival, as Orr points out, is both her personal aim and her aim for the reader. She constructs a story in which others may see and read their lives.

Repetition, then, may be seen as a struggle against disorder, a pattern most pronounced, perhaps, in *Let Evening Come.* "Three Songs at the End of Summer," a poem from that volume discussed more fully later in this study, illustrates the pattern. The first song opens with a listing of commonplace events at Eagle Pond Farm. The first stanza of the second song begins with an apparently optimistic repetition: "The days are bright/ and free, bright and free." Indeed they are. The narrator has just described them as such. The reader is lulled by the melody before the second stanza cracks like a whip:

> Then why did I cry today
> for an hour, with my whole
> body, the way babies cry?

The conflict between the bright day and her weeping accentuates her vulnerability.

This pattern continues throughout the volume. "Now Where?" shapes an eloquent dirge on melancholy, directed by three introductory repetitions:

clusion by picking up the varied sounds of the first two stanzas. A
Kenyon adds a few more deft touches. *For* in the final line picks ι
the regular interior rhyme of the first stanza. *Today* in the penult
mate line also closes off the poem by repeating that end-word fro
the first stanza.

"In Several Colors" does not stand alone in its careful use of me
ody. The last stanza of "Things" from *The Boat of Quiet Hours,* f
example, combines heavier *l* sounds with lighter *a* sounds to crea
a sense of falling. The play is perfect to the argument of the poen
all things fall into light. The drafts of Kenyon's poems do not sho
a sustained or even conscious effort to construct such melodic pa
terns. It seems an intuitive skill, the gift of a brilliantly tuned ear ar
the felicities of language sounds.

Kenyon uses repetition with the same seemingly intuitive skill. Sl
repeats lines or phrases to produce several powerful effects: to evol
a sense of supplication, to provide a sense of repose and acceptanc
or to express and try to understand a baffling struggle with difficu
events. In "Inertia" from *The Boat of Quiet Hours,* the initial repetitic
in the first line of the poem—"My head was heavy, heavy"—not on
evokes a mood for the poem but echoes the weighted vowel sound
onomatopoeia to encapsulate the mood itself. Not until line 21 is tl
repetition fulfilled in meaning: "muddled and heavy-hearted." He
the implied mood is specified to the narrator. A secondary patter
of repetition also moves through the poem, supporting the primai
mood of heaviness. In the first stanza the narrator comments th;
her hands are so heavy that "I had to ask two times/ before my han
would scratch my ear." In the second stanza she juxtaposes her hanc
with the "enterprising feelers" of the centipede that crawls out fron
the spine of her dictionary. In the third stanza she returns to her ow
befuddled and inept hands, then in the final stanza notes how quickl
the centipede slithers away. The repetition in the secondary pattern
disjunctive, underscoring the psychological distance of the narrato

In his essay "Our Lady of Sorrows," Gregory Orr says that Kenyon
use of repetition goes beyond poetic craftsmanship:

> It wakes when I wake, walks
> when I walk, turns back when I
> turn back. . . .

Similarly, the third stanza echoes "I lie down," "I lie down," as the narrator fights against succumbing.

The most notable use of repetition occurs, of course, in "Let Evening Come" itself. Here the rhetorical shadings of the lines are so supple that, although the repetition is obvious, the levels of connotative meaning emerge only after the lines have been savored many times. Here it is worth noting how Kenyon employs yet another shading of repetition to offer solace and benediction.

Melody in particular is directly linked to word choice, and an examination of Kenyon's poetic diction leads to surprising conclusions. In her writing workshops with her friends Joyce Peseroff and Alice Mattison, the three writers often searched for the "right" word. But what characterizes the right word? Appropriateness to context, surely. One might also mention the emotional weight of the word and its precision of description. For Kenyon, however, rightness went beyond these fundamental matters to an exact linguistic fittingness between word and image and hence between word and reader.

Marie Borroff's illuminating study *Language and the Poet* provides a helpful paradigm for considering Kenyon's selection of words and to what ends she uses them. Since the argument here will require some linguistic tabulation, I accept Borroff's caution: "It is not my view that tabulations of linguistic detail will of themselves yield an understanding of the all-important relationship between what a poem expresses and how it is expressed." That latter understanding is essentially a matter of style, meaning, and method, and includes such matters as imagery patterns, literary devices, character, and setting. Nevertheless, tabulation of word origins does reveal something of the poet's mind and art. Why this word instead of another that might work just as well? For a poet who labored as assiduously over revisions as Kenyon did, it is not an empty question.

Two defining qualities of Kenyon's language should be established to frame this discussion. First, readers are often struck by the conversational tone and accessible settings of the poems. The familiarity of language and setting, in fact, often disguises the sophisticated technical artistry. The reader moves into the story and is hardly aware of how he or she entered it. Borroff makes the same point about Robert Frost's poetry:

> We [readers] see that the story being told is "true" in the sense that it could have happened to us in the world as we know it. The scene in which it takes place is familiar to us, whether at first or second hand, and can be easily visualized. The manner of the telling is not realistic (the poem does not sound like a tape-recorded anecdote) . . . it is too clear and concise for that. Yet the details of the narrative are presented in a simple, down-to-earth manner, by a speaker who does not set himself apart from us.

These qualities apply almost uniformly to Kenyon's poetry. Even when we are in places that are not familiar to us, either by circumstance or by setting—such as in "Having It Out with Melancholy" and "Woman, Why Are You Weeping?"—the nature of Kenyon's clear, direct, realistic telling allows us intimate access to the events of the poem.

Second, the language of the poems—even when they deal with complex issues—appears to be quite simple. It is not bookish or erudite; it tends toward the vernacular. Clearly this lends emphasis to Kenyon's delight in the present experience. But a closer examination of the actual word stock she is using reveals the close deliberation involved in her language choices.

Simplicity in language can be defined in several ways. As Borroff points out, "The most obvious objective correlative of 'simplicity' in language is word length—the frequency, for instance, of lines made up wholly of monosyllables, and a corresponding infrequency of words of three syllables or more." Syllable count, however, is of limited worth in examining a poetic work, and only acquires relative merit when other technical elements are factored in. For example, *Credo,* section 8 of Kenyon's "Having It Out with Melancholy," has an unusually high percentage of monosyllabic words. The entire poem is spare as the emotions unravel, but this section strikes the reader as particularly jarring. Linking the spareness of worn emotions to the spareness of language appears to be an easy connection to make. "Credo" contains a total of 83 words. Of these, 63, or 75.9 percent, are monosyllabic; 17, or 20.5 percent, are disyllabic; and only 3, or 3.6 percent, are polysyllabic. The spareness of the syllabification is extraordinary.

In and of itself, however, syllable count is too limited a tool to be very useful in this analysis. It is when we look at syllable count in combination with something like word arrangement that it is more substantively revealing. The majority of the multisyllable words in *Credo,* for example, fall in the first stanza, starting with the long, five-syllable "Pharmaceutical" followed by the disyllabic "wonders." In the second stanza things fall apart at the predicted coming of the "Unholy ghost," and here the monosyllabic words pile up, in sharp, short phrases, verb structures, and descriptive units that hit like machine-gun fire. We meet the ghost through whiplash adjectives: "Coarse, mean." Then the narrator spits out the trinity of actions the ghost will take when it comes to possess her again:

> . . . you'll put your feet
> on the coffee table, lean back,
> and turn me into someone. . . .

Each of the verbs describing the ghost's actions are monosyllables. But what will the effect be on the narrator? She will be possessed by a being she doesn't want to be—a being with no being. The three negative verbs that follow match the monosyllabic action of the ghost: "can't take," "can't sleep," "can't read." It is the chant of hopelessness.

Merely counting syllables, then, is not enough. Many variables—such as the strategic placement of different-syllabled words, the author's use of rhythm and pacing, and internal conflicts—guide the poetic process and give it pattern. It is true, nonetheless, that Kenyon uses a slightly higher percentage of monosyllabic and disyllabic words to achieve a conversational tone. In this regard, she more closely resembles Robert Frost than, say, Wallace Stevens; more Elizabeth Bishop than Marianne Moore.

A more profitable way to define simplicity in poetry is according to word choice, particularly choices between the two primary contributors to our word stock: Old and Middle English on the one hand, and Romance and Latinate derivatives on the other. As one examines Kenyon's word choices, one discovers an overwhelming pattern of Old and Middle English derivations. In fact, the pattern is so striking that it almost seems that Kenyon deliberately screened the Romance-Latinate diction. Someone might point out that Kenyon was a French major at the University of Michigan before she became an English major. With that background, she would be aware enough of the word stock to screen it at will. Why would she want to? First, to mine the fundamental simplicity of the basic word stock of our language; and second, to use language with an elemental quality to match the elemental quality of her imagery. Kenyon's imagery is earth-rooted; so too is her poetic diction. According to Borroff, percentiles of ten or lower from Romance-Latinate stock indicate a very low or plain style—deliberately so in the modern era. Borroff says that such numbers represent the "extreme low." And this describes Kenyon's poetry: extremely high use of Old and Middle English derivations (with the exception of occasional use of Greek, Sanskrit, Old Norse, and other derivations), and extremely low use of Romance-Latinate stock.

"August Rain, After Haying" has a total of 101 words. Of these, 82 are Old English, 2 are Old English compounds, and 1 is Middle English—a total of 84.2 percent. Words with Romance-Latinate origins make up 10.9 percent. The percentages are in keeping with the elemental images of farm life described here, but also with the baptismal imagery of the middle and final stanzas. "Briefly It Enters, and Briefly Speaks" is an interesting poem linguistically because it reveals a substantially broader word base, including Greek, Sanskrit, and Gaelic. The total word count of 144, however, still includes 82.8 percent of Old and Middle English words and 11.1 percent of Romance-Latinate words. "Evening Sun," a poem evoking Kenyon's childhood and filled with the most elemental imagery and description, should not surprise us with its percentages of 81.4 for Old and Middle English and a scant 8.1 for Latinate words. Finally, the plaintive "Otherwise" creates its wistful tone with an elegant simplicity of idea and language. The poem moves through staggered accents and irregular lines, the longest of which is only seven syllables. One senses the feeling of mortality in its very structure. That feeling is reinforced by the language. Of the 103 words in the poem, 86.4 percent are Old English or Old English compounds, and a mere 7.8 percent are Latinate.

Several poetic tools, then, are critically important for Kenyon. Her imagery is inescapably earthbound, thus creating an accessible world for her readers to enter. The bridge to her poetic world is enhanced by the literary devices of simile and metaphor. And almost all of her poems reveal her skill with such devices as enjambment, caesura, assonance, consonance, and repetition to shape melodious patterns. Finally, Kenyon matches her diction to her imagery for a consistent poetic experience by relying heavily upon a "plain" style, marked predominately by an Old English and Middle English word stock. Instead of relying on the more refined and abstract Romance-Latinate diction, Kenyon derives the stunning power of her poems from the vivid image, the clear, cutting portrait, and the always inviting tone of her narrative voice.

STEVEN CRAMER

Home Alone: Self and Relation in Part I of *The Boat of Quiet Hours*

A decade after Jane Kenyon's death, many still find it hard to accept that we won't read new poems of hers. We offer tributes. We teach her work. We press her books into the hands of the uninitiated. We debate with those who find her poetry "too quiet," as does a friend of mine. We argue, as I have, that some poetic styles require us to lean in and listen—more like the RCA Victor Dog than the guy in the Maxell ad pressed back into his leather chair by the onrush of decibels from his stereo system. Of course, what we do most is reread, attending ever more closely. For years, I've listened to "Evening at a Country Inn," the first poem in Kenyon's second collection, *The Boat of Quiet Hours.* It strikes me as not only characteristic of her understated lyric strengths, but also—considered in the context of the section it introduces—of her architectural intelligence, alert to how a single poem can lend meaning to, and derive meaning from, the others in its neighborhood. So I listen again:

Evening at a Country Inn

From here I see a single red cloud
impaled on the Town Hall weather vane.
Now the horses are back in their stalls,
and the dogs are nowhere in sight
that made them run and buck
in the brittle morning light.

You laughed only once all day—
when the cat ate cucumbers
in Chekhov's story . . . and now you smoke
and pace the long hallways downstairs.

The cook is roasting meat for the evening meal,
and the smell rises to all the rooms.
Red-faced skiers stamp past you
on their way in; their hunger is Homeric.

I know you are thinking of the accident—
of picking the slivered glass from his hair.
Just now a truck loaded with hay
stopped at the village store to get gas.
I wish you would look at the hay—
the beautiful sane and solid bales of hay.

How innocent in tone is its title, even innocuous. We might picture heavy yellow curtains; plates of scones with tea at 4 p.m.; a hearth
with fire behind it (to warm our backsides after a winter hike); shelves
of worn paperbacks; the innkeeper devoted, perhaps too solicitously,
to our "making ourselves at home." Parsed into two events of connotative diction, however, the title registers a muted dissonance. On
the one hand, "evening" permits, without insisting upon, associations tending toward obscurity, solitude, introspection: "now comes
the evening of the mind," begins a poem by Donald Justice. That
tendency is corrected, as it were, by "country inn," which returns us
to that communal home away from home. Some might argue that to
read so much into a title is to read too much. If a title equaled a text,
I'd agree. But we have the poem, including its title, to reread—from
the top down and, because it's verse, from line to line.

Whatever hearthside coziness the title evokes the first two lines dis-
pel. The "single red cloud/ impaled on the Town Hall weather vane"—an
observer I'll presume female eyeing it "from here" (where?)—establishes

not just something seen but something felt. "Single" and "red" will need the poem that follows to release their full emotional charge. "Impaled," however, placed at the start of a line, juts into the path of our reading, sharp as the point it brings to mind. For reasons we don't yet apprehend, this speaker projects violence onto what she sees. I've often worried over "impaled"—too much too soon?—wondering if second thoughts occurred to Kenyon before she decided upon it. Ultimately, the choice persuades me as deliberate overstatement, its very self-consciousness an introduction to the speaker's hyperbolic mind-set. After all, something feels "off" about much in this first stanza. The "brittle morning light" resonates starkly with the soft, penetrable flesh of the cloud. More curiously, given the speaker's keen eyesight, we might wonder why she devotes three lines to horses and dogs she cannot see. Most disconcertingly, the stanza's sound and syntax, read out loud, overreach, as though the speaker struggled to find a natural way of talking. "Sight" and "light" strike a jarringly blatant rhyme jingle, and the sentence in which they chime betrays an ungainly organization. Ordered more naturally, it reads: *Now the horses are back in their stalls, and the dogs that made them run and buck in the brittle morning light are nowhere in sight.* My point here is not that Kenyon can't produce poetry "at least as well-written as prose." Rather, these "glitches," parts of a pattern, reveal a poet's confidence to use whatever necessary to achieve her aesthetic goals—in this case, to dramatize her speaker's instability under emotional pressure.

Paraphrasing "Evening at a Country Inn" clarifies what those pressures are. An intimate, anecdotal lyric cast in the vocative case—with a distinct, though not wholly determinate, backstory—the poem dramatizes a tense psychic stalemate between two people. The speaker carries on an internal argument with her presumably male companion, who grieves over an accident, possibly involving a car, which has seriously injured, and perhaps killed, someone close to him. We know he witnessed, up close, the immediate aftermath of the accident. We assume his attachment to the injured one is close, and can reasonably infer the same regarding the speaker. At the very least, we know that she empathizes strongly with her companion's grief.

In terms of plot, we know nothing else. As a "speech act"—Helen Vendler's useful term for the ways poetry imitates recognizable forms of social discourse—"Evening at a Country Inn" is an exhortation. Although the speaker doesn't plead *no more be grieved,* she does wish her companion could reconcile himself to the fact of the accident. She wishes he could laugh more than once in a day; start to take pleasure (in food, in community); brood less; and look more toward the healing confluence of nature and culture afforded by establishments like country inns.

As with so many of Kenyon's poems, charged details—inhering in verbs, nouns, and the strategically placed adjective—enact these psychic dynamics. Despite the companion's central role in the poem, passages involving him suggest a remote figure. Literature, not life, provokes his single laugh. He smokes and paces, motion without direction, as the skiers stamp past him toward that fire or food. Most tellingly, he "thinks," or rather "[is] thinking"—the present participle capturing the unrelieved blockade of his privacy. On the other hand, the speaker continually "sees" and keeps track, in her mind's eye, of what's not in sight: those dogs and horses, and most acutely, her companion pacing downstairs. Her sense of smell takes in the aroma of country cooking; a collaboration of sight and hearing apprehends the noisy, ruddy-faced skiers. In one of the poem's subtlest choices, an allusion to the skiers' hunger as "Homeric"—the first of two nonsensory adjectives—pegs her as a reader too. Her literary reference springs from beheld life, however, whereas her companion's bookishness shuts life out. In the poem's culminating image, she finds in what she sees—a truck piled high with tightly bound hay bales—emotional solidity, even sanity ("sane" being the poem's other abstract adjective). *To look is to heal; how I wish you'd give it a try.*

Might we accuse this speaker of complacency, her "wish you would look" a dismissive injunction to "get over it"? Listened to closely, the poem's prosody defends her against that charge. For instance, while we know the companion held the accident victim in his arms, "picking the slivered glass from his hair," and can reasonably presume the speaker did not, it's *her* auditory imagination that makes those glass shards "stick" with prickling assonance, consonance, and sibilance. Moreover, in her final wish that her companion look up from literature to life, she resorts, poignantly, to poetic literature's most audible embodiment of "solidity"—iambic pentameter: "The BEAU/tiful SANE/and SO/lid BALES/of HAY." She knows her mourning companion well enough to charge her last appeal with a rhythmic pulse that connects to his cellular memory.

"Beautiful, sane, solid"—those words might describe this poem, and much of Kenyon's work. But they don't do full justice to the paradoxes unsettling this introduction to a sequence that returns, again and again, to lost or last things. A friend of mine—a brilliant prose writer who reads poetry but didn't know Kenyon's work until I introduced him to "Evening at a Country Inn"—at first found its last line too pat. Then one day he came to me and said, "I've changed my mind, those bales loaded on that truck make the truck 'baleful'— what she wishes her sad companion to notice is no more sane or solid than the rest of the dangerous world in the poem." Would Kenyon have intended that pun? I find it a touch too fancy for this least fancy of poets. And yet, my friend's notion of a self-implicating, if unconscious, edginess to the speaker's appeal rings true. The very elegance of the last line's rhythm recalls, by contrast, that adroitly inarticulate first stanza. On further reflection, we might wonder why the speaker, engaged in a one-sided interior debate, leaves unspecified the details and outcome of the accident; such tact can only serve to protect herself. Finally, her insistence that she "knows" her companion is "thinking of the accident" constitutes a claim the poem proves to be true about *her*. Kenyon's empathic speaker doesn't quite "protest too much"—we believe she *has* made peace with the tragedy in ways he has not—yet the stance from which she wishes solidity for another is itself unstable. An exhortation to find equilibrium, the poem works hard to maintain its own balance.

Taken on its own, "Evening at a Country Inn" seems an unlikely poem with which to begin a book whose title includes the word "quiet." Imagine this solitary, nonhuman voice from "Briefly It Enters, and Briefly Speaks," the penultimate poem in *The Boat of Quiet Hours,* whispering the book's first words: "I am the blossom pressed in a book,/ found again after two hundred years. . . . // I am the maker, the lover, and the keeper. . . ." These lines establish an immediate link between reader and page, registering much more accessibly as the voice of a book, the one we are invited to read. Many less subtle poets begin their collections with a prologue poem of this sort, although few write one as good as "Briefly It Enters, and Briefly Speaks."

Instead, *The Boat of Quiet Hours* confronts us immediately with crisis and paradox. Its first section, titled "Walking Alone in Late Winter," begins with a poem that places us indoors, where only peripheral characters walk, and *inside* the mind of a stationary speaker painfully enmeshed in a lonely mental debate with another. Of the fourteen poems that follow, in only five do we encounter that speaker walking. The season is often specified as fall and, in only one case, as *late* winter. Furthermore, strictly speaking we rarely find the speaker alone. She repeatedly observes or engages with other people—house painters, hunters, a farmer, and various neighbors with memorable names like Archie Portigue. In a deeper way, however, the lyric protagonist we accompany through these poems has no company. Aside from a covert reference concluding "Deer Season"—"I plan our evening meal"—the companion central to "Evening at a Country Inn" drops out of the picture. One could read the section, for all its swerves into melancholy, as a much-needed detour *away* from that impenetrable brooder. When he reappears in the section's last poem, "Walking Alone in Late Winter"—one imagines Kenyon titling it with rueful pleasure in the ironies—her intention in naming the section becomes clear. From the start, we have been induced to look forward to some kind of companion piece to "Evening at a Country Inn," a cadence to its unresolved chords:

Walking Alone in Late Winter

How long the winter has lasted—like a Mahler
symphony, or an hour in the dentist's chair.
In the fields, the grasses are matted
and gray, making me think of June, when hay
and vetch burgeon in the heat, and a warm rain
swells the globed buds of the peony.

Ice on the pond breaks into huge planes. One
sticks like a barge gone awry at the neck
of the bridge. . . . The reeds
and shrubby brush along the shore
gleam with ice that shatters when the breeze
moves them. From beyond the bog
the sound of water rushing over trees
felled by the zealous beavers,
who bring them crashing down. . . . Sometimes
it seems they do it just for fun.

Those days of anger and remorse
come back to me; you fidgeting with your ring,
sliding it off, then jabbing it on again.

The wind is keen coming over the ice;
it carries the sound of breaking glass.
And the sun, bright but not warm,
has gone behind the hill. Chill, or the fear
of chill, sends me hurrying home.

But *does* this poem resolve the conflict scrutinized in "Evening
at a Country Inn," or simply reprise it? Its first two stanzas, beautifully attentive to the world renewing itself, present a speaker who has
certainly progressed toward emotional balance. She may still project

her inner life onto the natural world, but now she does so more affirmatively (those fun-loving beavers), and with a crucial awareness that her perceptions *are* projective—"Sometimes/ it seems"—as all perceptions are. Through the wit of analogy—winter as a symphony no one would wish longer, or as a root canal—she takes unalloyed pleasure in invention. These two stanzas imply throughout that if one works to be solid and sane as hay—its "burgeoning" now looked forward to—one can endure even the worst losses. Anything alive has some life left. The poem turns dramatically, of course, on its third stanza, which brings back "Those days of anger and remorse"; but what, in fact, has this pivot turned toward, or away from? In a brilliant stroke, Kenyon reveals that her speaker's earlier memory of the *accident* in "Evening at a Country Inn"—that poem's present tense swamped in the event's wake of grief—has receded, replaced in this stanza by her recollection of the *grief*. For the speaker, the accident itself has withdrawn by at least two removes of memory. Can we assume that, often enough now, she does *not* find her once-inconsolable companion "fidgeting with [his] ring,/ sliding it off, then jabbing it on again," that even he has reconciled himself to the event and its subsequent trauma? I think we can. But reconciliation doesn't equal immunization; there's no permanent "getting over it." Memories of grief can pierce almost as deeply as the losses we once grieved; they are keen as shards of broken glass, the sound of which this late-winter wind carries. Those days of anger and remorse occasionally catch us off guard, and we shudder, or perhaps we shudder out of fear that we will shudder, and flee back home—in this case to the home that's *not* away from home.

Home: a richly ironic word on which to conclude fifteen poems exploring the congenital aloneness that defines us in spite of, and perhaps because of, other people. A great deal of Kenyon's poetry wrestles with the dynamics between solitude and relation, how our thoughts and feelings fall within the closed circle of our own singularity, even as we try to "briefly enter, briefly speak," hoping to widen that circle and admit other selves. What sends the speaker hurrying home—"Chill, or the fear/ of chill"—captures even deeper fathoms about the self. For all her deserved acclaim as a master of the "natural object as the adequate symbol," it's often in minute *rhetorical* gestures like this that one recognizes in Kenyon's quiet lyricism the *gravitas* of tragedy. The word "chill" itself makes for a potent oxymoron: a mind recalling grief constitutes a kind of recurrent emotional flu. And the qualification that follows, spanning an enjambment charged with unrest, reminds us that humans, sentenced to self-consciousness, can't finally distinguish between a feeling and the feeling of a feeling. Walking alone or hurrying home (certainly to check on that "you"), we take ourselves with us, whoever we are, wherever we go.

WESLEY MCNAIR

A Government of Two

Several years ago, something happened to my friends Donald Hall and Jane Kenyon that I'd never seen in the literary world before. Up to that time each was well known to poetry audiences—he as a senior American poet and recent recipient of the National Book Critics Circle Award, she as a younger poet with a growing reputation. Then, their relationship itself became famous. Through their co-readings, their joint interviews in print and on the NPR show *Fresh Air,* and most importantly, their starring roles in the Bill Moyers special, *A Life Together,* millions of Americans came to know of the life in poetry the two shared as husband and wife in rural New Hampshire. Audiences also became aware of the couple's sorrows: Kenyon's lifelong struggle with depression, and Hall's colon cancer, which metastasized to the liver and despite a successful operation, seemed likely to return. Later on, of course, those who had followed the Hall-Kenyon story learned of its ironic and heartrending conclusion: fearing the fatal recurrence of his disease, the couple discovered a cancer growing in her—the leukemia that, despite a bonemarrow transplant, finally killed her, and left him with a grief that has lasted to this day.

The moving and ultimately tragic story of their life together has created a new interest in the poetry of Hall. It has created even more interest in Kenyon, whose death in midcareer has not only cast a spell upon many readers, but caused confusion about her work. I have heard readers attribute a variety of melancholy poems to her bout with leukemia, when, in fact, only one poem, "The Sick Wife," was written in the months of her fatal illness. Compounding the error, the review of her new and selected volume *Otherwise* in *Publishers Weekly* asserted that all of the book's new poems were about "her pending death." Yet if the legendary story of Kenyon and Hall makes her verse and his harder to see and assess, that story also suggests a new way to examine their poetry. For the truth is, their life together was vital to their development as poets, influencing everything from work methods to the content of work produced. In fact, it made their best poems possible.

To say so is only to repeat what these poets have suggested themselves. In a joint interview by Marian Blue printed in *AWP Chronicle* shortly before Kenyon's death, Hall remarked, "The great changes in my poetry, which my friends and the book reviewers find beginning in *Kicking the Leaves,* began after our marriage, while we were still in Ann Arbor; the move [to his family farmhouse] confirmed, enlarged, and extended those changes." And Kenyon declared: ". . . Whatever it is that I know about writing poems, I have learned most of it from being with Don, moving to his ancestral farm, keeping my ears open when his peers come to visit."

I became aware of their relationship when I visited that New Hampshire farm shortly after they moved in, drawn by hopes for my own poetry. Living nearby in New Hampshire, I knew that Hall had arrived at the place the year before, but I did not know much about Jane Kenyon, and neither did the friends who brought me there; it was the established poet and anthologist Donald Hall we had gone to see. However, Hall soon made it clear he was not the only writer living in the farmhouse. Inviting me back a couple of days later to discuss some poems I had left with him, he not only told me that Kenyon wrote poetry, but that she had her own assessment of my poems, which he, in her absence, passed on with obvious respect.

I should have sensed then how valuable she had become to him as a reader of his own work, but I thought mostly about how valuable he was to hers. The Jane Kenyon I became acquainted with at that time was, after all, very much like me—a young writer in formation who needed the kind of support an older writer like Hall, generous to a fault, offered—namely, the assurance that one had talent; the encouragement to use the talent; and honest, experienced appraisals of work in progress. Hall was helping both of us in these ways in the same period, and because he was supporting Kenyon financially, she had the additional luxury of free time.

"I think," he wrote to me recently, "I helped her in one big way, always: the hard work, the dedication, the stubbornness, the ambition." It is clear to me from my experience that he is right. When I met her, several years before "the Committee" (Kenyon's term for her workshop with Alice Mattison and Joyce Peseroff) first convened, she kept no regular writing schedule, but she was already beginning to write more than she had before. There is no doubt her new application came from watching Hall spend ten or more hours every day on poetry and prose, rain or shine, in hope and disappointment. Through him, she came to know how the writing life worked, and how the poems got done. "Don has so many poems, he could easily give several readings and never read the same poem twice," she told me as she was counting up poems for her first book, nearly complete. "All I have is these," she said. I see now that even as she measured her small output against Hall's, she was pondering the challenge of gathering more poems in her future. And when her first volume was at last ready and she had trouble placing it with a publisher, I heard Hall assure her that "It will happen" in a tone that suggested her own career in poetry would happen, too.

As Kenyon herself remarked, Hall's influence included the "peers" he introduced her to at his farm. One of these was Robert Bly, who advised her in the late 1970s to work on translations of the Russian poet Anna Akhmatova—probably the most important single piece of advice she ever received as a poet. Through Bly and another of Hall's friends, Louis Simpson, Kenyon located a translator, Vera Dunham, to help her with the project, publishing six Akhmatova poems in her first volume of poetry (1978), and more of them in *Twenty Poems of*

Anna Akhmatova (1980). As a result of her translations, Kenyon discovered the possibilities of the brief lyric, which she was to explore for the rest of her writing life.

In the introduction to *Twenty Poems* she describes not only Akhmatova's early poetry, but the verse she herself was now attempting. Interestingly, her description refers to John Keats, her other major influence at this time:

> As we remember [John] Keats for the beauty and intensity
> of his shorter poems, especially the odes and sonnets, so
> we revere Akhmatova for her early lyrics—brief, perfectly
> made verses of passion and feeling. Images build emotional
> pressure. . . . I love the sudden twists these poems take, often
> in the last line.

The poem Kenyon cites for illustration is one I heard her recite at a reading the two of us did together, with Hall in attendance, perhaps four years after *Twenty Poems* appeared:

> We walk along the hard crest of the snowdrift
> toward my white, mysterious house,
> both of us so quiet,
> keeping the silence as we go along.
> And sweeter even than the singing of songs
> is the dream, now becoming real:
> the swaying of branches brushed aside
> and the faint ringing of your spurs.

I recall how, in the question-and-answer session that followed our reading, she went back to the poem, taking pleasure in the "sudden twist" of its conclusion, where simple images are charged with eroticism. And I remember that she asked Hall at the restaurant we went to afterward about the poems she read from her first book *From Room to Room,* now several years old. He thought they had held up well, but Kenyon had her doubts. Of course, she had by that time experienced harrowing personal difficulties, including the death of her father and serious episodes of mania and depression—difficulties that changed her as a poet and must have altered her view of the earlier work. But I see now her doubts came also from her encounter with Akhmatova, who had changed the way she worked so much as to make some of her first poems seem foreign to her. I would discover the results of that encounter later on with the publication of her second book, *The Boat of Quiet Hours,* akin to Akhmatova's early work not only in its method but in its content: the allusive imagery drawn from nature or domestic life, the dreamy speech, the tone of anguish or melancholy.

Another thing I did not grasp at the time of our joint reading was the full meaning of Donald Hall's expression the whole time Jane read—a combination of the greatest pride and joy. It was the same expression I noticed at later readings when he sat in the audience; I took it then, as before, to be a sign of the pleasure her progress as a poet gave him, as it surely was. But reading this comment by Hall in the *AWP Chronicle's* interview makes me now suspect that the pleasure Hall took at her readings and in the letters he sent to me over the years praising her work, was more complicated than I initially thought, and related to his own progress as a poet:

> I know I have been encouraged and thrilled to watch Jane's
> own poetry develop, mature, become better and better. . . .
> Possibly in rivalry, possibly in mere joy, I think I have re-
> sponded to her own increasing ambition and excellence by
> trying even harder myself, or perhaps with more energy.

In fact, as I return to the poetry Hall started with *Kicking the Leaves,* no longer focusing on the older poet who guided both Kenyon and me but on a writer with his own need to change and grow, I see the help his wife gave him as an artist was every bit as valuable as the assistance he gave her. Even as he was providing a model for her as an older writer with long-term experience, she was presenting him with the model of a young writer developing and thriving. And just as he helped her by the discipline he brought to his craft, she helped him, as he put it to me in a letter, "by her own stubbornness and by the example of her overcoming obstacles, personal and emotional ones, to make art"—also "by her stubborn and beautiful love of the art of poetry."

It is now clear to me, moreover, that whereas Hall's influence on the content of Kenyon's poetry was limited, Kenyon's influence on the content of his was profound. Only through his relationship with her in his ancestral farmhouse was he able to imagine the connection with Kate and Wesley Wells and their agrarian past that is essential to *Kicking the Leaves*. It is Kenyon, after all, with whom he dunks his finger into the quart of syrup in the central poem "Maple Syrup," the two of them bonding through that gesture with the grandfather and the past; and it is Kenyon he refers to in "Flies" when he says, "We live in the house left behind; we sleep in the bed where they whispered together at night." That "we," linked in the book's last poem "Stone Walls" to a vision of family and community, nature, and religious belief, is what brings the sense of place Hall celebrates into being.

In their *AWP Chronicle* interview, Hall speaks of Kenyon's influence on the "Sister" poems of his next book, *The Happy Man,* as well: "my closeness to Jane," he says, "gave me the courage to try writing in a female voice." It seems likely that Kenyon's impact on *The Happy Man* was even more extensive and began with certain poems in her first volume *From Room to Room*. In this book Kenyon identifies—through verses like "The Thimble," "Finding a Long Gray Hair," and "Hanging Pictures in Granny's Room"—with the women who have lived on Hall's ancestral farm. Reading such poems one by one as Kenyon wrote them, Hall was no doubt better able to imagine an alternative, feminine view of his new place and of the world—the view that he presents in *The Happy Man*. Thus, there is an irony in the title of this volume that critics have not yet noticed: his collection is not finally so much about a man or the masculine self as it is about a woman and the power of femininity.

Hall's female principle in the book is associated with the idea of repose, a word that recurs in the poems of the last section, "Sisters," and that is defined in the section's epigraph (from Meister Eckhart) as "what the soul [looks] for" and "what all creatures [want], in all their natural efforts and motions." The male principle, on the other hand, as announced in the section titled "Men Driving Cars," has to do with compulsive motion and the submergence of the emotional and intuitive life. It is significant that men in this section, clearly the weaker sex, are disconnected from women; for the ideal the book advances in spite of its darknesses is a linking of the masculine and feminine selves, appearing in poems about grandfather and grandmother, mother and father, uncle and niece, and couples engaged and married. It should be no surprise that among the volume's couples, those most often referred to are the author himself and Jane Kenyon, the wife and poet who initiated the collection's feminine themes. Making a first appearance in *Kicking the Leaves,* this "we" has played a crucial role in every Hall book since.

In Donald Hall's next volume, *The One Day,* a book-length poem about America's spiritual corruption, he casts his couple as exemplars bound so closely in their love and their work of writing that "the day is double" and their eyes "gaze not at each other but a third thing" they have created together: "work's paradise." The poem's recurrent scenes of himself and Kenyon in their farmhouse are the more moving for being placed in the context of the lovelessness and unfulfilling work of American society. Linking his life with Kenyon to the life of the nation in *The One Day,* Hall was never before so affirmative about their relationship or more encompassing in his poetic vision. And Kenyon, who had provided him with the real-life version of the poem's relationship, helped him bring the ambitious poem forth. As his first reader, she was the one who listened to him read the poem aloud in an early draft; it was she too who supported him in his long struggle with the book, understanding its importance.

"Don has been working on a different kind of poetry now that shows all his wisdom," she told me shortly after the book was done. By that time I had moved from New Hampshire to the University of Maine at Farmington, where I had invited her to read her poems. Walking together to a class for discussion of her work before the reading, she and I made quite a pair: I was depressed about a long poem in progress that wasn't working out, and she, worse off, had undergone a period of clinical depression. "I haven't been feeling well for a long time," she told me. "The poems of the book I've just finished are very melancholy, very dark," she added, shaking her head and pressing her lips together as she always did when she was distressed. "You'll see when I read them tonight."

At the reading some of the poems from the new book, *Let Evening Come,* seemed to have their own wisdom, suggesting that while her husband had been working on the poetry she praised for being wise, she had been expanding the brief lyric to include a wisdom of her own. One of these was "The Pear":

> There is a moment in middle age
> when you grow bored, angered
> by your middling mind,
> afraid.
>
> That day the sun
> burns hot and bright,
> making you more desolate.
>
> It happens subtly, as when a pear
> spoils from the inside out,
> and you may not be aware
> until things have gone too far.

There were other new variations in the work of *Let Evening Come,* clearer to me as I read it now, several years later. The associations of certain poems—some imitating the form of notes and letters, others involving vignettes and thoughts about travel—were more complex. Moreover, in poems like "On the Aisle" and "At the Public Market Museum: Charleston, South Carolina," Kenyon had begun to deal with concerns in the world outside of her inner struggles. Finally, there were hints in her handling of narration of the deepening influence of Chekhov, and a new, Bishop-like way of addressing the reader as a confidante.

Yet just as she had warned, the poems also had a great sorrow in them—a sorrow also evident in *The Boat of Quiet Hours* and her fourth collection, *Constance*. Notwithstanding their moments of lightness and their moving mysticism, all of these books contain themes of terminal illness and death, depression, detachment from the body, and alienation from social life. All reach back to a childhood troubled by psychological stress and the misunderstanding of others. Their narrators often speak with a child's innocence, too, offering the disturbance they feel so calmly and simply; the poems are the more unsettling as we ponder them. A friend who knew Kenyon once told me that when she asked the poet to describe her process of writing, Kenyon told her it was always "gut-wrenching." Given the dark content of the poems and Kenyon's attempt in many of them to deal with extreme personal difficulties, this description is not hard to believe. It seems likely to me that the enormous stability and understanding she found in her relationship with Hall helped her persist with such difficult subject matter.

But she got even more help from her remarkable determination— what Hall termed her "example of overcoming obstacles, personal and emotional ones." That determination is never more clearly seen than in *Constance,* where, in addition to returning to the subject of her father's death, first taken up in *The Boat of Quiet Hours,* she confronted the more serious personal and emotional obstacles she ever experienced: her lifelong depression and her fear of Donald Hall's cancer. The result was some of her most poignant poems: "Chrysanthemums," the nine-part "Having It Out with Melancholy," and "Pharaoh." One can only imagine how difficult it was for Kenyon to write the concluding stanza of "Pharaoh," conceding, as it does, the possibility of Hall's death:

> I woke in the night to see your
> diminished bulk lying beside me—
> you on your back, like a sarcophagus
> as your feet held up the covers. . . .
> The things you might need in the next
> life surrounded you—your comb and glasses,
> water, a book and a pen.

In the meantime, Hall continued to write about Kenyon, this time in *The Museum of Clear Ideas,* which was released in the same year *Constance* was published. In some of the sections of Hall's title poem, he attempts to quiet Kenyon's anxiety about him, giving a reader of the two books the odd and moving impression of a dialogue taking place between the two poets, across volumes. The most affecting example is "Mount Kearsarge Shines," where the speaker uses images of weather to discuss with "Camilla" (Kenyon's name in the title poem) the possible recurrence of his cancer and to qualify its threat:

> Storms stop when they stop, no sooner,
>   leaving the birches glossy
>
> with ice and bent glittering to rimy ground.
> We'll avoid the programmed weatherman grinning
>   from the box, cheerful with tempest,
>   and take the day as it comes,
>
> one day at a time, the way everyone says.
> These hours are the best because we hold them close
>   in our uxorious nation.
>   Soon we'll walk—when days turn fair

and frost stays off—over old roads, listening
for peepers as spring comes on, never to miss
the day's offering of pleasure
for the government of two.

As it was in *The One Day,* the relationship between Hall and
Kenyon is extremely important to Hall's title poem in *The Museum
of Clear Ideas;* for the stability of that relationship helps the poem's
narrator to stand apart from the world in which he lives and to view
it with distance and clarity. Yet our awareness of what his precarious
health might do to the "government of two" threatens the equanimity
of the speaker's vision, occasionally jiggling the lens. Thus, the same
Camilla sections that help the narrator achieve his distance also suggest a vulnerability and humanity that temper his remoteness, making the view he offers easier to accept.

But alas, we live in a world where governments fail and nations disappear, sometimes in the least predictable ways; it was Jane Kenyon,
not Donald Hall, who got the cancer, and she who died of it. I remember going to dinner with them just after Christmas in New
Hampshire, where the three of us exchanged and signed volumes of
poetry, each having published one earlier in the year. I recall, too, the
apprehension just beneath our festivity about Hall's health. So when
I received a note Hall sent less than two months later, I was shocked
to read its news of Kenyon's leukemia.

During her illness and their attempts to cure it through a bone
marrow transplant operation, Hall worked to complete a new book—
his twelfth volume, *The Old Life*—which bears more of Kenyon's
influence than ever. Like every collection Hall ever wrote after his
marriage to Kenyon, this one is dedicated to her and includes, among
other poems, verse about their life together. But unlike the other
volumes, *The Old Life,* a poem in eighty-odd parts, contains a series
of brief lyrics that closely resemble Kenyon's in their form, the images and events of each gathering toward a concluding disclosure or

epiphany. As in Kenyon, Hall's disclosure sometimes comes by surprise out of events that predicted it all along:

> We walked in the white house
> like ghosts among ghosts who cherished us.
> Everything we looked at
> exalted and raptured out spirits:—
> full moon, pale blue
> asters, swamp maples Chinese red, ghost birches,
> stone walls, cellar holes,
> and lopsided stretched farmhouses like ours.
> The old tenants watched us
> settle in, five years, and then the house
> shifted on its two-hundred-
> year-old sills, and became our house.

Sometimes the concluding disclosure is less predictable, as in this lyric about Kenyon's depressions:

> Curled on the sofa
> in the fetal position, Jane wept day
> and night, night and day.
> I could not touch her; I could do nothing.
> Melancholia fell
> like rain on Ireland for weeks
> without end.
>   I never
> belittled her sorrows or joshed at
> her dreads and miseries.
> How admirable I found myself.

However the conclusion is handled, the result is the sudden twist Kenyon admired in the poems of Akhmatova.

In the days just before Kenyon's death, the two worked to assemble her last volume *Otherwise,* a collection of new and selected verse. The book's new poems were among the best she had ever done, striking in their variety and their coherence. Continuing to explore the short lyric (the majority of the poems were half a page long or less), she dealt with dark themes familiar from earlier books—her father's dying and Hall's cancer—adding poems about the death of her mother-in-law. Yet there was a new range of emotional tone, which included both sorrow and happiness, "Happiness" being, in fact, the title of one of the poems. Moreover, Kenyon was less tied to autobiographical detail, exercising a new freedom of invention, and using the third person to deal with events and issues in the world around her. Finally, there was a new integration of religious belief and poetic observation, showing us how strongly faith guided Kenyon and shaped her view of the world.

Of this last work, the only poem written during Kenyon's illness was "The Sick Wife," on which, as Hall says in his afterword to *Otherwise,* she "would have made more changes if she had lived." This poem features Kenyon and Hall, as many earlier ones do. Yet while the earlier pieces are often love poems, "The Sick Wife" speaks of love's absence. Since the husband of the piece has gone for groceries, the wife, helpless in her illness, is left to watch "even the old and relatively infirm" move outside in the parking lot and the cars alongside of her pull "away so briskly/ that it . . . [makes] her sick at heart." Whereas the Kenyon of the earlier poems is at home in the place where love and work happen, the sick wife is in all ways displaced, neither at home, nor able to join the world's traffic. Choosing the third person to portray the wife in this poem, Kenyon stands eerily outside of herself, observing not only the verse's moment but her own finite history.

Yet in spite of "The Sick Wife" the love poems about Kenyon and Hall continue, because in his grief, Donald Hall goes on writing about his mate, and even—in the concluding poems of his volume *Without*—to her. In an interview on the NPR program *Fresh Air* done while he was completing *Without,* Hall declared that everything he had done as a poet seemed to him a preparation for the poetry he is now involved with. Then he read a sample, "Weeds and Peonies," one of his most beautiful elegies, where he paces between the weedy garden Kenyon left behind and her newly blossoming peonies by the porch of the ancestral farmhouse. Watching their petals blow across the abandoned garden, he imagines Kenyon vanishing into snow-flakes; looking up at Mt. Kearsarge, he thinks of the words he spoke when she went off for a day of climbing: "Hurry back"—words that are useless now. Hall's elegy is the more poignant for the way it inter-weaves words and images from Kenyon's poems, as if to illustrate the interdependency that sustained the two poets in their life together. There are references to Kenyon's walking with Gus, the dog that ap-pears in her third and fourth volumes, and to snowflakes as particles, a metaphor used first in her poem "Winter Lambs." Describing the peonies, a favorite subject in Kenyon's work, Hall uses the words "prodigies," "heads," and "topple"—all found in earlier Kenyon poems and releasing a range of sorrowful meanings best appreciated by studying the original sources and the new context Hall's elegy has pro-vided. In one of its lines "Weeds and Peonies" even refers to a poem Hall included in his first New Hampshire book, "Old Roses"—a love poem to Kenyon that spoke of the beauty of the old roses around the Wilmot farmhouse and, ironically, how quickly they perish.

No doubt this allusive and moving poem, and the interview dur-ing which Donald Hall read it, will continue to spread the legendary story of two poets, drawing readers to the work of Hall and Kenyon, and at the same time distorting that work and making it more dif-ficult to assess. But there will be time in the future for such assess-ments. For now, we may simply be grateful for the abundance of poetry these two have written over the last twenty-five years—poems both local and universal in their subjects, which range from despair to celebration. And we may give thanks for the unique relationship that brought such poetry to us.

MOLLY PEACOCK

from

A Comfort Poem

On a winter day near the solstice, I met Jane Kenyon for tea. Nearly all the lights in New York City were on, and it was only 4:30 in the afternoon. I had hurried through the dusk, late, and stood catching my breath in the doorway of the Upper East Side tearoom. There, among cups as pink as the cheeks of the royals on the *Majesty* magazines placed at each table, Jane sat, in a mahogany chair. She'd come in earlier from her home, Eagle Pond, her husband, the poet Donald Hall's, family farm in New Hampshire. Still and composed, she rested there almost as if she were a portrait of herself, the cloud of her dark hair suspended over her hand-knit sweater. Though it was only a few hours past its middle, the day lay in dusk outside the large window she stared through—behind her, the room in a heated glow.

As I heaved off my coat and barged toward her—we'd never had a face-to-face meeting before, and I was late and a bit nervous—I thought of her poem "Let Evening Come," in which dusk comes to a midsummer day, on almost the opposite side of the calendar. In her poem, the end of the day is almost statuesque, just like Jane.

The slow comfort of her poem's lyric voice is a tonic I use to settle myself. Whenever I summon the poem up, its pacing seems to slow down my breathing. But *what* inside Jane Kenyon's words would give the effect of actually regulating the diaphragm? How does the body of language that a poem assembles seem to change the pacing of the human body receiving it? One of the loveliest—and most ancient—of pacemakers is repetition, and when Kenyon repeats *Let* in "Let Evening

Come," the pulse of that syllable becomes a New Hampshire mantra. She uses the oldest of ways we have to coax ourselves into relaxation: murmuring the same word again and again to create a chant, a late-twentieth-century litany.

I plopped down in a needlepoint chair and gushed, "How was China?" She answered serenely, "I took your poem 'The Lull' there."

"The Lull." Was there ever a lull in my own life now? I rushed from teaching children in the daytime to teaching a graduate course at night, cramming my social life like sweaters crushed, last-minute, into a bursting suitcase.

"What did they think of your work, the Chinese?"

"Oh," Jane hesitated, ever truthful, "I couldn't tell, really."

Although this was our first meeting, Jane and I spoke as though we knew each other well. That is because, in a few postcards and brief calls, we had realized that we knew each other's writing very well. I'd read just about everything she had published. I remember one of my teachers at Johns Hopkins, Cynthia Macdonald, saying to our class that nothing would ever be as important to us as the work of our peers, and certainly this was true in my relationship to Jane Kenyon's work.

"How are you doing with the depression poem?" I asked in our strange, literary intimacy. Jane endured lifelong depressions as well as the drugs used to treat them, which she revealed in a poem called "Having It Out with Melancholy." But our talk was about words, not about bipolar disorder. We settled down in the rhythms of the writing community of two. Editors, publishers, bites of cucumber sandwiches, magazines, nut bread, what we wanted for our art . . . the day sank around us. The ritual of our murmurings and the pouring of tea served as our form of vespers.

If you read "Let Evening Come" aloud, you can feel a vespers resonance. The rhythm of the dozen *Lets* Jane Kenyon uses can lull you into an attitude of prayer. Yet her poem provides the liveliest kind of devotion because the language both repeats *and* quickens with change. Like the mottled light of dusk, the *Lets* move in a scattered pattern, like most patterns in nature.

By the time I reach the end of "Let Evening Come," when she states that God does not leave us comfortless, I completely believe her. But what in Kenyon's plain vocabulary would be responsible for the raptness—and immediacy—of not only my belief but that of most people who read her? Harbored in the poem is the steady pulse of the hymn line, or common measure. It is a loosely constructed hymn, counting often—though not always—eight syllables per line, generally with four beats of emphasis. (*"It CAME upON the MIDnight CLEAR,"* begins the Christmas carol.) Jane, herself a churchgoer, understood intuitively how music underpins the power of a poem's emotion. We can think of the beat beneath the hymn line as loudness and softness alternating. She puts the loud syllable first: *LET the CRICKet TAKE up CHAFing.*

If you are in a hurry, your internal rhythm accelerates till all the syllables inside your head are loud. Your mental pulse imitates the loud buzz of fear. Being inside frenetic activity is like being, rhythmically, in the staccato grip of fear. Each syllable of your life seems stressed. By removing half the loudness, by equalizing its emphasis with softness, Kenyon creates a steadiness—or the exact opposite of an adrenaline surge. Fear has a rhythm of overemphasis. By de-emphasizing the fear state, in which your heart pounds in your ears, the poem regulates your in- and exhalations, slowing your breathing.

The stress of overemphasis is partly responsible for what destroys our perspective in life. When we are too consumed by tasks, our mental vista shrinks. Unmitigated emphasis closes the world in on us. De-emphasis actually opens mental space. Quieting sound creates a visual horizon. Kenyon's simple images shine because the musical system has opened up the mental space we need to connect to them. The alternating rhythm clarifies by literally clearing the air, allowing us to breathe with the deep and regular inhalations and exhalations that sustain life.

Our sense of the poem's spirituality comes from this alternating emphasis—or music—moving through each line as its breath. "Spirit," it is nice to remember, *means* breath. Sound, the most subliminal aspect of poetry (though it can be consciously manipulated) carries emotion in a poem in a nearly kinesthetic way. How the poem feels to your tongue and teeth—the consonants, the vowels, the loudness and softness of syllables—is the embodiment of the feelings that sounds evoke. We think poems are about life in language, but they are, as importantly, about nonlanguage, the preverbal experience of emotion, of *being*. One of the reasons we surprise ourselves with our primitive reactions to poetry is that it often recalls us to a preverbal place. Our whole preverbal life, alight with curiosity and interest in everything, occurs *before* we speak recognizable words. The rhythms of lines, as opposed to sentences, can walk the sharpest yet most *unnameable* feelings through the poem. Lines move in ways we are unaware of—just as we move through space without awareness of the momentum of our bones.

While the line is drumming a musical baseline, the sentence, that most conscious of linguistic constructions, is making music, too. In fact, you can see and hear both kinds of music working in "Let Evening Come." The first stanza is a sentence in itself:

> Let the light of late afternoon
> shine through chinks in the barn, moving
> up the bales as the sun moves down.

But the second stanza is two sentences, and so is the third. Though each sentence begins with *Let*, Kenyon places them differently, creating a sentence rhythm with each stanza. And this is what stanzas are all about. Although they sometimes act as paragraphs, and even look like them, they don't always signal or elaborate new ideas the way prose paragraphs do. They are musical groups. *Stanza*, in Italian, means room; you can think of stanzas as musical chambers, as the chambers of a shell. In this poem they are just as pearly and luminous as natural objects because they are both symmetrical *and* asymmetrical. Part of what I think defines beauty in poetry (and this has nothing to do with whether a poet is writing about something pretty or something ugly) is the shimmering verge between what's regularized (in this case, each stanza has three lines, and each sentence, at least in the beginning, starts with *Let*) and what emerges from the regularity—the bump in the shell wall, the mercurial pearl of the color (in this case, the way the sentences move irregularly through the stanzas). The poem's unevenness in spite of its evenness displays a delicious tension between the predictable and the surprising. It is as if someone decided to build a picket fence with varying fence posts, so that the line of the fence becomes a wave.

When the title of the poem pops up at the end of the second stanza in its own sentence, it makes you realize that the title itself is a complete thought, with its own subject and verb. The subject is You (understood). Oh my goodness, is the subject God? Or is it Us? Is it *we* who are to relax enough to let evening come? Is it *we* who are to slow our breathing so that things might end with the pace that belongs to them? Oh dear, the whole universe is here, and we are only nine lines down:

> Let the cricket take up chafing
> as a woman takes up her needles
> and her yarn. Let evening come.
>
> Let dew collect on the hoe abandoned
> in long grass. Let the stars appear
> and the moon disclose her silver horn.

The soothing "l" sound that begins the first word of the first line, like an arm slipped around a shoulder, also begins the second and third stanzas, then appears in the middle of the third line of the second stanza and the second line of the third stanza, interrupting the pattern, making it more complex. After that comes the fourth verse, when the poet rubs four *Lets* through the stanza—as if that arm around us were rubbing our shoulders.

Let the fox go back to its sandy den.
Let the wind die down. Let the shed
go black inside. Let evening come.

Now another aspect of rhythm besides regularity comes into the poem. It is pacing. Human beings have subtle responses—and the mechanisms that operate in poetry are subtle, too. Pacing takes that alternating hymn rhythm and colors it with individual response. In the line *Let the FOX go BACK to its SANdy DEN,* the loudness shifts. The hymn line, eight syllables, stretches to ten. The regularity of how syllables alternate soft and loud in common measure also stretches, expanding and contracting in this line, because even though there are two extra syllables there are still the same four beats. Those two extra unstressed syllables, like soft breaths, introduce the fox. After the fox enters the poem, the next line goes right back to eight syllables. Yet because the next two sentences end midline, the pacing shifts again. The periods at each midpoint give these two lines a clipped quality. There's a quickening—evening is coming faster.

But it is two tiny, lowercase *lets* in the last two stanzas that trigger the little miracles of this poem. In the fifth stanza *let* seems at first nowhere to be found—then we discover it—protruding its lowercase head.

To the bottle in the ditch, to the scoop
in the oats, to air in the lung
let evening come.

Kenyon's withholding of the *let* until the last line of the stanza internalizes it. It is deep inside its sentence, as air is deep in the lung, or the scoop is deep in the oats. How specific and shiningly individual she makes the bottle by placing it *in the ditch* so familiarly that we are included in her perspective—of course, we know what ditch it is; now we too are part of the everyday evening landscape she inhabits. Lowering the case lowers the poet's voice. Jane herself had a low, calm voice. As the voice of another enters us—slowly, just as the evening comes—our own biology seems to change. Another breath is inside us. When people feel inexplicably changed by—charged by—poetry, part of that inexplicability is this bodily mystery.

It is lovely to remember that the preposition is supposed to have been Gertrude Stein's favorite part of speech. Prepositions are our most private speech parts. They achieve intimacy by showing relations, relationships, and meeting places, sometimes so secret that we forget them. *To the bottle in the ditch, to the scoop / in the oats, to air in the lung:* in two short lines are six prepositions, each showing another slip of relation, another sliver of closeness. As readers of these prepositions, we grow more deeply intimate with the evening—and with the poem itself—becoming more aware of our own biology; finally it is possible to feel ourselves *in* that lung, even as the rhythm of the poem is *in* us. Both the bottle and the scoop are in positions of rest, lying down in their environments, ready for the miracle of restoration that is sleep, or the closure that dissolves the known world and that is death.

There really are only two subjects of lyric poetry, and these are the two things that most rivet our attention: love and death. They are locked by a link of language—*and*—which is an example of my own favorite part of speech, the conjunction. In the presence of the absence that this poem portends grows a mild-mannered, seemingly insignificant word: *so.*

> Let it come, as it will, and don't
> be afraid. God does not leave us
> comfortless, so let evening come.

So is a conjunction; it joins ideas, healing ruptures. As prepositions show us relations, conjunctions make unions. They marry ideas; they are stable and encompassing. And snugly familiar. We almost don't notice them. In the last stanza, before the conjunction slips in, the address of the *Let* changes. *Let it come,* she says in a kind of acceptance tinged with resignation, *as it will.* Then follow the most reassuring words in English, *don't be afraid.* For any work of art to supply an answer—as it is not at all obligated to do—is a thing of satisfaction so complete that it sends roots into the soul.

Here is the moment when we realize how much the music of the poem, with its injection of a soft syllable between most louder syllables, has diminished the constant stress of everyday being. The *un*stressed syllables have slowed and calmed the lines. When Kenyon says *don't be afraid,* we are prepared to let go of our fear because we have been abandoning the rhythm of fear through the regularity of our breathing. We can accept the idea that we don't have to be afraid because we have slowed down, re-attuned ourselves to the intake and exhalation of our breath and the beating of our hearts.

Then she has the kindness to tell us the reason we are not to be afraid. *God does not leave us /comfortless,* she writes, following the line with a comma, that little curve of a pause, itself like a scoop, before she pronounces the ultimate conjunction, *so. So* unites the twelfth and last repetition of *let* with our perception that yes, darkness *will* fall—and it will be all right now, with all of us, even the darkness of death that is part of the pattern.

When I wake up in the middle of the night, as I often do, "Let Evening Come" is one of the poems I turn to. In the face of my roused anxieties, it reinforces my need to let things shut down, and I find the poem's rhythms deeply restoring. Yet there is always a place in a poem where repetition becomes oppressive, and the poem must seek a change. When I come to the penultimate stanza of "Let Evening Come," I feel how Kenyon quickens the language, growing the poem off the trellis of its pattern. It is like throwing off the weight of too many blankets. She quietly shows that there must be a shift from pattern to conclusion, an opening into what is beyond the scaffolding that repetition makes yet can be discovered only because limits are set: the sudden perspective of grace.

JUDITH HARRIS

Discerning Cherishment in Jane Kenyon's Poetry: A Psychoanalytic Approach

Jane Kenyon maintained throughout her career that "the natural object is always the adequate symbol." In other words, language has a libidinal adhesion to the object it represents, and this adhesion is always already laden with natural affect. The object is not a symbol of another "truth" that leaps out it the way religious meanings leapt out of natural objects in seventeenth-century poetry, giving the form a static, but securable content. For some contemporary poets, nature is in itself an adequate sign of emotion and transcendent meaning. The message is not separable from the image, but is always implicit. Poetic perception is a matter of bringing the two sources (poet and feeling object) into alignment. As Kenyon stated in a lecture, "Everything I Know About Writing Poetry":

> There's the need to make sense of life behind the impulse to write. We celebrate the world by writing about it . . . we feel the pressure of emotion and thought, and we need to find, among the many things of this world a way to body forth our feeling. It's metaphor, the engine of poetry, that does the work. Metaphor is simply talking about one thing in terms of another. Poems are where the inner world is revealed in terms of the outer world—revealed in terms of things . . .

One of the goals of both therapy and poetry writing is self-elucidation and self-understanding. Paradoxically, self-understanding may be one way of liberating one's self from one's self. In Elisabeth Young-Bruehl and Faith Bethelard's *Cherishment: A Psychology of the Heart,* the authors assert that there are moments in therapy when patients' needs emerge in what they term "cherishment scenes," like those moments of "sacred truth" in the *Iliad.* The authors refer to receptive moments, when hatred "relents" because it understands, for a moment, its own inception, its own origin as something that erupts from a lack of love, affection, or cherishment. It is a moment when the deep-seated disappointments and fears of dependency that keep so many of us from forming healthy relationships are finally confronted, and when a patient and therapist are able to stand together on the edge of suffering, sharing it. It is also a moment in which the patient is able to arm herself with compassion not only for herself, and her specific history, but also for others, and what brings them into relatedness.

The principle of sharing, and mutual reliance, can be redefined as one of co-creation in both literary activity and psychoanalytic exchange. When one reads a poem, the reader creates his or her own particular interpretation of the written word, or, one might say, he or she creates an object relationship with the words on the page. In my view, the co-created meaning (a matrix of writer and reader's) forms a third virtual space, or analytic "third" that joins both the patient and analyst, writer and reader. Kenyon was particularly predisposed to working through her own affective disorders by focusing on objects in the natural world. Her facing off with "melancholy," through the writing of poems about illness and despair, is an extraordinary example of self-recognition and self-understanding. Through nature, Kenyon breaks through isolation and despair, recognizing and affirming the beauty of valued objects that claim their own emotionally magnetic field. Or as the authors of *Cherishment* might define it, Kenyon's process is an affectionate current that brings with it the expectation to be loved, or cherished by someone who can validate one's need to be recognized, a current that reflects the broader needs and gratifications of all human beings.

In this essay, I wish to show how cherishment (as a psychoanalytic and therapeutic concept) functions in a Kenyon's work. Kenyon suffered from a bipolar disorder and endured long periods of depression, consoled by beauty, by the dramatic enactment of the need to be cherished, and to tend, and be tended by, her object-related world. Sadness was often a wellspring for the birth of the poem. As Kenyon said in an interview with Bill Moyers, " . . . it's odd but true that there really is consolation from sad poems, and it's hard to know how that happens. There's the pleasure of the thing itself, and somehow that works against the sadness." By inviting melancholy, and "researching" it introspectively, she broke with the older ways of naming and thinking about mental illness as primarily a disease of the soul rather than body.

Although there has been a long poetic tradition that has romanticized melancholy—as in Edgar Allan Poe, John Keats, and Edward Thomas, and, more recently, confessional writers—Kenyon's concept of melancholy and its felt expression in poetry is innate and incessant and chemically produced by the brain rather than by the soul. Kenyon's melancholy is not a romantic condition, often venerated by poets who assume its visitations to be inspiring, nor it is a metaphorically profound, religious perspective on the human condition. Depression must be contended with until it relents ("What hurt me so terribly/all my life until this moment?"). Sad moods compete with life but also deepen the poet's need and capacity for consolation.

Far from accepting a condition of chronic depression, Kenyon found relief in the concreteness of antidepressants and the ordinary contentment of observing things in the world that might go unnoticed if it had not been for the fact that she was searching for some reminder of what seemed securable and constant in a nature outside her own mercurial moods. She saw her life and work as a "psychology of heart"—as a means of fostering and bodying forth the earth's body through rhetoricity, one to be dressed in the colors of its own light (light, in fact, was the mead of her vernacular, as was her use of color as an attribute of light). In "April Chores," as in so many of her poems written out of daily experience, Kenyon resigns herself to the forces that are outside of her control. The important moment comes when the mind can concentrate on itself and on the object in nature long enough, and with enough intensity, that the right revelation comes to it, turning it "up" like a rhubarb leaf shooting through loam. Like Rilke's, Kenyon's poems insist on an inner necessity that will impel their own destiny:

> When I take the chilly tools
> from the shed's darkness, I come
> out to a world made new
> by heat and light.
> . . . .
> Like a mad red brain
> the involute rhubarb leaf
> thinks its way up
> through loam

Kenyon made important contributions to poetry by cultivating realism in her work, and drawing on the phenomenological implications of a processing self. Hence, the mood of each poem changes with the mood of the speaker, while place, setting, time, and characters stay relatively the same. In other words, Kenyon did not concern herself with artifice; rather, she devoted herself to introspective changes and reflections on her felt experience. Her poems, especially "Having It Out with Melancholy," parallel Edward Taylor's or Anne Bradstreet's Puritan meditations and spiritual writings, explicating strategies for emotional survival in the poem, and how these can be applied by the poet to her own psychological condition. (*From the Nursery*, the first section of "Having it Out with Melancholy," shows how the modern idea of mental illness as an affliction has its roots in religious affliction, but now, the idea of the tormented soul is replaced by the theory of biochemical imbalance. Pills become the palliative and antidote.) "Having It Out with Melancholy" is thus divided between an impulse to defend against melancholy as something to be warded off and a hope that insight can transform melancholy into something to be accepted rather than cured, or in which cure and disease are mutually intertwined. The fifth section, coming at the midpoint of the nine-part poem, recalls a moment of visionary wholeness: "Once, in my early thirties, I saw/ that I was a speck of light in the great/ river of light that undulates through time./ I was floating with the whole/ human family."

This description of floating surrender nonetheless recalls language associated in other poems with illness or depression, as in the last line of "Sick at Summer's End": "I'm falling upward, nothing to hold me down." Resisting the fall, resisting the loss is what sickens the poet's heart and motivates grief, or the recognition of grief. When antidepressive medications set in, ". . . the pain stops/ abruptly" and the poet is astonished by the fact she has forgotten what the hurt was, since she no longer hurts, and pain is not memorable. Stepping outside of herself, she is graced with a renewed interest in objects, and notes a bird with its "small, swiftly/ beating heart . . . / singing in the great maples;/ its bright, unequivocal eye." The bird's eye is not mercurial, but absolute. Unclouded by bias, untouched by tremor of mania, or terror of depression, the bird sings in its strange certitude, an emblem of equanimity.

But perhaps what is more important for contemporary readers is that the poem offers the poet a self-therapeutic solution to the afflicted psyche's condition. In "Having It Out with Melancholy," the poet fends off depression by acknowledging its power over her; she gives into it, not as a disease but as a divine incubus, an unholy ghost, that holds her and releases her. Her only option for fighting it is to do what Young-Bruehl and Bethelard suggest as salvation for the wounded child still nursing her wounds; she turns toward her dependency on nature, seeking in its objects some consolation, some unequivocal beauty that cannot be destroyed by depression. The patient, like the speaker, wants and demands love, and the fear that love will not be available to her, is what causes her to want to hate and destroy. This is what causes the cherishment scene's reprieve. In an "exchange of looks" described by Young-Bruehl and Bethelard, the two (they can be patient and analyst, melancholy and speaker) see each other not as targets worth destroying, but as equals in a universal drama of defying death with love, and "the frail and obstinate will...to flower and bear fruit...is restored." What truth springs forth is that human beings, like trees, are rooted underneath and linked to one another although they appear separate in space.

Relatedness, in its underground invisibility, is discovered not only between patient and therapist, but also between poet and the objects of nature she draws, willingly, or unwillingly, into comprehension. As in the Romantic tradition, depression is not only personified but also apostrophized:

> When I was born, you waited
> behind a pile of linen in the nursery
> and when we were alone, you lay down
> on top of me, pressing
> the bile of desolation into every pore.
>
> And from that day on
> everything under the sun and moon
> made me sad—even the yellow
> wooden beads that slid and spun
> along a spindle on by crib.

From this point on in the poem, Kenyon struggles against melancholy, bringing to the surface her anger at its hold over her. Depression, melancholy, the dark embrace of the negative state, has, in Kenyon's words, impaired her ability to engage or sustain a needed passion long enough to want to write: "You taught me to exist without gratitude./ You ruined my manners toward God." The melancholic, or clinical depressive is at a loss when it comes to praise: existence itself seems overrated. But as much as sorrow is an affliction, it is, for Kenyon,

still enacting a necessary identification with Christ and his martyr-
dom; it is still claiming its share of inexplicable torment that keeps
one close to God. In the battle, the poet acknowledges her bond
with others who are similarly afflicted. Young-Bruehl and Bethelard
call this empathy, an allusion to the Greek pathos: a feeling or emotion into others—an in-feeling. As Sexton remarked, "Any poem is
therapy. The art of writing is therapy." My contention is that resolution to Kenyon's lyric, which is a substitute for therapy, comes only
after clash or struggle between hatred and love, light and darkness,
silence and sound. Affirmatively, the poet must concede, just as the
therapist does, that there are things in life that must endured that are
all but unendurable.

One of the primary functions of poetry *and* psychotherapy is expressive; both seek to bring about an affective reaction, usually on
the part of the speaker and hopefully the reader. But first we have to
understand affect and how it operates. Contemporary poetic theory
has yet to articulate a vocabulary that allows it to deal adequately
with emotion. Sexton and Plath "created" or dramatized emotions
and embellished the surface of their poems, co-opting realities in
imaginative sweeps. But Kenyon's investment in the natural world
demanded concentration, a more self-analytic and studied stance.
Affects bring about and change others' feelings by demonstrating
something to them. To *affect* is to change a person's emotions in some
usually specified way. Hence, a poet may be experiencing an emotion, but her task is to persuade her reader to feel that emotion, to
assume, or to imitate it. This is how poets "touch" others with their
feelings, and this is the empathetic moment Young-Bruehl specifies
in the cherishment scene.

Affects, unlike emotions, are the feelings we identify within the
social forum, rather than what we experience on a nonverbal level.
They exist at the juncture of the physiological response and the cultural codes that make this response intelligible. Kenyon's genuine-
ness, her effort to be genuine, or truthful, is far more inventive, and
less confessional, than many readers realize. Kenyon's feminism, for

instance, rests on her exposing the various messages of the culture that tell women to feel a certain way, and not another. For example, in "Winter Lambs" Kenyon shows ambivalence about pregnancy: "I have a friend who is pregnant—/ plans gone awry— and not altogether/ pleased. I don't say she should/ be pleased." Or, in the poem "Fat," the speaker mocks her "fashionable friends" who will diet on "seaweed milkshakes" while the starving "maintain/ the current standard of beauty without effort."

In another poem entitled "Peonies at Dusk," Kenyon's affect is one of a caretaker and nurturer; one who is cherishing her own dependency on the outer garden that makes clear sense of her own symptoms. While waiting for her depression to lift she strolls out to oversee her garden beds and finds the peonies at dusk, "Outrageous flowers as big as human/ heads!" She observes them as being "staggered/ by their own luxuriance," so heavy that she must prop them up and support them. In them, she sees her own vulnerability and failure to understand the origin of what the moist air must do to them, heightening their scent—which is key to their language, their means of "signifying" something human in their pain that may pertain to her own. She writes her last stanza, by characteristically taking in the whole scene yet again as if to suggest to her reader, and to herself, that nothing can be understood fully in isolation. It is not just the flower; it is the flower in its overluxuriance that makes it want to slump or sleep because of its weight. It has toppled itself over; and out of sympathy and identification, she "draws" one near in order to grasp what affect it is displaying to her, and with which she can readily find in-dwelling in her own feelings:

> In the darkening June evening
> I draw a blossom near, and bending close
> search it as a woman searches
> a loved one's face.

Asked about this poem, Kenyon talked about the importance of pay-
ing attention. She said, "I suppose the men with white coats would
come and get me if they could hear me in my garden talking to my
plants and saying, 'What is it you need, my dear? What's the problem?' When the roses are blooming and the peonies are blooming, I
literally just say, 'My beauties.' I talk to them . . . it's nuts. . . ." Here
Kenyon inverts the cultural codes that instruct women to be the
subordinate object to male subjectivity and intuition; knowledge is
subordinate to feeling, and true empathy is in "search" of what tran-
scends the boundaries of the self—the object.

"One of the functions of poetry is to keep the memory of people
and places and things and happenings alive," Kenyon said in that
same interview. Keeping the memory of things alive is an intrigu-
ing prospect for the poet who is in many ways always a mourner;
but again, Kenyon's existential position allowed her to "ask the questions" and bracket the answers. She kept space in the poem to speculate. Because emotions tend to reveal their opposites as they are being
processed interdependently, Kenyon's view of mourning may not
be so different from her view of nurturing. The poet talks to her
plants because she has the ability to relate to them as objects, and to
"transplant" her own inner emptiness, her lack of being, into what
their being "lacks." The inner world of a poet is an image-making
world. An experience of emptiness not only informs painful memories of lost people, but also paradoxically cultivates subtle aspects
of self-experience, in this case through the peonies. Mourning not
only informs the emptiness of the things we imagine to be lost but
also supports the substantiality of the things we imagine to be present. Being exists everywhere lack is avoided; being is the desire to
fill a lack. Psychoanalysis emphasizes that we have plenitude, or being, only insofar as desire constructs for us an internal self-image
that denies an inner emptiness. Hence, Kenyon searches the faces of
the flowers for a response, an affirmation of being, which she feels is
missing in herself. The beauty of the flowers console and suffice.

Another way to approach the variousness of affect and mourning is through Kenyon's translation of another poet's sadness or affect. In a poem written by Anna Akhmatova, Kenyon translates the Russian poet's grief into her own vernacular:

> Like a white stone in a deep well
> one memory lies inside me.
> I cannot and will not fight against it:
> it is joy and it is pain.
>
> It seems to me that anyone who looks
> into my eyes will notice it immediately,
> becoming sadder and more pensive
> than someone listening to a melancholy tale.
>
> I remember how the gods turned people
> into things, not killing their consciousness.
> And now, to keep these glorious sorrows alive,
> you have turned into my memory of you.

In Akhmatova's poem, the first stanza attempts to give the reader an object that might substitute for the abstraction of memory, which is now a marker of what has been lost. It exists; it is a joy and something that fills the well. However, because it exists in place of another object that can no longer be experienced in reality, it is a weight that drops endlessly to the bottom of the well. Of course, the well has no bottom as long as there is a weight being dropped to its end. It has no physical dimension but is something that exists for the observer, who will recognize it as something sadder and more pensive than "someone listening to a melancholy tale." One may read the lines in a way that suggests that the one who looks into the speaker's eyes sees profound pain there that is sadder and more silent than what might be seen or heard if she were to tell the tale. Indeed, the emotion is clearly distinct from the story that produced it, and it is self-sustaining. The emotion must be mirrored in the other's eyes in order to keep itself from falling to an endpoint and diminishing to a stop. The deferral of any end-point, which a "tale" would have to reach, is one strategy that keeps the memory alive.

With regard to this poem, a mourner's labor of grief is not in the fact of not having the beloved, but in trying to withdraw libido from the thing that in some imaginary sense has already been possessed and now is lost. In this way, the person and the internal thought about the person are synonymous. People and beliefs are not simple signifiers but part of a network of signifiers that forms a system that supports the sense of self. Although we assume we mourn something outside the self, it is clear that mourning is also an internal process.

Indeed, mourning is an emptiness signified by the depth of the well; but inside the emptiness lies a weight that can't be "fought" against. "Fought" was probably Kenyon's word choice for the translation, since "fighting" against the weight of melancholy or depression was her most consistent theme. It is interesting that the passive object of the stone, which is simply taking up the space of emptiness, is experienced by the sufferer as hostile or threatening, causing her to have to fend it off. Still, the mourning that is done in isolation has no real meaning until it is brought into relation to the body, and to other people's bodies. Hence, the grief must be apparent to "anyone" who looks into the speaker's eyes, and when it is "noticed" it will become sadder and more pensive as it creates that effect on the observer. Both the grief and the observer of the grief will become sadder than "someone listening to a melancholy tale": they will see the object and not its context; just as the dead figure will be transformed into an object of memory, which is identifiable as itself, but never itself in the sense that it can be regained in the environment.

Hence the bereaved speaker's expression is one of sorrow, but it is still gloriously sorrowful. Sorrow must have its sorrow just as weight needs gravity. In "Thoughts on the Gifts of Art," Kenyon justifies the need for art in troubled economic times by asserting that artists report on the inner life, and the inner life distinguishes us from "centipedes" (although Kenyon concedes that she may "underestimate centipedes").

"We cannot afford to ignore our inner lives, our imaginations, for when we do, we become capable of extreme cruelty and destruction. Tenderness toward existence is what we lose when we lose art, or fail to value it properly."

But why write poems? Emotions are not words; but they are what give us our affects; our ways of communicating to others how we feel, and what is consistent about our feeling a way others might feel. Feeling is an inward state, like the center of mourning in Akhmatova's poem, but it can only be convincing as an object that another person can recognize and acknowledge—the stone lodged at the bottom of the well; the desolation of not being able to lift the weight of emptiness, nor fathom its depth.

For Kenyon, and for the authors of *Cherishment,* pain has its redemptive power, when its birth in poverty is finally admitted to. Its redemptive power is in the affirmative, restoring and recreating hope out of an inherent sadness that is suddenly, and inexplicably, made bearable. The self, shaken, emerges from under layers of disguises and defenses; it has reached the nascent bottom of its own indwelling feeling. And yet, as Kenyon remarks, there is a sense that there is some goodness, something to be cherished in the fact of relatedness itself. Emotion, and affect, are fostered by human wonder. Kenyon's faith is mounted on the unconditional. "Why, when there could have been nothing, is there something? How, when there could have been nothing, does it happen that there is love, kindness, and feeling?"

PAUL BRESLIN

Jane Kenyon's "Manners Toward God": Gratitude and the "Anti-urge"

Reviewing *Otherwise* for *Poetry* in July 1997, I noted how Jane Kenyon's attention to the physical world, which in her earliest work could seem mere description for description's sake, came to have deeper significance as a counterforce to the world-dissolving powers of depression. I want to trace more carefully the tension between descriptive noticing and depressive obliviousness in "Having It Out with Melancholy," her most extensive poetic engagement with the consequences of depression for her art and life. To do so requires a more nuanced description of that tension than the earlier essay could provide.

Kenyon's title avoids the modern, clinical word "depression," replacing it with "Melancholy," as in Burton's *Anatomy* of same. For Burton, Melancholy was closely allied to the vocations of poet, artist, and scholar; it was above all else an affliction of a "hurt and misaffected" imagination. A powerful imagination was found in "melancholy men" and in "poets and painters." Moreover, the affliction was not always experienced as pain; his "Author's Abstract" claims that among all joys, there is "Naught so sweet as Melancholy," though there are also no griefs "so damn'd." Burton's Melancholy is not yet the enemy of the poetic. Almost two centuries later, Keats, in his ode on the subject, could affirm that "in the very temple of Delight/ Veiled Melancholy has her sov'reign shrine"; its "wakeful anguish of the soul" was to be cultivated, not avoided. But the telling word is "wakeful": the kind of melancholy Jane Kenyon struggles against does not stay awake. Against

Keats's advice, it goes to Lethe, it twists "wolfbane, tight-rooted, for its poisonous wine." Melancholy has become "the anti-urge,/ the mutilator of souls," rather than a power whose "might" sustains those elect spirits who are able to "taste" its "sadness." Instead of enabling poetry, this kind of melancholy impairs it: "You taught me to exist without gratitude./ You ruined my manners toward God."

The idea that gratitude is an important source of poetry is familiar. *"O sage, Dichter, was du tust?—Ich rühme,"* said Rilke. But a late-twentieth-century poet usually leaves God out of the account. Gratitude for the world as given may inspire praise, but it entails no further obligations. "God" and "manners" have been losing adherents steadily for at least a hundred years. By 1965, Elizabeth Bishop's poem "Manners" treats its subject nostalgically, as a charming but hopelessly obsolete code, expounded by grandparents "for a child of 1918." As for God, most poets of recent times have been more inclined to complain of His discourtesy to us than to worry about theirs to Him. "I'm cross with God who has wrecked this generation," wrote John Berryman, brooding on the fate of Delmore Schwartz and other self-destructive contemporaries, not least himself. Plath's Lady Lazarus sees God as a patriarchal monster, scarcely distinguishable from His adversary: "Herr Gott, Herr Lucifer,/ Beware/ Beware." So there is something disarming and almost quaint about Kenyon's regret for her lost "manners toward God." The "Suggestion from a Friend" in Section Three, that belief in God might cure depression, is never altogether dismissed.

The poem's implied plot is something like a Protestant conversion narrative: the recognition of sin, the search for repentance, an unexpected "pardon" that has not been earned (though with the Dickinsonian, and subversive, suggestion that the guilt was not earned either), enabling the pardoned one to love and praise. If that plot were explicit, or if it had not been translated convincingly into this-worldly terms, it would be sentimental or merely quaint. If allowed to slide into available secularized conversion-rhetoric, such as that of twelve-step programs, it would be hopelessly banal. But Kenyon has managed to draw on a narrative that resonates deeply as a sustained metaphor without insisting on its literal commitments. What she has found is a way of reconciling the categories of modern medicine—in which a biochemically produced psyche has replaced the soul, so that monoamine oxidase inhibitors inspire more confidence than meditation—with older ways of naming and thinking about mental illness, as primarily a disease of soul rather than body.

The poem seems divided between an impulse to defend against melancholy, treating it as a disease to be warded off, and a hope that insight can transform melancholy into something humanly and po-etically sustainable, treating it as a quality of spiritual temperament to be accepted rather than cured, or in which cure and disease are mutually intertwined. The fifth section, coming at the midpoint of the nine-part poem, recalls a moment of visionary wholeness:

> Once, in my early thirties, I saw
> that I was a speck of light in the great
> river of light that undulates through time.
> I was floating with the whole
> human family.

This description of floating surrender nonetheless recalls language associated in other poems with illness or depression, as in the last lines of "Sick at Summer's End": "I'm falling upward, nothing to hold me down," or the moment in "Evening Sun" when the lyrical evocation of "the ochre light/ of an early June evening" only brings the realization "that I would have to live, and go on/ living: what a sorrow it was." After the momentary immersion in the "river of light," Melancholy reclaims her errant child, portraying herself as res-cuer: "'I'll hold you up. I never let my dear/ ones drown.'" To the extent that Melancholy is a personified aspect of the speaker's own consciousness, it would seem that Kenyon is suspicious of her own vision: to give way to such dreams of belonging and well-being is to fall for a seductive illusion. Which is needed, surrender or defense?

One thinks of another Keats ode, the one to the Nightingale, where the moment of union with the bird's song is either a long-awaited glimpse of a deeper reality or a dangerously seductive dream: "Fled is that music—Do I wake or sleep?"

The defensive gestures begin with the allegorizing personification of Melancholy as a separate being. She appears first as a sort of succubus or night-hag: "when we were alone, you lay down/ on top of me, pressing/ the bile of desolation into every pore." By this means she takes possession of the child from infancy: "I only appeared to belong to my mother." The second section opens with a litany of antidepressant drugs, as if to marshal forces against the enemy. The pharmaceutical list also recalls, by poignant contrast, earlier, more Whitmanian catalogs of the natural world, like the one that opens "Now That We Live":

> Fat spider by the door.
>
> Brow of hayfield, blue
> eye of pond.
> Sky at night like an open well.

One of Melancholy's anti-poetic symptoms is the contraction of attention to the unease of the self: instead of the sights of earth and sky, an arsenal of drugs. And, as the epigraph from Chekhov reminds us, "If many remedies are prescribed for an illness, you may be certain that the illness has no cure." The strategy of defense may prove to be futile.

So the poetic expansion of attention becomes an alternative to modern medicine—and yet, the object of poetic attention in this poem, until the closing section, is the phenomenology of depression itself. It is not quite enough to say that outward-directed noticing and poetic description are the antidotes to depression. Rather, the poem undertakes the seemingly impossible task of lifting itself by its own bootstraps. If "Melancholy" in Kenyon's sense is the enemy of noticing, then she undertakes in this poem a noticing description of a condition whose most distressing symptom is a diminished desire to notice. From the day that Melancholy first pressed down on her in the nursery, she says,

> everything under the sun and moon
> made me sad—even the yellow
> wooden beads that slid and spun
> along a spindle on my crib.

The clear evocation of the wooden beads does not remove them from Melancholy's domain. The beads, placed there as one of the infant's first toys, to delight and to stimulate curiosity, become subsumed as emblems of sadness. That the poem can catalog the child's domestic surroundings cannot heal her alienation from them; they are where she "appeared . . . / to live" but, in fact, did not. Already she had been stolen away from the "blocks," "cotton undershirts/ with snaps," the "red tin lunch boxes/ and report cards in ugly brown slipcases." The catalog ranges with unobtrusive precision over the most important areas of a child's life: the blocks are her toys, the undershirts the clothes she wears on her body, the lunch boxes carriers of the food that sustains her, the report cards a judgment on her intellectual and social progress. The poet recalls her childhood self as surrounded by but disaffected from these objects; only the mature poet's responsibility to see and record can hold them in memory. They are not numinous objects or Proustian doorways into lost time, only blank particulars scrupulously preserved.

The early parts of the poem, despite the suggestion of strenuous combat in its title, are remarkable for what might be called a disciplined neutrality. The language refrains from abandoning itself to feeling: even the epiphanic moment of the fifth section lies in the past and is reported from the outside, as a memory, not a rekindled vision. In the fourth section, a sense of decorum, of what "seems adult," postpones the depressed urge to go to bed early. Instead of elaborating on the "massive pain in sleep's/ frail wicker coracle," the poem focuses on the defense against it, the strategy of going to bed early "in order to push away/ from" it.

The recollected floating vision of section 5 lies far in the past, and the fall back into Melancholy is cruelly steep. Yet the recollection initiates a turn outward that continues in section 6, although this time the scale is so much smaller that one may not at first recognize a connection. The speaker, having withdrawn from the first floor of the house, has not sought any comfort. But

> The dog searches until he finds me
> upstairs, lies down with a clatter
> of elbows, puts his head on my foot.
>
> Sometimes the sound of his breathing
> saves my life—in and out, in
> and out; a pause, a long sigh. . . .

The dog's unexpected arrival might be taken as a miniaturized emblem of grace. His breathing becomes a metaphor of interaction with the world: to live, we take in air from outside the body, and then we give it back. But whatever the dog represents has still not entered the speaker's being. It is one thing to take comfort from the animal's warm, breathing body, and another to sustain that well-being from within. As if in recoil, the alienation from surroundings we found in the first half of the poem returns intensified in section 7, as an alienation from self:

> A piece of burned meat
> wears my clothes, speaks
> in my voice, dispatches obligations
> haltingly, or not at all.
> It is tired of trying.

"I" has become an object among objects. As "burned meat," it exists for consumption by others, but, being overcooked, it is not even palatable. The external manifestations of personhood—clothing, speech, performance of "obligations"—have no self behind them. And yet even this piece of meat impersonating a human being has exhausted itself "trying/ to be stouthearted." The gestures of resistance, of keeping up appearances, that permeate the poem up to this point reach a dead end. They have been dutiful, joyless, and futile.

The closing lines of section 7 return us to the shelf of drugs introduced in Section Two. The "monoamine/ oxidase inhibitors" for once bring an end to "the pain," though they do not bring a cure. They do, however, enable a change in the poet's attitude toward Melancholy. In addition to whatever biochemical benefits the drugs provide, the fact that they can so markedly change her state of mind absolves her from feeling responsible for her illness, and that is a great benefit in itself. She feels instead "the wonder/ and bitterness of someone pardoned/ for a crime she did not commit." (Lurking somewhere behind these lines, I hear Emily Dickinson's "Of God we ask one favor,/ That we may be forgiven—/ For what, he is presumed to know—/ The Crime, from us, is hidden"). The return to the "human family" rests on precarious ground; to be "pardoned" is not the same as being exonerated. But it is finally possible to

> come back to marriage and friends,
> to pink-fringed hollyhocks; come back
> to my desk, books, and chair.

The "desk, books, and chair" are the first objects in the poem (apart from "my crib" in the first section) to be claimed with a possessive modifier. As the objects most necessary to a writer, they confirm the role of poetry in regaining the world. But only with the help of a drug can it perform that office. Poetry no longer has the insupportable burden of being solely responsible for hauling the poet out of her anti-poetic misery. The language here remains cautious, not celebratory. Apart from the "pink-fringed hollyhocks," the items on the list do not evoke memorable images, they merely catalog. The syntax still holds to matter-of-fact statement, as if elation might be premature.

The eighth section, titled "Credo," arrives at such resolution as the poem will allow. Despite the "[p]harmaceutical wonders . . . at work," the poet can "believe only in this moment/ of well-being," for the "[u]nholy ghost" is "certain to come again." Once again, Melancholy is a personified enemy. It can "turn" her into "someone" else once more, and most insidiously, into someone who can't resist, who will not "call/ for an appointment to help." The last lines of the section confess: "There is nothing I can do/ against your coming./ *When I awake, I am still with thee.*" She has accepted a middle state, between defeat and cure, in which there will be moments of well-being, but the other moments also. That acceptance relieves her of the desperate resolve to escape Melancholy altogether (as in the remembered vision of the "river of light"), which brought a depressive rebound after each failed attempt.

Yet if the poem had ended there, it would be too good, too gray, too resigned. The ninth section finds a stopping place for joy within resignation. It is called *Wood Thrush,* recalling the hermit thrush that sang to Walt Whitman in "Out of the Cradle Endlessly Rocking" and "When Lilacs Last in the Dooryard Bloom'd"; Kenyon's thrush, like Whitman's, is "a solitary singer, projecting" the poet's self at a moment of insight. This ending offers a very traditional, familiar gesture of identification with a natural symbol, yet in the context of the preceding eight stanzas, it seems anything but a lazy relapse into outworn poetic habits. Rather, it stands as an archetypal emblem of the poetic act of imagination, precisely the kind of empathic noticing without which lyric poetry cannot happen at all, the kind that Melancholy had threatened to annihilate. The enabling conditions of this moment owe something to Nardil and something to the June light, to recent pharmaceutical wonders and the age-old restorative interplay of nature and imagination. In contrast to the cosmic light-river of section 5, this is a scene of "ordinary contentment," yet one so intense the speaker is "overcome." The reticent neutrality that has dominated so much of the poem gives way to the exclamatory "How I love the small, swiftly/ beating heart of the bird/ singing in the great maples;/ its bright, unequivocal eye." The bird will stop singing, and the poet will have other bouts of melancholy. Yet the poem ends in hope, for if this moment can come once, it can also come again. There will be other thrushes.

LYNN STRONGIN

A Faith That Blessed Through Sorrow: Meditations on Jane Kenyon's Poetry

She was our Akhmatova, a priestess of song, Jane Kenyon who died at forty-seven from leukemia. Before the crush of illness she wrote some of her most incandescent poems.

Her work at first glance can pass us by, it is so unassuming. Then, detail upon detail, emotion upon emotion, these poems are etched clean as blue and white Delft tiles. We are swept away by one-of-a-kind beauty. Is her hook upon us Russian impressionism? That love which induces melancholy? There is a Russian saying, "We must bless life, darling, even as we weep." The Russian sensibility, especially Akhmatova's, magnetized Kenyon. She was immediately captured when, in her late twenties she took up Anna Akhmatova. Only Chekhov did she love more. Donald Hall wrote in a letter:

> I don't think that Jane became obsessed with Akhmatova
> until she was almost thirty years old. She was immediately
> overcome by Akhmatova.

Although Kenyon realized that translation is an impossible task, she knew that the nexus of lyric poetry, imagery, is the *one thing* that can survive translation. Kenyon said, "We revere Akhmatova for her early lyrics—brief, perfectly made verses of passion and feeling." In this, she found Akhmatova comparable to Keats, another poet she adored. Akhmatova wrote:

There is a certain hour every day
so troubled and heavy . . .
I speak to melancholy in a loud voice
not bothering to open my sleepy eyes.
And it pulses like blood

AKHMATOVA

Unholy ghost,
you are certain to come again.

KENYON

When a medication works, Kenyon is overcome "by ordinary contentment," loving the wood thrush "singing in the great maples;/ its bright, unequivocal eye."

At opposite ends of the century, each poet writes, casting irony's light upon the proximity of pain with love. Both Akhmatova and Kenyon learned young that often anguish is mute. "Act as though you had faith," Kenyon quoted Isaac Bashevis Singer in "The Mud Will Dry." "Faith will come afterward." If Kenyon's last poems were about "the other side," her early ones glistened with the light of a blue Russian winter. In looking at her last two books, I will focus primarily upon *how* she arrived at that particular faith which blessed life through sorrow.

She began with a difficult childhood darkened by a fire-and-brimstone preaching grandmother. She moved forward through young womanhood in which she became enthralled by Keats, to a maturity enraptured by Akhmatova. She was a colorist, fascinated by the things of this earth. Donald Hall writes in his "Afterword:" "Her poetry gathered resonance and beauty as she studied the art of the luminous particular." She loved blue, white, burgundy. Above all blues and all its shades—indigo, cobalt, azure—were her touchstone.

Kenyon's *oeuvre* encompasses all seasons. But like Wallace Stevens, hers was predominantly a mind of winter, its iconography drawn from nature and the Bible.

In paradise, it will always be Sunday. Eden—how lonely it would be on bright weekday afternoons, says Dickinson. Dickinson and Kenyon shared elements of the anchorite: Dickinson, no convinced Christian, was known to be reclusive. Kenyon, like Emily, contained both mystic and visionary. Consider "Who":

> These lines are written
> by an animal, an angel,
> . . . .
> Who is it who asks me to find
> language for the sound
> a sheep's hoof makes when it strikes
> a stone?

Both are enamored of blizzards: mystically, snow takes over and transforms roads in glassy tracks. Like the poet of the Eighth Psalm, Kenyon sees man "a little lower than the angels." The spirit hungers for love: sustenance. Set Dickinson's "I Never felt at Home—Below," beside the opening quatrain of Kenyon's "Twilight: After Haying." One discovers a kind of Boolean algebra: earthly time overlapping with heavenly creating two circles, a shaded area in common. These two circles are animal and angel. Kenyon's angel dictates lines of poetry that become food for her body. The overlapping, shaded area is human activity. For Dickinson, the two circles are bright Wednesdays and Paradise. Kenyon writes about shadows going out, evoking time beyond clock time. "Yes, long shadows go out/ from the bales; and yes, the soul/ must part from the body."

The long shadows become soul leaving body. Daily life is reflected in "bales," and workers, "tips of their cigarettes" that "blaze like small roses/ in the night air." In "Rain in January," Kenyon says, "I woke before dawn, still/ in a body."

In her prose, Kenyon relaxes somewhat her visionary intensity.

She loves to frequent old five-and-dime stores, the country church; loves the old white lilacs that lean over the car oozing sap each spring. Kenyon's descriptions remind me of Colette. Although their length was determined by the newspaper column, they are saturated with poetry. "Like the tides, white envelopes go out and come in again. Almost everything important that happens to us happens through the mail." ("Poetry and the Mail.") Rejected, "we begin the vigil, waiting for the sound of the mail-carrier's car." Her landscape is hardscrabble Yankee soil; the humor is a wry way of seeing things in Concord, and Wilmot. A painterly sun slides behind cloud laying the land bare, metallic, an engraving. "How well I remember standing in the September morning fog, waiting for the yellow bulk of the school bus." The wide-eyed, round-faced child "had math anxiety . . .Numbers had such strange proclivities. Even geometry . . . bollixed me."

Kenyon wrote these shards of memory before her own illness. "Tonight before the storm I went out with . . . kitchen shears . . . I cut every full-open peony in sight . . . I knew the rain would shatter the flowers." Winter arrives and "Good-bye to flesh." Turtlenecks and woolens come out of drawers. Now come "the . . . sober activities in a cold climate—little deaths . . . [which] we confront [by] planting burgundy lilies." Now "We come inside, where the evenings are long and silent. . . . sleep until the white-throated sparrow, with its coarse and cheerful song, calls me out of the dark."

Her telescoping, philosophic mind of winter is more cheerful and shares with Stevens a stoic lyricism and detachment. Little did she realize that within four or five short years she would be out of earshot of the coarse, cheerful sparrow, although her "bright unequivocal eye" will not be put out. The duration of winter is "like a Mahler symphony." A cold sun, like one of his final cadences illumines the scene.

> A ledge of ice slides from the eaves,
> piercing the crusted drift. Astonishing
> how even a little violence
> eases the mind.

The opening to "Bright Sun After Heavy Snow" is dazzling in its perception of a violence that comforts. It its "extreme state of light/ everything seems flawed." In the final stanza smoke is rising from the chimney like the clothesline rising in wind: "One/ wooden pin is left, solitary as a finger:/ it, too, rises and falls." We are painted an Andrew Wyeth world, bright and brittle.

When *The Boat of Quiet Hours* was published, Jane was thirty-nine. The curtain lines went to *Constance,* published two years before her death. "The Pond at Dusk" begins quietly, a fly wounding water in summer dusk. Green haze suggests fire, but this is a false alarm, merely smoke-mist of apple blossoms over a neighbor's barn.

> But sometimes what looks like disaster
> *is* disaster: the day comes at last,
> and the men struggle with the casket
> just clearing the pews.

What prepares us for a casket? Nothing. Yet, the final day comes; men barely clear church pews with casket. No church is bodied forth, nor any religious imagery put in place. "The Pond at Dusk," almost a languid poem, ends with the trauma of death.

———

All major illness is transformational. Depression had been Kenyon's Achilles' heel. Trapped by Methodist guilt, as a girl she was boxed in by a Midwestern childhood in addition to an inherited tendency on her father's side toward melancholy. Despite her recurring bouts of having it out with melancholy, at rare times life's beauty got her between the eyes. "Happiness," is "like a prodigal/ who comes back to the dust at your feet." She asks, "[H]ow can you not forgive?" when ". . . you weep night and day/ to know that you were not abandoned/ that happiness saved its most extreme form/ for you alone." Incandescent happiness is that which "finds you asleep midafternoons." Donald Hall wrote:

There was one patch, of three or four weeks, when she was
well enough to do some revisions. . . . All I can think of that
she changed was to arrive at that beautiful ending by cutting
out several other, parallel imaginings of happiness. The only
poem she wrote during leukemia was "Eating the Cookies,"
one month into Jane's illness. She wrote nothing about, or
affected by, her leukemia.

In 1951, after colliding with something visible only under a micro-
scope, I found myself on my back, paralyzed from the waist down,
in a large New York hospital overlooking the East River. I had been
transformed from a child who couldn't be contained to one a few
feet from an iron lung. Mother read me the Jewish mystic, Simone
Weil. (At that time, Jane was a four-year-old Methodist child in Ann
Arbor, Michigan, her grandmother inflicting on her a fire and brim-
stone version of hell.) My life altered: a sombre pewter light shone
from that summer sky of 1951 when polio brought me to the outer
rim of the circle.

If Dickinson envisioned a soul at *white* heat, Kenyon's light was
blue: those milky dawns of Michigan winter, or New England. Her
compass pointed to true North; melancholy was waiting for her when
she was born. True North embodied song, lyrical and stoic. Kenyon's
memories are sharply picked out. Even the bright "yellow wooden
beads that slid and spin/ along a spindle" on her crib made her sad.
Shiny colors of picture books on clay-based papers were dulled by
despondency, which spilled a kind of dust over them. In "Having
It Out with Melancholy," Kenyon writes, "You ruined my manners
toward God." Like Plath, Kenyon said she early belonged to "the
anti-urge,/ the mutilator of souls." Though the colors remind one of
childhood—yellow, red, brown—the tone does not. She waits until
it is dark to go to bed, as long as it seems an adult ought to wait. . . .
Unlike Plath, Kenyon utters remarkable awe in a passage from section 5, *Once There Was Light:*

> . . . I saw
> that I was a speck of light in the great
> river of light that undulates through time.
> I was floating with the whole
> human family.

Finally, a medication works, allowing her to "come back to marriage and friends, to . . . desk, books, and chair" from a pervasive gloom that rusts the very light till light itself flakes and peels like worn paint. This woman says, "I believe only in this moment/ of well-being. Unholy ghost,/ you are certain to come again." Plath could never say this, nor could Sexton. While all three poets are confessional, Plath and Sexton spit out their pain like pits, while Kenyon is tugged by things of this earth.

Colors being her ignition, we are given sky purple eggplant, we see sky turning "from gray to pale apricot," as sun rises on Main Street in Andover. The cat's face, upon being studied, reveals a trace of white around each eye, as though made up for a part in an opera. In these poems, relieved, for a heartbeat, of that stark desolation in which she is startled by her shadow, and the fear of the body being a dwelling place for the Holy Ghost, Kenyon reaches out for others, community.

Given stone more often than bread, the child Jane stands up to the frightening grandmother, "No! NO! How is it good to be dead?" If her grandmother lacks pity, her father doesn't. "The Stroller" is fresh every time I read it. She portrays her stroller at different years in her history.

1949

> It was copen blue, strong and bright,
> and the metal back looked like caning

on a chair. The peanut-shaped tray
had a bar with sliding beads:
red, yellow, blue, green, white.

Kenyon has perfect visual pitch, from copen blue to "peanut-shaped tray." Her mother now old and moving out, son and daughter sort "through fifty years' accumulations," among them "a portfolio of Father's drawings/ from his brief career in Architecture/ School, exercises in light and shadow. . . . I come upon/ a drawing of my stroller, precisely to scale,/ just as I remember it."

In the letter of May 2003, Donald Hall wrote me, ""I just want to tell you: Jane's father's drawing of the stroller is framed on the wall of her study. Still." I can come up with few other poems in the canon of modern American poetry that convey an action or object pictorially with the intensity and detail of Kenyon's, reminiscent of a Dürer engraving. (Auden's "Musée des Beaux Arts," and Marianne Moore's "The Steeple-jack" come to mind.) At last we see the stroller drawn "on tracing paper, diaphanous." This adds a ghostly touch, which reminds Kenyon of a mirror. She sees not only her own eyes, but also someone else's: Father comes "to interrogate" his child's "wounds." I can picture this delicate drawing whose tracery is reminiscent of those architectural sketches her father must have executed as a student. More elegiac, again treating of family relations and stepping stones, "In the Nursing Home," is among Kenyon's last poems. It is about Hall's mother. Writes Hall,

The day after we discovered that Jane would die, when we set about working to choose the poems for *Otherwise,* she told me where to find the twenty new (uncollected poems) that are printed at the front of the book. She had forgotten this one. She said, "I never thought that little thing would amount to anything." When I read it aloud to her, I had never seen it either, and I loved it. When she heard me read it, she changed her mind and agreed with . . . me.

> She is like a horse grazing
> a hill pasture that someone makes
> smaller by coming every night
> to pull the fences in and in.

The repetition of *in* is comforting like an Amen. Kenyon carries through the simile of old woman with horse, continuing to emboss her pastoral with references to the Twenty-third Psalm. She has "stopped running wide loops,/ stopped even the tight circles." The one-syllable words are like hatchet strokes but they do not cleave, they bind. "No," too, is written with a sense of last things.

> The last prayer had been said,
> and it was time to turn away
> from the casket, poised on its silver
> scaffolding over the open hole
> that smelled like a harrowed field.

In progressively increasing silence,

> . . . I heard a noise that seemed
> not to be human.

"Dutch Interiors" is one of my favorite poems among the twenty final poems, only outshone by "Happiness." Here, Kenyon takes the clichés "done to death/ in the cold reaches of northern Europe" of Christ, bread, cheese, a pewter beaker of beer and asserts defiantly: "Now tell me that the Holy Ghost/ does not reside in the play of light/ on cutlery!" Kenyon achieves a Vermeer-like calm. Hers is not a glass sea, but rough textured. The illumination is in a woman lace-making, the companionable dog and the ever-present light in its eyes, the yellow gown. And most especially in the adjectives Kenyon chooses to describe pleasure: balanced, wary. Physical details are vivid, tactile: black ink, jonquil jacket, red-cheeked girl. Every time I read the poem it is "the air of cautious pleasure" that confers the stroke of genius.

How ironic that in what were to be *her* final years, she went with Donald Hall through *his* cancer. In "Coats," light passes as through glass:

> I saw him leaving the hospital
> with a woman's coat over his arm.
> Clearly she would not need it.
> The sunglasses he wore could not
> conceal his wet face, his bafflement.

This is poetry of a translucency, almost transparency at times. Coat, sunglasses, air, hood. These poems "are not Protestant-work-ethic flowers. . . ." Donald Hall wrote me, "In 'Happiness' she is talking about mania, as she is in 'Notes from the Other Side.' Well, not talking about it, goodness knows, but writing out of it. All the great mystics—St. John of the Cross, Hopkins—have these extreme ups and downs. If God works on the human spirit, why would God not use brain chemistry?"

With the illumination of hindsight, one can trace one's way back to the beginning of a life, a career, the road gaining a sort of inevitability. Take the titles of those books of Akhamatova's excerpted in *A Hundred White Daffodils* (*Evening*, (1912) *Rosary*, (1914), and *White Flock*, 1917), and you get the iconography of Jane Kenyon's soulscape. *White Flock* suggests to me albino landscapes: the color often associated with Russia: snow, white nights. Once Kenyon showed her husband a poem printed in her first book, "Full Moon in Winter," fearing that it was more Anna than Jane. The *world* was the icon to which both poets gave undivided attention: "the luminous particular."

If the "luminous particular" was the nuclear rod of emotion for Kenyon, religion was what struck her dumb. In 1980, Hall says he returned from some days away to find Jane "in a quiet, exalted, shining mood . . . something extraordinary had happened while I was away. She had felt a presence with her in the room that lingered . . . associated it with the holy Spirit . . . it seemed . . . female." She announced an extraordinary experience but became speechless when she tried to name it. All that she could convey was the timelessness of childhood. "I lived," she writes, "in terror of letting it slip." But she just holds on; whether ironing or studying a beaver in December at the pool, Kenyon moves spiritually, rowing in a boat of quiet but dark hours, toward "thoughts/ in an unconflicted mind."

"She will be read and remembered here as Akhmatova is over there," said Hayden Carruth.

In "Last Days," a black cloud, "truly black," appears, "Then horizontal rain began, and apples fell/ before their time." This is preternatural. Doors open and close on their own. Lights flicker off, then back on. Kenyon is with someone dying, in "a room made small/ by the paraphernalia of the mortally ill." She paints the scene with unerring brush, ranging "ranks of brown bottles from the pharmacy" (they must be brown). "Looking at Stars" makes clear that if we are to receive any help, it won't come from God, but from the son.

At the end, Kenyon courageously battled her husband's cancer, then her own. She lived in an exhausted body. Donald Hall wrote in a letter:

> She was never well, from diagnosis until death, except a little bit—hell, she was not well!—when she could work for about half an hour a day, in June of 1994. . . . There was one afternoon when she and I walked Gus together, probably about three hundred yards, one afternoon in March about a month before the leukemia returned. We chose the place where we walked him because it was flat . . . and it was a triumph, those three hundred yards!"

In "Notes from the Other Side," she can conceive of its being otherwise. If Kenyon wrote with Akhmatova's hand guiding her in her apprenticeship, Kenyon's pen alone composes "Notes from the Other Side."—"I divested myself of despair/ and fear when I came here." Now indeed, the evening of life may come.

In closing, I'd like to couple the lyrics "Otherwise" and "Let Evening Come." The self is stripped. Evening approaches. The dry-eyed lament of life is over. "Don't/ be afraid. God does not leave us/ comfortless." The match is struck to waver, blue, in a brown room. No longer hostage to fortune, the poet welcomes news from the other side where there is "no illness" and "the poor we no longer have with us." I see the light as copen blue. These are hypnotically quiet poems. Turning back, one discerns a special beauty. "It's not just more flowers I want, it's more light." When Donald Hall came home to discover Jane in an untranslatable state, she was trembling on the brink of words. A vision probably had left her "in a quiet, exalted, shining mood." One feels in her last poems that she has come to a place where she has been "divested" of fear. In *Constance,* she addresses her husband. Waking at night, she sights him in the powerful night beside her. Here are the things he "might need in the next/ life . . . glasses, water, a book and a pen."

Shorter Pieces and Reviews

HAYDEN CARRUTH

from

Poets on the Fringe

From Room to Room is Jane Kenyon's first book, written, moreover, in the casual, low-toned poetry I have deplored elsewhere. But I include her in this company of her elders because her poems, the best of them, really are expressive in the way intended by other young poets, so often unavailingly. It is a question of topic, I think. Kenyon has something deeply felt to write about, her emigration from her native Midwest to a home on a New England farmstead. Through the small details, natural and social, of her new life, she evokes indirectly her bewilderment, her gradual settling in, her recognition of the moral and psychological and cultural values of her new environment. The poems are charming. Taken altogether they are more: poignant, ultimately joyful. I expect before long Kenyon will find her own voice more firmly and the structures that will reinforce it. Meanwhile she has given poems that are a pleasure to read and a pleasure to hear—fully successful within their acknowledged limits. Her book also contains six translations of poems by Anna Akhmatova, which come nearer than others I have seen to showing my ignorance why that woman has been placed so high in the judgment and affection of her Russian readers.

This review was written before I met Jane or her husband, Donald Hall. Later we all became good friends. I have tried to remember how Jane's book came to me, but that detail has gone from my memory. I was doing a lot of reviews at that time, however, and publishers routinely sent me review copies of their new books of poetry. Probably the explanation is as simple as this.

Jane and I met shortly after this review was published, when she came to give a reading of her poems at Syracuse University, where I was teaching. I was assigned to be her host. We had an extremely cordial and happy luncheon before her reading, which was, according to Syracuse tradition, in the afternoon.

from

Shape-Changing in Contemporary Poetry

Jane Kenyon's second book, *The Boat of Quiet Hours,* is a significant development over *From Room to Room,* itself a most eloquent state-ment of the uneasiness of a woman who leaves the security of her own family ("My people are not here, my mother/ and father, my brother. I talk/ to the cats about weather.") for a house filled with "five generations" of a husband's family's memorabilia. (She feels clumsy ". . . among photographs/ of your ancestors, their hymnbooks and old/ shoes.")

The world of the first book persists into the second, of course: the house, the husband, the cats, and especially the rural landscape (not too far from town) that in *From Room to Room* had offered something like solace from bouts of depression. But in her new book, the house has changes—and dramatically. The first stanza of "Back from the City" makes that clear:

> After three days and nights of rich food
> and late talks in overheated rooms,
> of walks between mounds of garbage
> and human forms bedded down for the night
> under rags, I come back to my dooryard,
> to my own wooden step.

Now the house not only is hers, it has also grown friendly, as have the fields and the neighbors. "At the Summer Solstice," for example, is ostensibly in celebration of the haying prowess of their neighbor's son who is "turning the hay—turning it with flourishes," but it is equally celebratory of the loved landscape itself: "the low clovery place/ where melt from the mountain/ comes down in the spring, and wild/ lupine grows." It is a poem full of luxurious detail and of luxurious sensuality:

> So hot, so hot today. . . . I will stay in our room
> with the shades drawn, waiting for you
> to come with sleepy eyes, and pass your fingers
> lightly, lightly up my thighs.

The artistry is essentially one of concealments in a poem of this sort: inconspicuous repetitions (when you think of it, the purest form of rhyme) move through from top to bottom, but even in these last few lines we can feel their presence (hot/hot; lightly, lightly) along with the hidden internal rhymes and partial rhymes (today/stay/ shades; room/you; eyes/my/thighs) that account for the most definable elements of its quiet, satisfying music.

The title of the book is an adaptation of a phrase from Keats's *Endymion,* and the casual echoes of Keats and two direct references to him punctuate the poems. In "Ice Storm" Kenyon is aware of tree branches breaking—"For the hemlocks and broad-leafed evergreens/ a beautiful and precarious state of being." But suddenly, a visitor in a sleeping household, she is swept by longing: "It could be for beauty—/ I mean what Keats was panting after,/ for which I love and honor him." The second mention of Keats is in the title and substance of a poem called "Reading Late of the Death of Keats" that is the first of five poems dealing with the death of her father, poems that are among the most memorable in the book.

The important thing to say, of course, is that where she herself resembles Keats is not in language or technique but rather in a shining awareness of the mortality of all things—and in a capacity to manipulate time to memorialize the discrete instants of life. (In one of her poems, she literally stops the clock: "Through time and space we come/ to Maine Street—three days before Labor Day, 1984, 4:47 in the afternoon.") Like Keats, also, she is able to step back from the meticulously observed scene to make a grand generalization: "Everyone longs for love's tense joys and red delights" ("Thinking of Madame Bovary"; "the soul's bliss/ and suffering are bound together/ like the grasses" ("Twilight After Haying").

In "Things," the last poem in the book, she speaks of the sound a hen makes as it tosses a small stone onto a red leaf, of a lichen-scarred juncture of twig and branch, of the mouse that chews a hole through the blue star of a hundred-year-old quilt. And then she offers the necessary statement that we need if we are to accept, mourn, and live with a world that changes but that does not end:

> Things: simply lasting, then
> failing to last: water, a blue heron's
> eye, and the light passing
> between them: into light all things
> must fall, glad at last to have fallen.

CAROL MUSKE

The Boat of Quiet Hours

Jane Kenyon's new book seems more a condition of thought than a collection of separate poems. If she is indebted to Keats beyond her book's title—a paraphrase of a passage from *Endymion*—it is because she discovers, in the attitude of mind he called "negative capability" (a poet's acclimatization to states of doubt and mystery), her life. Sometimes this life is stitched plain as a sampler's koan:

>   And I knew then
>   that I would have to live, and go on
>   living: what a sorrow it was; and still
>   what sorrow burns
>   but does not destroy my heart.

Sometimes she identifies, egoless, with the object of her contemplation—as when she writes that beavers in a nearby pond move "like thoughts/ in an unconflicted mind." Nest-building in the hoary reaches of negative capability offers further shelter for homeless thought—and a "longing" comes over her:

>   It could be for beauty—
>   I mean what Keats was panting after,
>   for which I love and honor him;
>   it could be for the promises of God;
>   or for oblivion, *nada;* or some condition even more
>   extreme, which I intuit, but can't quite name.

And the morning after oblivion: "I woke before dawn, still/ in a body."

In "The Sandy Hole," Ms. Kenyon seems to hover above the tiny grave at an infant's funeral and provide, in the untouchable silence of the young father, a contemporary counterpoint to the brutal talk of the husband and wife in Frost's "Home Burial"—*her* father stares at a coffin "no bigger than a flightbag," and is sealed in his grief, beyond human discourse.

These poems surprise beauty at every turn and capture truth at its familiar New England slant. Here, in Keats's terms, is a capable poet.

ALFRED CORN

from

Plural Perspectives, Heightened Perceptions

Let Evening Come, Jane Kenyon's third collection, shows her at the height of her powers. Reading these five dozen first-person lyrics will stir again a wish felt by almost any poet at some time: wouldn't it be wonderful if all I needed to do was write about myself in moments of heightened perception, confronted by the world and some of its inhabitants? But people would say the perspective was too narrow, wouldn't they? What's more, Ms. Kenyon lives in New Hampshire, so she has to expect routine pigeonholing as a regional poet. The fact is, however, that this book holds one's attention and promotes identification with the author's sensitive and forthright temperament.

This is a "sunset" collection, unified around the themes of nightfall, the sense of endings, the death of family and friends, and implicitly, the maturing of a poetic talent. Fairly early in the volume we are familiar with the poet's daily round. Like Emily Dickinson, she might say, "I started early—took my dog," for Ms. Kenyon likes to range around the countryside with her faithful companion. It comes to represent everything in her identity that is physical, spontaneous, untrammeled by tragic knowledge.

> Time to head home. I wait
> until we're nearly out to the main road
> to put him back on the leash, and he
> —the designated optimist—
> imagines to the end that he is free.

That poem gains resonance from an earlier one in which the poet takes a similar walk after having received news of her father's incurable relapse as a cancer patient. His death is recalled in "We Let the Boat Drift":

> Once we talked about the life to come.
> I took the Bible from the nightstand
> and offered John 14: "I go to prepare
> a place for you." "Fine. Good," he said.
> "But what about Matthew? 'You, therefore,
> must be perfect, as your heavenly Father
> is perfect.'" And he wept.

Jane Kenyon's descriptive skills are as notable as her dramatic ones. Her rendering of natural settings, in lines of well-judged rhythm and simple syntax, contribute to the memorableness of the poems, a late adaptation of Poundian Imagism:

> Spring rain, relentless as obsession:
> the mountain streams run swift and full.
> The red tassels of blossoming maples
> hang bright against wet black bark.

In the title poem, after a series of details vividly presented in declining light, the poet summons the end of day: "God does not leave us/ comfortless, so let evening come." Among the comforts, we can guess, is the ability to see things clearly and to find verbal equivalents for them. The volume's last poem, not incidentally, pictures the poet on one of her walks, dog ranging along ahead of her; the time of day is sunrise.

ROBERT PINSKY

from

Tidings of Comfort and Dread:
Poetry and the Dark Beauty of Christmas

Alert to the seasonal space between desire and possession, between display and reality, here is a passage from Jane Kenyon's poem "Christmas Away from Home:"

> In the hiatus between mayors
> the city has left leaves in the gutters
> and passing cars lift them in maelstroms.
>
> We pass the house two doors down, the one
> with the wildest lights in the neighborhood,
> an establishment without irony.
> All summer their *putto* empties a water jar
> their St. Francis feeds the birds.
> Now it's angels, festoons, waist-high
> candles, and swans pulling sleighs.

The poet is a country person, spending Christmas in an alien suburb because someone is sick. The meaningless, ungoverned maelstrom of dead leaves is associated with the equally wild activity of the swans, the saints, and giant candles on someone's property. The time of year seems to demand more than this. Though the poet doesn't tell us what gestures of religion, community, or irony would suffice, the yearning beyond this confident display of symbols becomes associated, as the poem progresses, with yearning for home.

On a less delicate level, that well of feeling is pumped by the song "I'll be Home for Christmas." The title cheers us, but also maybe reminds us that to be home is a relative matter, as in Hardy's poem "The Oxen":

> Christmas Eve, and twelve of the clock.
>   "Now they are all on their knees,"
> An elder said as we sat in a flock
>   By the embers in hearthside ease.
>
> We pictured the meek mild creatures where
>   They dwelt in their strawy pen,
> Nor did it occur to one of us there
>   To doubt they were kneeling then.
>
> So fair a fancy few would weave
>   In these years! Yet, I feel,
> If someone said on Christmas Eve,
>   "Come; see the oxen kneel
>
> "In the lonely barton by yonder coomb
>   Our childhood used to know,"
> I should go with him in the gloom,
>   Hoping it might be so.

He is near the coomb, the barton, the oxen, but he is no longer with the "flock" of people who sat in "hearthside ease." Kenyon too is an alien in the world of a naïve Christianity, in her case gazing at the foreign Christmas gestures not with Hardy's nostalgia, exactly, but with a respectful, calm, not-quite-wistful irony that is characteristic of her. She sees the suburban ritual gestures and misses the cold North Country, "the black shade of pines," and her charitable, clear-eyed judgment is provisional, distinct, reticent.

MARIE HOWE

Jane Kenyon's *Constance*

Nothing extraordinary seems to happen in Jane Kenyon's fourth book of poems, *Constance:* snow falls; a woman drives to the village store; a dog settles down on a wooden floor, breathing; somebody can't sleep; somebody throws away a potato; somebody cuts up a nightgown for rags; somebody becomes ill; somebody dies in a grove of trees; somebody looks for a lace-trimmed pillowcase in a chest of drawers. And taken together these events form only "A Portion of History," as Kenyon calls it in the poem of that name:

> The sweet breath of someone's laundry
> spews from a dryer vent. A screen door
> slams. "Carry it?"—a woman's voice—
> "You're going to *carry* it!?" Now I hear
> the sound of casters on the sidewalk.

And real life pours across the page: ordinary, messy, tragic, sweet, and a reader's heart begins to beat in recognition—I live there—as if one were looking at a painting or a map to right here, right now.

> Car doors close softly, engines
> turn over and catch. A boy on his bike
> delivers papers. I hear the smack
> of the *New York Times* in its blue plastic
> sheath, hitting the wooden porches.

"Pretty plain," my friend the poet Tony Hoagland says, and he's right—very few metaphors or similes, no words you have to look up, no extravagant poetic gestures, nothing extraordinary: merely a soul deeply present to the world, a consciousness in a deep and fluid relationship to reality, and a desire to be clear.

—·—

Like Elizabeth Bishop, one of Kenyon's influences, Kenyon trusts that the actual world will provide all the "situation" she needs. Bishop catches an old fish, then lets it go—where's the poem but within the mutual if intermittent gaze of woman and fish? And so Kenyon listens to and looks at the world, not that she sees the world as a metaphor for the human condition—the world is not in service to her or to her poems. Rather the poet lives within a web of presences, correspondences, her soul in constant relationship to the soul of the world—and the dialogue within that relationship, when it surfaces and becomes audible, is the flesh and blood of these poems.

"Things," Rilke wrote to his friend Lou Andrea Salome, "not plastic written things but realities that rise out of the craft itself." The craft is so subtle in "A Portion of History," for example, that one hardly notices how this "plight" is expressed not only in the details but in the play of sound within the chosen words, a mix of violence and human comfort, a small symphony within a poem that appears, at first glance, to be plain and simple. The sweet breath of laundry, as it turns out, *spews.* The screen door *slams.* And the sound of casters reminds us of both a laundry cart and coffin. "Carry it?" a woman asks, engines *catch,* newspapers *smack,* hitting the porches. In the concluding stanza:

> In the next street a garbage truck cries out.
> A woman jogs by, thrusting a child
> in a stroller ahead of her, her arms
> straight as shafts, the baby's fair
> head bobbing wildly on its frail stem.

the line breaks, the verbs, the adjectives, the similes and metaphor all present an experience of durability and frailty, violence and care.

———

> "Whither shall I go from thy spirit?
>   or whither shall I flee from thy presence?"

Kenyon has used an excerpt from Psalm 139 as a kind of prologue, and like the rest of the book it's both calming and terrifying. "The darkness and the light are both alike to thee . . ." is a terrible irony for one to whom the darkness and light are not at all the same. Kenyon has spoken, on television with Bill Moyers, at public readings, and now here in these poems about her personal struggle with clinical depression. Within such suffering how can one have faith? Kenyon does have faith, she's a frankly spiritual poet with a Christian heart—referring to parables like some of us refer to pop culture or family stories—a faithful creature, and veined deep in the body of the creature self is faith's antithesis; a flattening despair that wants everything dead and finished.

"Having It Out with Melancholy," a poem in nine parts, placed in the center of the book, gives voice to the varying voices within that physiological/spiritual struggle. In the first section, *From the Nursery*, the assonance underscores the sense of correspondences:

> When I was born, you waited
> behind a pile of linen in the nursery,
> and when we were alone, you lay down
> on top of me, pressing
> the bile of desolation into every pore.

"Born" and "alone," "down," "desolation" and "pore" enact, within the ear, the cell-deep connection. The parallel syntax and assonance between "pile of linen" and "bile of desolation" link the details of domesticity with despair.

> And from that day on
> everything under the sun and moon
> made me sad—even the yellow
> wooden beads that slid and spun
> along a spindle on my crib.

"That day on" is linked with "sun and moon" and "spun"—the *u* and *o* sounds like the yellow wooden beads themselves sliding on the speaker's spindle. The assonance between "sad" and "crib" enacts, within the sound itself, depression's origin.

This ambitious poem is a wonder: each section provides a glimpse into the physiological reality of the illness. Insights are provided not only in the contents of each section, but in the varying strategies each section employs: a catalog of medications in section 2 (like an anti-litany of saints); a flat and understated remark from a friend in section 3; a lyrical epiphany recorded in section 5; a moment of sensual comfort in section 6.

What saves this poem and the entire book from sounding like mere complaint is its lack of self-pity. Kenyon gazes at depression as intently as Bishop gazes at the fish she will eventually drop back into the water, with increasingly compassionate interest. But it's erotic energy that fuels the writing of the poems. It's this energy that illuminates the love the speaker feels for the specific world of creatures ("the beating heart of the bird/ singing in the great maples") and that fuels the understated humor, quietly evident in many of the poems—a humor born from suffering and compassion for every other living creature that like the speaker must suffer and die.

One of the funniest, most heartbreaking poems in the book is "Not Here," a celebration of the mortal dance of temporary survival, reprieve, and interdependence:

> Searching for pillowcases trimmed
> with lace that my mother-in-law
> once made, I open the chest of drawers

> upstairs to find that mice
> have chewed the blue and white linen
> dishtowels to make their nest
> and bedded themselves
> among embroidered dresser scarves
> and fingertip towels.

These mice, who never make an appearance, are the most hilarious characters in the book.

> A couple of hickory nuts
> roll around as I lift out
> the linens, while a hail of black
> sunflower shells
> falls on the pillowcases,
> yellow with age, but intact.

Those *o's* and *u's* in "a couple of hickory nuts roll around" are the sound of those nuts in the drawer—we can hear them—and their incongruity makes them funny. The nuts and mouse shit among the lacy things are funny too, comic in the deepest sense because alive. "Tufts of fibers, droppings like black/ caraway seeds"; Kenyon compares their droppings to food, "the stains of birth/ and afterbirth." The mice have survived their winter—and with little harm done, the dishtowels, those daily workhorses, ruined admittedly, but the more precious pillowcases saved, "yellow with age, but intact." Kenyon loves those mice, she calls them "the bright-eyed squatters" and depicts them as heroic, courageous as G-men, and imagines them scuttling in for winter

> along the wall, from chair
> to skirted chair, making themselves
> flat and scarce while the cat

dozed with her paws in the air,
and we read the mail
or evening paper, unaware.

The rhyme of "chair," "air," and "unaware" connects all would-be
contenders in their common mortality and struggle.
This survivor's glee is humanly celebrated in the poem "Back":

We try a new drug, a new combination
of drugs, and suddenly
I fall into my life again

like a vole picked up by a storm
then dropped three valleys
and two mountains away from home.

I can find my way back. I know
I will recognize the store
where I used to buy milk and gas.

The syntax is straightforward, the tone confident and direct, and
the details increasingly more specific:

I remember the house and barn,
the rake, the blue cups and plates,
the Russian novels I loved so much,

and even more specific:

and the black silk nightgown
that he once thrust
into the toe of my Christmas stocking.

Three lines are given to that nightgown, which must be silky indeed to fit into the toe of a stocking. And that sexy exhilarating "he once thrust"!

This relationship to detail is the erotic heart of the book. I want to quote so many poems here, but there's only room for one last essential one: the empathetic rendering of the last minutes of a young man's life, a soldier who's shot during the famous Battle of Gettysburg, another "portion of history." In Kenyon's rendering of his dying, within her close gaze, so close as to enter into his imagined experience, eros triumphs over thanatos even as death commences and wins. Understatement, irony, and a refusal to condescend or pity allow the overblown and historical to become ordinary, life-size, and precious:

> The young man, hardly more
> than a boy, who fired the shot
> had looked at him with an air
> not of anger but of concentration,
> as if he were surveying a road,
> or feeding a length of wood into a saw:
> It had to be done just so.

The gaze of the shooter is the gaze also of the poet: concentration unmuddied by sentimentality. Kenyon's restraint allows us to gaze at the young soldier and not look away, and her empathy allows us entry into what is happening to him as it happens:

> The bullet passed through
> his upper chest, below the collarbone.
> The pain was not what he might
> have feared. Strangely exhilarated
> he staggered out of the pasture
> and into a grove of trees.

Look how we are brought nearer to the boy in the next stanza:

> He pressed and pressed
> the wound, trying to stanch
> the blood, but he could only press
> what he could reach, and he could
> not reach his back, where the bullet
> had exited.

So close, then even closer: "How good the earth smelled" the boy thinks, falling. "[M]usty and damp and cool"; "A cowbird razzed from a rail fence"; "Stray bullets nicked the oaks / overhead. Leaves and splinters fell."

Like "A Portion of History" life here is recorded in its minute particulars, a swell of images; life, sex, and death at once. Somewhere between the last two stanzas the soldier dies so quietly we don't notice it at first. "A streak of sun climbed the rough/ trunk of a tree": we're busy watching *that.*

The world is ordinary and precious and terrible at once, this single loss palpable and unendurable, even as the erotic presence of the world itself is imminent, strong, and enduring.

> "Carry it?"—a woman's voice—
> "You're going to *carry* it!?"

The movement of the entire book is evident within these lines: between that first "Carry it?" with its incredulous question mark, and the second "*carry* it!?" with its exclamation. And in between "a woman's voice" speaking from eye level, from the world where we live now.

I love all of Jane Kenyon's poems, from the first book, *From Room to Room,* to *The Boat of Quiet Hours,* to *Let Evening Come,* because of the qualities in *Constance*—this abiding love of the world and the creatures in it, the compassion, humor, honesty, and clarity. There's great pain in many of the poems in this book, which are perhaps the most painful Jane Kenyon has written. Nevertheless, she has written them—like the mice she has survived the winter—and the poems are a tribute to her spirit and the spirit of poetry. It might have been "Otherwise" as she herself writes in the penultimate poem in this book:

> I got out of bed
> on two strong legs.
> It might have been
> otherwise. I ate
> cereal, sweet
> milk, ripe, flawless
> peach. It might
> have been otherwise.
> I took the dog uphill
> to the birch wood.
> All morning I did
> the work I love.

LUCIA PERILLO

Notes from the Other Side

Everyone knows that women poets are loonies: a roll call of America's most beloved female practitioners would not necessarily undermine this conventional wisdom. We've all heard, for example, the life stories of Sylvia Plath and Anne Sexton, frequently cited as cautionary tales about what happens when "poetesses" fall too much in love with their own depressive illnesses. But curiously, though these women were adept at putting their emotional pitches and swoops to the service of art, they did not engage in much glossing on these interior states. For both Plath and Sexton, psychic upheaval functioned as a given an initiating premise, neither woman was particularly interested in mediating between her distress and an exterior, "objective" world.

This mediation is one of the projects of Jane Kenyon's *Constance,* which lays stress on the poet's battle with depression, a disease that, says Kenyon, "ruined my manners toward God." Followers of Kenyon's work may be disoriented if not entirely surprised by the revelation of Kenyon's illness: earlier books like *The Boat of Quiet Hours* and *Let Evening Come* demonstrated Kenyon's gift for rendering the natural world in poems that were scrupulously detailed but equally scrupulous in their refusal to turn their lens toward the poet herself. This made reading Kenyon a ticklish experience, at least for me—I greatly admired the craft of her poems but also suspected that something was being withheld, something that would account for the poems' pervasive and haunting sadness.

Constance comes clean not only about its author's depression but also the encroaching mortalities of her closest allies (Kenyon's husband, Donald Hall, has written extensively about his ongoing bouts with cancer). To announce that Kenyon twines her own illness with a tally of deaths nearby or impending might scare off potential readers; it's easy to fear such a book's being too moribund to bear. The remarkable thing is that one emerges from *Constance* exhilarated by the poet's emphasis on the life lived in the face of death. Kenyon pushes her subject matter toward redemption by balancing decay against the body's potential vigor, whether that be climbing a mountain with another woman or simply walking the dog.

The centerpiece of this new volume is an ambitious, multisectioned poem called "Having It Out with Melancholy," which nods to Keats's famous ode on the same theme. Kenyon effectively exorcises the word *melancholy*'s nineteenth-century century specters, in part by emphasizing modern technology's management of the disease. I was startled to see Kenyon make space for terminology like "monoamine oxidase inhibitors" and "Ludiomil." Yet this kind of attentiveness to physical and pharmaceutical detail is what allows Kenyon to skirt the charges most often launched against so-called confessional poetry—namely that poets (and here the implication is women) who have attempted to speak about their illnesses (i.e., mental) have failed to engage a world beyond their own (here read pejoratively) *feelings*.

Kenyon turns this criticism on its ear by showing us *how* depression cuts its subject off from the external world, at the same time keeping her naturalist's eye trained on what surrounds her, as when Kenyon describes a moment of epiphany unleashed by one of her disease's sudden (and temporary) remissions:

> High on Nardil and June light
> I wake at four,
> waiting greedily for the first
> note of the wood thrush. Easeful air
> presses through the screen

with the wild, complex song
of the bird, and I am overcome

by ordinary contentment.

By persistently hewing to the world's concrete details, Kenyon frees herself from the tired abstractions of suffering. A friend's elegy, for example, finds its central image in a doe that, after pausing in the roadway, bolts straight for the speaker's car, "glancing off the hood with a crash,/ into a field of corn stubble." A short poem that has the speaker observing a man stepping outside, presumably after attending his wife's sickbed, makes no comment about grief but instead studies the woman's coat draped over his arm. The man himself, Kenyon writes, "had zipped his own coat and tied/ the hood under his chin, preparing/ for irremediable cold."

When she becomes involuntary witness to her husband's cancer diagnosis, Kenyon applies this same method of precise description: "The surgeon,/ when I asked how big your tumor was,/ held forth his substantial fist/ with its globed class ring." Given less to philosophy than service, Kenyon works the transitional terrain between life and death by engaging in the necessary labor of caregiving, whether it be cleaning up after the ambulance attendants ("Litter") or pressing the bolus to administer her husband's morphine ("Chrysanthemums") or preparing "the things you might need in the next/ life" (Pharaoh").

Constance is a short book, and its poems are terse and at times zen-like in their reflections on nature. Yet Kenyon steers her imagery clear of the stock complacency of the "nature poem." Rather, the landscape Kenyon works is often harrowing. The same natural world full of wood thrushes and flowers will eventually reveal its sinister underside to the keen observer: deer rush at cars, peonies are as big as human heads, mice take up residence for winter in the writer's house and leave behind "droppings like black/ caraway seeds and the stains of birth/ and afterbirth [that] give off the strong/ attar of mouse."

In previous books, this method of working solely with the world of real things at hand imposed limitations on Kenyon's range; it didn't, for example, allow her a voice capacious enough to accommodate history or politics. This new work shows Kenyon stretching the scope of her poems without losing either the credibility of their voice or the immediacy of their detailed focus. Instead the small things of this world grow large in unexpected ways: a meditation on an old nightgown becomes a vigil for civilians killed in the Persian Gulf, a lightweight ode to a spoiled potato turns into an indictment of American waste. As a rural resident who shuns much of consumerist culture, Kenyon could have easily slipped into the lopsided voice of polemic. But she negotiates this new territory with grace, never excusing herself from complicity in our collective social ills.

Personal pain continues to be a recalcitrant subject for writers, despite its prominence in American poetry for more than fifty years. Perhaps this is because, at bottom, grief and depression remain narcissistic experiences, difficult to translate to those who, unlike the poet, are not inside. Yet Kenyon's sense of complicity with a broad and imperfect spectrum of humanity also allows her to speak about the private regions of her psyche, without the self-absorbed tunnel vision that critics have faulted in confessional verse. Instead Kenyon speaks of herself "floating with the whole/ human family. We were all colors—those/ who are living now, those who have died,/ those who are not born." It may sound odd to describe as energetic the writing found in a book that takes depression for its foreground, and yet this paradox is one of the things that makes reading Jane Kenyon's new poetry such an extraordinary experience.

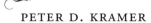

PETER D. KRAMER

Unequivocal Eye

After giving my talk, speaking with readers, signing some books—this was at the Miami International Book Fair last November—I slipped back into the auditorium to hear what the next authors had to say.

There were two, a man and a woman. The man, in his middle sixties, spoke in a storyteller's voice, modest and with a sense of pleasures shared, in the manner of a more open Robert Frost. Despite the poet's public demeanor, the words he read were by no means simple. He was unafraid of high seriousness.

Alternating readings with him was a woman many years his junior. Her face was warm but strained, and she had done nothing to camouflage a shock of white hair that hinted at troubles seen. She appeared to be utterly self-aware, appealing in the manner of someone who has dealt with pain and manages now to meet the world straight on. She gave, as part of a friendly stage manner, an impression of daunting honesty—a woman who has little truck with small talk or false manners. And yet certain of her poems concerned the small pleasures of life.

In their poetry, the two—they were obviously husband and wife—began to comment on each other, and on each other's ailments, she on his metastatic cancer, he on her depression. It dawned on me that I knew who these poets were. The man was Donald Hall. I had recently read a review of his latest nonfiction book, *Life Work,* a meditation on the labor of Hall's grandparents, subsistence farmers, and his own labors as a poet on the same stony New England land.

The woman was, of course, Jane Kenyon, whom Hall in his writing has identified as manic-depressive, mainly depressive. The scene came together for me when she read one of her most affecting poems, "Pharaoh." Hall has returned home from a hospital treatment for his cancer; waking, Kenyon looks at her sleeping husband and sees the bedclothes as a sarcophagus:

> The things you might need in the next
> life surround you—your comb and glasses,
> water, a book and pen.

Kenyon read from another poem I admired, one that is the occasion for this column. "Having It Out with Melancholy" is a meditation on depression.

There is, of course, an extensive poetry of depression. We may think immediately of English poet John Keats, not only the "Ode on Melancholy," but also the "Ode to a Nightingale" ("My heart aches, and a drowsy numbness pains/ My sense . . .") and many other odes and sonnets. Kay Redfield Jamison, in *Touched with Fire* (Free Press), her encyclopedic study of depression and creativity, catalogs thirty-six mood-disordered or suicidal eighteenth-century English-language poets, many of whom made melancholy their subject.

Their successors frequently approached this theme. In correspondence, Jamison has introduced me to the World War I lyrical poet Edward Thomas (1878–1917), whose "Melancholy" ("What I desired I knew not, but whate'er my choice/ Vain must it be") can be considered representative of a substantial tradition. In her book, Jamison names more than eighty major poets who suffered with, and for the most part wrote about, mood disorder.

Modern poets must take into account a daunting tradition when approaching melancholy as a subject. And yet there is great need for a contemporary approach. Though the illness of depression remains more or less a constant, each generation has its own apprehension of the affliction, ours colored by biological research and the availability of often effective biological treatments.

I have written at length, in this column and elsewhere, of the ways in which medication shapes our understanding of temperament and personality. To experience depression as objective, biologically caused or maintained, partly heritable, recurrent and relapsing is not just a scientific posture; for the sufferer, this vantage constitutes a specific sense of self. Nowhere ought this influence be more evident than in the person of the depressed artist. I thought I heard in Jane Kenyon's poem indications of the new perspective.

I do not refer only to *Bottles,* although the first lines of that section speak to a different form of natural surround for the melancholic poet:

> Elavil, Ludiomil, Doxepin,
> Norpramin, Prozac, Lithium, Xanax,
> Wellbutrin, Parnate, Nardil, Zoloft.

The objects named are identifiers of a unique moment and particular sort of life in that moment.

But they are not all that differentiates this consideration of melancholy from that of, say, Keats or Thomas. A distinctive perspective is evident from the poem's first lines: "When I was born, you waited/ behind a pile of linen in the nursery . . ." The verse continues: "And from that day on/ everything under the sun and moon/ made me sad . . ." Here is a new sort of depression, one that is innate and incessant, and also a new sort of childhood, standing in marked contrast to the carefree youth of the Romantics. Though she appears to live among playthings, the child belongs not to her mother but to this enemy.

There is throughout an understanding of depression as recurrent, almost constant. When medicated, the poet feels well-being, she still understands: "Unholy ghost,/ you are certain to come again." And, at the end of this sonnet-like "Credo," more eerily: *"When I awake, I am still with thee."*

Medication is more than a series of exotic names. It is characterized (perhaps along with a seasonal change) as the instrument of pardon from a hell imposed by an incomprehensible god. "We move on to the monoamine/ oxidase inhibitors," and the pain ceases. What the poet experiences is not the Romantics' Lethe and Nepenthe but a sense of well-being, a return to life, albeit with side effects and perhaps a tendency to overshoot. Thomas's poem ends as elegy, with the song of a distant cuckoo. Kenyon's does, too, as she hears the wood thrush, but only because she is "High on Nardil and June light."

This last distinction is perhaps the most important. Thomas's depression is in the Romantic tradition: "Yet naught did my despair/ But sweeten the strange sweetness..." The romanticization of melancholy, and its close relatives suicide and alcoholism, has remained a theme in this half-century: think of Dylan Thomas, Sylvia Plath, Anne Sexton. Kenyon's depression is something new: ". . . the anti-urge,/ the mutilator of souls." Kenyon does not elegize melancholy, she bears witness to a scourge, as survivors bear witness to political and moral outrages. The poem is both art and a public act on behalf of fellow sufferers.

After the reading, I purchased *Constance,* the volume in which "Having it Out with Melancholy" appears. I then had the pleasure of reading the book on the flight home, along with Hall's wonderful new collection, *The Museum of Clear Ideas.*

The hub-and-spoke system being what it is, Hall, Kenyon, and I were on the same flight out of Dade County and so had a chance to talk between connections. I asked Kenyon then whether *Psychiatric Times* might reprint the poem, and she said that she had encouraged the publisher to allow it to be circulated widely.

On my return home, I chanced to hear Donald Hall on *All Things Considered* and then to see both poets on a Bill Moyers special on public television. In the television interview, filmed earlier, Kenyon spoke frankly about depression. She was shown reading "Having It Out . . ." to a local New Hampshire audience, and read "Pharaoh" for Moyers.

The program showcases Hall as a wise, humorous rural poet. The broader truth is that Hall is a literary man of astonishing range. Look on your bookshelf, and you are sure to find an anthology—of children's verse, of literary anecdotes, of midcentury poetry—by Hall. He has written of his acquaintance with Thomas, Frost, T. S. Eliot, Ezra Pound, and others. Hall is an exact contemporary of James Merrill, Adrienne Rich, and Allen Ginsberg, and his work shares the classical referents and the tendency toward surrealism as well as the common-language accessibility of his contemporaries' output.

But it would not surprise me if Hall, if he maintains his health, were to assume the mantle of Frost, another New England poet and Harvard man whose homespun, "artless" image belied the subtlety of his work. If so, it may be Hall and Kenyon together who become identified with poetry in the popular mind, an occurrence that would be fortunate both for lovers of the literature and those who care about the perception of mental illness.

Like her wood thrush, Kenyon does not equivocate. She speaks with a straightforwardness that serves to reclaim the dignity of stigmatized sufferers from depression. She bears an affliction, one she does not flinch from naming and depicting, and one she cannot help embodying. It strikes me that her poems signal the transformation of a trope. For Kenyon, melancholy is not a romantic condition, like one of Samuel Coleridge's or Thomas De Quincey's opiated states, nor is it only a profound perspective on the human condition. It is also pure hell—in the exact sense, torture without mitigating benefit. "A piece of burned meat/ wears my clothes . . ."

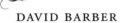

DAVID BARBER

Constance

Jane Kenyon possesses one of our day's most scrupulously transparent idioms. Deliberate, fastidious, disarmingly bare of adornments and conceits, her poems' colloquial surfaces can at first seem too artless to contain much in the way of sustaining depth or weight. But modesty of means is not the same thing, of course, as simplicity of apprehension. Kenyon's resolute absence of affect in articulating local and quotidian instance enables her best work to assume a palpable moral aspect that would be overbearing in a more elevated manner and unconvincing in a less taciturn mode. In her hands the home truth becomes both more pertinent and more inscrutable than readers weaned on urbane indeterminacies might otherwise have supposed.

The inscrutable side of Kenyon's poems lies in their welled-up irresolutions rather than anything remotely resembling willful obscurity. Their calm decorum harbors thorny qualms. Writing from "north of Boston" maple and birch country where Frost waged his lover's quarrel with the world, Kenyon, too, in her most recent collections has seemed to carry on an understated dispute with the seasonal and domestic exigencies of the latitude she's embraced. Kenyon's framing occasions more often than not are rural-route commonplaces; but commonplaces made uncommonly perceptible by the poet's meticulous sensitivity to the exposing detail, the arrested moment, the implicit emotion. *Constance* certainly marks no break with these habits of mind and elements of style, but the book gives off an atmosphere of urgency that seems to chafe more intensely than in the past against Kenyon's sparing and chary quietude. The book's epigraph is a fragment from Psalm 189 ("O Lord, thou hast searched me . . .") and Kenyon's opening poem doesn't hesitate in starkly introducing what New England's Puritan divines would have branded a crisis in faith:

> Even at noon the house is dark.
> In my room under the eaves
> I hear the steady benevolence
> of water washing dust
> raised by the haying
> from porch and car and garden
> chair. We are shorn
> and purified, as if tonsured.
>
> The grass resolves to grow again,
> receiving rain to that end,
> but my disordered soul thirsts
> after something it cannot name.

It's more than a little perilous, in writerly terms, to leave oneself this aesthetically unprotected, this shorn. "August Rain, after Haying" is as far removed as one could likely get from the cagey and crusty sagacity of Frost; nor could the distance be much vaster between Kenyon's "disordered soul" and the charged metaphysical intricacies that give the spiritual hungers of a Dickinson or a Herbert such transfiguring power. But what Kenyon divests herself of in terms of ostensible wit and wisdom she tends to gain back in suggestive gradations of sense and sensibility. Her poems stake almost everything on tone. Catching that tone exactly takes work and amply assures the reader of the complications that underlie any given poem's deceptively casual feel. "Winter Lambs" begins, as so many of Kenyon's poems do, with a muted declarative description of wholly unremarkable circumstance: "All night snow came upon us/ with unwavering intent—/ small flakes not meandering/ but driving thickly down. We woke/ to see the yard, the car and road/ heaped unrecognizably." The

tenor of near-detachment continues in the next stanza, heightened
though it is by a touch of country drama ("The neighbors' ewes are
lambing/ in this stormy weather") before Kenyon makes one of her
characteristically sharp pivots in the final stanza that overturns the
picturesque drift of her scene and leaches any residual innocence out
of the phrases "unwavering intent" and "heaped unrecognizably":

> I have a friend who is pregnant—
> plans gone awry—and not altogether
> pleased. I don't say she should
> be pleased. We are creation's
> property, its particles, its clay
> as we fall into this life,
> agree or disagree.

Constance asks to be read as a series of confrontations with faith
and doubt, though Kenyon's abiding sense of proportion is such that
her poems never seem enslaved to their premises and themes. Even
when Kenyon takes on more expansive subjects or more extended
forms, there's no dilution in the concentrated quickenings of perception that give her poems a probing immediacy amid their overarching
solemnity. Despite their more evident orchestration, works like "The
Stroller" (a five-section narrative monologue that's both an elegy to
Kenyon's father and a grapple with childhood nostalgia), "Having It
Out with Melancholy" (a poem in nine movements about Kenyon's
lifelong battle with clinical depression), or "Chrysanthemums" (a
chronicle of husband Donald Hall's cancer operation) are distinctive less for their scope than for what they share with Kenyon's compact pieces: an expressive acuity and economy, a personal directness
that's neither cramped nor swamped by personality. However heavy-
hearted, she makes it her sedulous business to remain clearheaded
and sharp-eyed.

The extent to which Kenyon's incisive introspection and unobtrusive prose virtues have become her most formidable artistic strengths

is neatly encapsulated in the sequence of poems that make up the last of her book's four sections, whose subtitle ("Watch Ye, Watch Ye") is borrowed from the first line of a Shaker hymn. The first five poems here principally aspire to historical and social conscience rather than to self-reflection: Kenyon listens "to news/ from the war, of torture where the air/ is black at noon with burning oil" ("Three Small Oranges"), notes "the smack/ of the *New York Times* in its blue plastic/ sheath, hitting the wooden porches" ("A Portion of History"), and imagines, in a curiously cinematic set piece, a young Civil War soldier's death throes ("Gettysburg: July 1, 1863"). Although skillfully composed and customarily unlabored ("Potato" in particular displays a light-fingered puckish charm), these poems come off as somewhat worked up, almost as if Kenyon felt obligated to enlarge her range of feeling by broadening her frame of reference. The book's final three offerings, however, demonstrate just how much emotional resonance she's capable of achieving when she cleaves to her contained meditative temper. "Pharaoh" is perhaps the book's single most memorable poem—a prologue to an elegy, one wants to call it—by virtue of managing to be at once quietly unnerving, profoundly intimate, and manifestly humane. And "Otherwise" and "Notes from the Other Side," yoked across the book's final facing pages, are both written in that most vestigial of verse forms, the prayer.

The devotional courage that Kenyon draws from what Marianne Moore called "the unanswered question,/ the resolute doubt" may not win our assent but it does earn our trust. Her planed-down honesty and clarity are not just virtues, but powers.

DEBORAH GARRISON

Simply Lasting

I never knew Jane Kenyon, who died last year, of leukemia, at the age of forty-seven, but I feel as though I did because her poems are so frankly confiding, and the materials of her daily life, which were also the materials of her poetry, fall into a classic American genre that makes her world instantly recognizable to a newcomer. The sound of hammering coming from somewhere down the road, the sadness of newly mown hayfields, a casket being carried between narrow pews: Kenyon's existence, at least in her poetry, has a timeless, "North of Boston" quality. *Otherwise: New & Selected Poems,* a volume containing twenty new poems and selected works from her four previous collections, confirms this sense of her as a good literary neighbor—a poet with absolutely no airs. She and her husband, the poet Donald Hall, lived on a New Hampshire farm that had been in his family for four generations, and there is something of the farmer's plainsong in Kenyon's approach to her surroundings. In "After the Hurricane," she walks out to the pond at the edge of the property with her dog, who races ahead:

> In the full, still pond the likeness
> of golden birch leaves and the light they emit
> shines exact. When the dog sees himself
> his hackles rise. I stir away his trouble
> with a stick.

Kenyon's approach to the world (to poetry) is summed up in that gesture, the slightly humorous but ingenious use of the stick. Her farmhouse pragmatism—she lives in nature but isn't afraid to muss it up, if need be—is just as fitting in town, at the dime store or the church fair; even her passing thoughts are conveniently lasting and useful, like the wooden clothes pins she still has a need for in the 1990s, or the small silver berry pails she remembers carrying into the Michigan woods as a girl. Yet Kenyon refuses to sentimentalize the sense of material American solidity that she conveys, and often undercuts it, as when she writes, in "Things," of how objects we love have a way of "simply lasting, then / failing to last," and roots for the mouse that is living on the batting in a hundred-year-old quilt: "She chewed a hole in a blue star / to get it, and now she thrives. . . . / Now is her time to thrive."

Kenyon's evenness of tone—her ability to mirror in the simplest language all that she sees—is the kind of smooth, dark ice that conceals wildly rushing waters. Like the dog who's spooked by his own reflection, she is the victim of her mind's constructions, of emotions coursing just under the surface of her linguistic composure. In "The Appointment," she is worrying over a visit to the doctor by her husband:

> It might have been the finest day of the summer—
> the hay was rich and dry, and the breeze
> made the heart-shaped leaves of the birch
> tell all their secrets,
> though they were lost on me. . . .
> . . . .
>
>   If you
> had turned into the drive just then, even
> with cheerful news, I doubt
> I could have heard what you had to say.

This is perhaps Kenyon's central subject: the way what troubles the mind spreads outward to trouble the world, so that the two seem to vibrate in unison, in the same minor key. Her awareness of this crossing of wires, however, allows her not only to transmit signals but to receive incoming ones. During a heavy snowstorm, she lies in bed as though buried in a drift herself, picking up both the lethargy and the pleasure of the snow's will: "It falls on the vole, nosing somewhere / through weeds, and on the open / eye of the pond. It makes the mail / come late. . . . I'm sleepy and benign in the dark. / There's nothing I want." At the end of winter, she is equally suggestible in the opposite direction:

> As late as yesterday ice preoccupied
> the pond—dark, half-melted, waterlogged.
> Then it sank in the night, one piece,
> taking winter with it. And afterward
> everything seems simple and good.

Changes in the weather, both mental and actual, affect us all; indeed, Kenyon's gift is a reminder that there's a fine line between describing your day and writing lyric poetry. (Only rarely, at the end of a poem, does she insist on a note of description that is one degree too plain and keeps the lines from achieving poetic liftoff.) Her feel for the chemistry of our everyday moods is most evident in her writing about clinical depression, which she apparently suffered from throughout her life. In "Now Where?" she writes of the ubiquity of the thing that haunts her, that

> wakes when I wake, walks
> when I walk, turns back when I
> turn back, beating me to the door.
> . . . .

And so, like a widow, I lie down
after supper. If I lie down
or sit up it's all the same:

the days and nights bear me along.

Her honesty about things pharmaceutical is an ironic (and, again, characteristically pragmatic) touch in the context of country life:

High on Nardil and June light
I wake at four,
waiting greedily for the first
notes of the wood thrush. Easeful air
presses through the screen
with the wild, complex song
of the bird, and I am overcome

by ordinary contentment.
What hurt me so terribly
all my life until this moment?

Kenyon shows her affinity with Anna Akhmatova, whose work she translated, when she is grappling with herself this way; oddly, the depression brings with it a Russian-like, spur-ringing passion for life—or, at least, the memory of such passion, which lurks in Kenyon's voice even when she sounds as though she can't go on. My favorite of all her poems, "Back," evokes that marriage of depression and passion, in a meeting-it-head-on tone that's uniquely hers. "[S]uddenly / I fall into my life again," she writes, expressing her faith that the observing mind, which regularly betrays us, will return us to the things we cared about in better times:

I can find my way back. I know
I will recognize the store
where I used to buy milk and gas.

I remember the house and barn,
the rake, the blue cups and plates,
the Russian novels I loved so much,

and the black silk nightgown
that he once thrust
into the toe of my Christmas stocking.

ROBERT HASS

from

Poet's Choice

The book I've been living with this last month is *Otherwise* by Jane Kenyon. Kenyon wrote in the plain style—something of Frost, though her poems are much more interior, and something of the Russian poet Anna Akhmatova, though Akhmatova had an imperious and dramatic quality very different from Kenyon's reflective, almost workmanlike attention to daily life. She seems to have struggled all her life with depression and this, instead of making her poems seem dark and unhappy, gives them a luminous gravity. Here's one of the later poems, atypical because it looks out of New England at the larger world.

Mosaic of the Nativity: Serbia, Winter 1993

On the domed ceiling God
is thinking:
I made them my joy,
and everything else I created
I made to bless them.
But see what they do!
I know their hearts
and arguments:

"We're descended from
Cain. Evil is nothing new,
so what does it matter now
if we shell the infirmary,
and the well where the fearful
and rash alike must
come for water?"

God thinks Mary into being.
Suspended at the apogee
of the golden dome,
she curls in a brown pod,
and inside her the mind
of Christ, cloaked in blood,
lodges and begins to grow.

When I read this poem, I was struck at first by her imagination of—what do they call the birth of gods?—theogony, the coming into being of the Christ of suffering. But what stayed in my mind was the phrase about our common condition: "the well where the fearful and rash alike must come for water." This is the way her poems work on me. Some phrase or image that I almost don't notice on first reading settles in and haunts.

MICHAEL DIRDA

from

The Gift of Being Simple

Last summer I reviewed, quite favorably, a collection of essays by poet Donald Hall, and a few weeks later, a note appeared from the man himself, just a few words of thanks. When I turned the postcard over, I found a poem—printed in blue type—by Jane Kenyon: it was entitled "Man Eating." At the time I had never read any of Kenyon's poetry, but I remembered that she was Hall's wife, and that she had died earlier that spring from leukemia. I now know, in part through her husband's restrained Afterword to *Otherwise,* that she would have been forty-nine in May of 1996.

Like many people, I tend to glance rather dutifully at unfamiliar poems, whether in magazines or on the back of postcards. So I skimmed "Man Eating" quickly, then paused and read it again, more slowly. I have now reread it at least a score of times, each time with increased pleasure. It is, I think, exceptionally beautiful, utterly unforced in its simple diction but made with careful artistry:

> The man at the table across from mine
> is eating yogurt. His eyes, following
> the progress of the spoon, cross briefly
> each time it nears his face. Time,
>
> and the world with all its principalities,
> might come to an end as prophesied

by the Apostle John, but what about
this man, so completely present

to the little carton with its cool,
sweet food, which has caused no animal
to suffer, and which he is eating
with a pearl-white plastic spoon.

In a loose sense, one can say that poets tend to use language in two ways: the artful or the natural. They either transmute their thoughts through metaphor, striking imagery or unusual syntax into something rich and strange; or they pack their meaning into the kind of language really used by men and women. On the one hand, Wallace Stevens, Gerard Manley Hopkins, and Jorie Graham; on the other, William Carlos Williams, Archilocus, and Philip Levine. Most poets probably opt for flash and filigree—after all, "the multitudinous seas incarnadine" *sounds* like poetry. It takes real confidence, and a sure judgment, to set down words as simple, and deeply moving in their context, as "Pray, undo this button."

Kenyon is obviously a writer of the second sort. In "Man Eating" every word falls like a light hammer tap; no distracting metaphors intrude; the language is simple, clear; the tone of quiet thoughtfulness. Single-syllable words predominate, and there are no rhymes, nor an obvious meter. One admires this poem for the way it conveys, almost effortlessly, a glimpse of unity and peacefulness: a Zen epiphany. Kenyon's art, as Hall notes, aims for the "luminous particular."

And yet the closer one looks into these dozen lines, the more one finds. Consider the wit of the title: "Man Eating" might suggest ravenous tigers and bloody meat rather than this clean world of whiteness, innocence, and purity. Note the skeins of alliteration and assonance that tie the poem together, most obviously the *p's* (progress, principalities, prophesied, present, pearl-white, plastic) but also the *m's* (man, mine, might, man) and the last stanza's *c's* (carton, cool, caused) and double *o's* (cool, food, spoon). Many of the lines hover around nine syllables, though each stanza's last line has only seven; note, too, the half-rhymes of mine and Time, cool and spoon. The poem's rhythms are carefully established, building to a Biblical flourish with the multisyllabic "principalities." Though depicting a scene from ordinary life, a man concentrating on eating yogurt, Kenyon invests this moment with unsuspected spiritual significance: by truly doing what you are doing, by focusing all your energies on the task at hand, by being, in short, "so completely present/ to the little carton," you may triumph over time, achieve transcendence.

Such Buddhist implications seem appropriate to a poem tonally akin to haiku and much early Japanese literature. But there is also a possible sense, a bit tangled by the syntax, that the man may escape the Christian Last Judgment or have nothing to fear from it. Kenyon's sole literary allusion—to the Apostle John prophesying the end of time—doubtless refers to the Book of Revelation, with its final apportioning of souls to Hell and Heaven. The yogurt-eater has "caused no animal to suffer," and his pearl-white spoon already links him to a kind of unblemished purity. Not least, Kenyon's "cool, sweet food" from a "little" carton echoes one of the most powerfully symbolic moments in John's vision (Revelation 10:10): "And I took the little book out of the angel's hand, and ate it up; and it was in my mouth sweet as honey."

CONSTANCE MERRITT

Jane Kenyon, *Otherwise*

Although her name does not appear among those "certain authors" that Donald Hall, in his Afterword to Kenyon's posthumously published *Otherwise: New & Selected Poems,* tells us "she read and reread . . . with excitement and devotion" (Keats, Akhmatova, Bishop, Chekhov), Emily Dickinson is no less a presence here. Beyond shared themes—death, depression, hard grappling with God—and a shared subject matter—daily domestic life in a New England village, intimacies with flowers, beasts and birds, the cycle of seasons, of daylight and darkness, and companionable rambles with a cherished dog—it is the intricate equilibrium struck between evanescence and durability, gravity and grace, between "that joy so violent/ it [is] hard to distinguish from pain" and "the Hour of Lead" that weds her work to a singular tradition. And if Kenyon is not one of Dickinson's self-appointed apprentices, it is perhaps because, by virtue of landscape, temperament, and lifestyle, she comes by the inheritance naturally.

Together with generous, well-chosen selections from four previous collections of poems, *Otherwise* offers twenty new poems—many of them extraordinary. Though Kenyon was born in Ann Arbor, Michigan, and educated there, it is Eagle Pond Farm that provides the dominant landscape for these poems. In selections from *From Room to Room* (1978), we witness Kenyon's first "clumsy" attempts at negotiating the new space, searching out her place among the "five generations" of ancestors—particularly the women—and the rooms, crowded with thickly inhabited things:

My people are not here, my mother
and father, my brother. I talk
to the cats about weather.

"Blessed be the tie that binds . . ."
we sing in the church down the road.
And how does it go from there? The tie . . .

the tether, the hose carrying
oxygen to the astronaut,
turning, turning outside the hatch,
taking a look around.

("From Room to Room")

Note the precision with which the image of the "astronaut,/ turning, turning outside the hatch" conveys, at once, the perceived alienness of the new surroundings and the poet's disorientation and unshieldedness, untethered (recently hatched) from the place of *her* people and birth. But also notice how the casual diction of "taking a look around" opens up a new space in the poem—cautious, curious, tentative. Similarly, in "Here," the poem that follows "From Room to Room," Kenyon is able to weigh her own self-consciousness ("I'm the one who worries/ if I fit I with the furniture") against the landscape's egalitarian hospitality ("Already the curves in the road/ are familiar to me, and the mountain/ in all kinds of light,/ treating all people the same.") without slighting her own loss or the possibility of healing ("I feel my life start up again/ like a cutting when it grows/ the first pale and tentative/ root hair in a glass of water").

Becoming at home in a new landscape, as in the world, requires an innocence, an openness to things, a willingness to let one's self be taken in (*embraced,* and possibly *deceived*) that self-consciousness disallows. Looking at things unguardedly and being favored by their answering gaze becomes one hallmark of Kenyon's poems. "Now tell me," she writes in "Dutch Interiors," one of the volume's strong new poems, "that the Holy Ghost/ does not reside in the play of light/ on cutlery!" And sure enough, by the grace of her eyes, even hardened skeptics begin to see a trace of . . . *something* in a thimble, a clothes pin, a shirt, a grandmother's damask tablecloth—or rather, in *this one, the luminous particular one.* Perhaps more than anything else— more than all the things I have mentioned heretofore, it is Kenyon's unselfconscious use of personification, that most suspect of figures, that so immediately brings Dickinson to mind. In the idiom of these poems, "feeding the stove-animal," "the clock's heart/beat[ing] in its wooden chest," "brow of hayfield, blue/ eye of pond," "the moon mov[ing] around the barn/ to find out what [a new scent in the air] is coming from" seem wholly commonplace and natural; as do these lines from "Afternoon in the House":

> The geranium leans this way
> to see if I'm writing about her:
> head all petals, brown
> stalks, and those green fans.
> So you see,
> I am writing about you.
> . . . .
> The house settles down on its haunches
> for a doze.
> I know you are with me, plants,
> and cats—and even so, I'm frightened,
> sitting in the middle of perfect
> possibility.

And with all the trouble in the world (private and historical)— though we do not like to admit it, not even to ourselves—there is good cause to be frightened. Add to the pot of common woe: posses- sion from infancy by the "unholy ghost" of melancholy and a grandmother's ardent instructions in the ways of her "vengeful God," and we can begin to see the horns of the dilemma that Kenyon, throughout her work, struggles to gain a purchase on. In part a response—nay, a rebuke—to Elizabeth Bishop's much-anthologized "One Art," "The Pond at Dusk" is one of the most startling poems in the collection. Neither its placement in the volume nor its own bucolic mien prepares us for the final stanza's spring:

> A fly wounds the water but the wound
> soon heals . . .
> . . . .
>
> The green haze on the trees changes
> into leaves, and what looks like smoke
> floating over the neighbor's barn
> is only apple blossoms.
>
> But sometimes what looks like disaster
> *is* disaster: the day comes at last,
> and the men struggle with the casket
> just clearing the pews.

Rather than focusing, as Bishop does, on loss, which simply points to an absence and thus remains immaterial and vague, Kenyon cruelly confronts us with death's considerable and unwieldy weight. Most good writers not only choose kindred precursors to whom they may willingly submit, but also congenial sparring partners to actively resist; for Kenyon, it seems, Bishop is such a one. Consider "The Argument," Kenyon's counterpart to Bishop's "First Death in Nova Scotia," but without the latter's ironic distance or restraint:

> "All things work together for the good
> for those who love God," . . . [Grandmother] said
> to comfort me at Uncle Hazen's funeral,
> where Father held me up to see

the maroon gladiolus that trembled
as we approached the bier, the elaborate
shirred satin, brass fittings, anything,

oh, anything but Uncle's squelched
and made-up face.
"No! NO! How is it good to be dead?"
I cried afterward, wild-eyed and flushed.
"God's ways are not our ways,"
she said then out of pity
and the wish to forestall the argument.

Due, at least in part, to the lack of self-consciousness mentioned earlier, here, little distance separates the adult poet from the child she recollects. In fact, it is "woodsmoke" drifting through the rolled-up windows of the poet's car ("insinuating that I might . . . have been made for unquenchable/fire.") that occasions the childhood recollection. In contrast to the romantic trappings of Bishop's poem—"the gracious royal couples," Arthur's coffin as "a little frosted cake," "the Maple Leaf (Forever)," and "Jack Frost"—here, the context is starkly religious and staunchly moral—the tension between the two intimately conflicting positions, exquisitely balanced across the lines "all things work together for the good/for those who love God" and "No! NO! How is it *good* to be dead?" The grandmother worships an incomprehensible God who swoops out of the clouds at whim and chooses and rejects and avails Himself of means too inhuman to be justified by any imaginable good end.

For Kenyon, as with Dickinson before her, death belies the notion of a just and loving God. "You wouldn't be so depressed," a friend suggests in "Having It Out with Melancholy," "if you really believed in God." But unbelief is not the problem. Like Dickinson, Kenyon *believes* in God and feels herself and her loved ones answerable to His laws and vulnerable to His whims. It is the Dickinsonian paradox all over again: a wholehearted belief in God—His threats, His perils—without faith in His beneficence, hope in His promises, consolation in His gilded words. We feel this last point most poignantly in Kenyon's writing about the life and death of her father in lines like these from "We Let the Boat Drift":

> Once we talked about the life to come.
> I took the Bible from the nightstand
> and offered John 14: "I go to prepare
> a place for you." "Fine. Good," he said.
> "But what about Matthew? 'You, therefore,
> must be perfect, as your heavenly Father
> is perfect.'" And he wept.

Writing in a similar vein, Kenyon exclaims, "A person/ simply vanishes!" Here, the incredulity appears to cut two ways: first, toward the incomprehensible annihilation of personhood and consciousness expressed earlier in "We Let the Boat Drift"; but it is also this very incomprehension that mandates belief, despite our keenest doubts, in a life to come, where loved ones are restored not only to each other, but first and foremost, to themselves. Thus, in "With the Dog at Sunrise," seeking words of consolation for a newly widowed friend, Kenyon ends by offering things she sees (how "the poplars/ growing along the ravine/ shine pink in the light of winter dawn") and doesn't see, but knows ("Far up in the woods where no one goes/ deer take their ease under the great/ pines, nose to steaming nose"). Similarly, in "Reading Aloud to My Father," the final new poem in this collection, emblematic truth and vision provide a proof against doubt and desolation where conventional faith and dogma have utterly failed. The poem opens with the poet "haphazard[ly]" choosing a book to read to her dying father and her almost instantaneous knowledge that she has chosen wrong as she begins to read from Nabokov: *"The cradle rocks above an abyss . . ."* She stops, but with everything it is the same: even Chopin disturbs her musician-father in the midst of his dying. Again, in that canny way of hers, what Kenyon sees becomes her vision:

> But to return to the cradle rocking. I think
> Nabokov had it wrong. This is the abyss.
> That's why babies howl at birth,
> and why the dying so often reach
> for something only they can apprehend.
>
> At the end they don't want their hands
> to be under the covers, and if you should put
> your hand on theirs in a tentative gesture
> of solidarity, they'll pull the hand free;
> and you must honor that desire,
> and let them pull it free.

What keeps all of this—death, depression, hard grappling with God—from being unbearable and hopelessly grim is Kenyon's keen joy in the creation; a sense of well-being arising from being at once firmly rooted in a sheltering place and open to all weathers, freely borne along by seasons and days; and music, sometimes subtle, sometimes (as here, in "Spring Evening") dense:

> Again the thrush affirms
> both dusk and dawn. The frog
> releases spawn in the warm
> inlet of the pond. Ferns
> rise with the crescent moon,
> and the old farmer
> waits to sow his corn.

from

Intimations of Mortality

When Jane Kenyon died in the spring of 1995, she had published four volumes of poetry and one book of translations. She was mourned widely as a poet whose creative arc was cut short just as it deepened into her most affecting work. Kenyon's quiet, intense poems are praised for their precise imagery of everyday, yet extraordinary, moments of pain and beauty—a quality her husband, Donald Hall, calls "the luminous particular."

What some admirers of Kenyon's poetry may not know is that she also wrote prose—even newspaper columns—with the same startling accuracy, honesty, and deep, unsentimental feeling. *A Hundred White Daffodils* is assembled around a series of columns she wrote for the *Concord Monitor* about life in her rural New Hampshire community.

Several short essays demonstrate her mastery of the form. In all cases, Kenyon reveals herself as passionate about the simple pleasures, daily mysteries, and spiritual lessons of place and community living, measuring how deeply connected she felt to the farm and neighborhood where she lived for nearly twenty years.

Kenyon's prose reveals a refreshing sense of humor, which may surprise readers of her poetry. In "The Moment of Peonies" she writes, in perfect northern New England celebration of the showy blooms, "These are not Protestant-work-ethic flowers. They loll about in gorgeousness; they live for art; they believe in excess. They are not *quite* decent, to tell the truth."

Several years before her death, Kenyon was persuaded to write newspaper columns as a way of talking to neighbors. She wrote about ordinary chores and events in a way that made them profound: the spiritual necessity of planting spring bulbs, the joys of rural mail delivery, walks with a beloved dog, and ways to keep the faith in mud season. She anticipates the ritual opening of a summer camp, and the natural rhythms of the church calendar. Of a nativity play she says, "Different children fill the roles over the years, but the play goes on, renewing itself like a compost infinitely rich and life-giving."

"The Honey Wagon" tells of having the septic system pumped: "A gray, putrid, frothing glop coursed into the hose—the residue of *nouvelle cuisine,* of glasses of wine taken with friends. It was our washwater, our blood, sweat, and tears. All is vanity."

Again and again in these essays, as in her poems, Kenyon leads us to the simple facts, honest about what hurts, exulting in what lifts the heart. In her mix of compost wit and poetic contemplation, Kenyon makes ordinary acts of rural living unforgettable. Always, she seems aware of the turning of the seasons, of imminent, sometimes frightening, change.

A strong thread of sadness runs through Kenyon's work, and with reason. In her last decades she contended with her own illnesses, her husband's bouts with cancer, the illness and death of a parent, and her lifelong, recurring depression. In one of her most moving columns, "The Shadows," she writes of facing bad times. "This is what we are trying to do at our house: simplify, appreciate, stay close, be kind, tell the truth, work as we are able, rest." She finds solace in nature's abundance: "Tonight before the storm I went out with the kitchen shears and a basket. I cut every full-open peony in sight, quantities that I would never permit myself under other circumstances. . . . Pick them, something told me, pick them and fill the house. . . ."

JOYCE PESEROFF is the author of four books of poems and a recipient of grants from the National Endowment for the Arts and the Massachusetts Artists Foundation. She grew up in New York City and currently resides in Massachusetts, where she is on the faculty of the University of Massachusetts, Boston.

The text of *Simply Lasting* has been set in Adobe Garamond Pro, a typeface drawn by Robert Slimbach and based on type cut by Claude Garamond in the sixteenth century. Book design by Wendy Holdman. Composition at Prism Publishing Center. Manufactured by Sheridan Books on acid-free paper.